nickelodeon

AVATAR

THE LAST AIRBENDER

THE OFFICIAL BOOK OF

AMIGURUMI

nickelodeon

AVATAR
THE LAST AIRBENDER

THE OFFICIAL BOOK OF

AMIGURUMI

Written by
LEE SARTORI

INSIGHT EDITIONS

SAN RAFAEL • LOS ANGELES • LONDON

DEDICATION

This book is dedicated to my husband, Sean, and my sons, Noël and Conan. Thanks for introducing me to Avatar so many years ago and for being excited about this project with me.

CONTENTS

BEGINNER PROJECTS

EASY PROJECTS

INTERMEDIATE PROJECTS

ADVANCED PROJECTS

SCAN HERE FOR AN EXCLUSIVE AMIGURUMI PATTERN!

INTRODUCTION

Water. Earth. Fire. Air. Long ago, the Four Nations lived together in harmony. Then everything changed when the Fire Nation attacked. Only the Avatar, master of all four elements, could stop them, but when the world needed him most, he vanished. A hundred years passed, and my brother and I discovered the new Avatar: an Airbender named Aang. And although his airbending skills are great, he still has a lot to learn before he's ready to save anyone. But I believe Aang can save the world.

In *Avatar: The Last Airbender*, Aang sets out to master the four elements and save the world. Along with his friends, he makes mistakes, and in doing so, he experiences joy, the pain of loss, and the satisfaction of learning.

On our crochet journeys, we experience something similar. We set out to master the main stitches of crochet, starting with chains, moving on to single crochets, half-double, double, and eventually manipulating those stitches to make fascinating things! I remember when I first learned how to crochet. I started out at a little local shop, in a class with a handful of students eager to learn from an experienced teacher. As I listened and learned from her, I came away with a love for something new and exciting. A craft that offers endless possibilities and opportunities for discovery.

We also experience the joys of friendship when we meet up with other crocheters and knitters. We share the frustration of learning and the pride of succeeding. And life happens along the way as we work on our projects: the pain of loss, the joy of new beginnings, and the simple pleasures of days moving past us. Working on this book with my fellow guest designers felt a lot like that. While we worked on this book together, we felt the joy of time spent with family, as well as the fear that came with living in an area of Eastern Canada going through wildfires (that's me). One of the guest designers had a kitchen accident that took away her ability to crochet for a time while she healed. Through the love of our craft, we were able to come together and create something fun and beautiful in this book, bringing all our experience with us on the journey.

Aang sets out to learn, to help, and to enjoy what life has to offer him. And I feel that in our lives as crocheters, we are on that journey ourselves. Enjoy, learn, and be open to what life has in store for you. Let past crochet teachers guide you in your skills and be willing to teach others. That's the way of the Avatar.

—LEE SARTORI

APPA

Designed by
LEE SARTORI

Skill Level:
BEGINNER

The sky bison Appa is the loving and powerful lifetime companion of Avatar Aang, the last Airbender. When Aang finds out he was the Avatar and runs away on Appa, he becomes frozen in ice for a century after a violent storm, and upon emerging, he's relieved to see his massive six-legged friend still by his side. Groggy and confused, Appa takes his time getting in the air again, and when he does, he and Aang set off to solve the mystery of what happened to the other Airbenders during their long absence.

Now you can crochet your very own Appa, complete with soft fur and six legs! This crocheted companion might not be able to fly, but he is always available for cuddles! Yip yip!

"Choose well. A sky bison is a companion for life."

—SISTER IIO (Book 2, Episode 16)

FINISHED MEASUREMENTS
Height: 10 in. / 25.5 cm • Length: 20 in. / 51 cm

YARN
Worsted weight (#4, Medium), shown in Lion Brand *Chenille Appeal* (100% Polyester, 284 yd. / 260 m per 3.5 oz. / 100 g ball)
Color A: 099Z Coconut, 4 balls
And worsted weight (#4, Medium), shown in Lion Brand *Lazy Days* (100% Polyester, 179 yd. / 164 m per 3.5 oz. / 100 g ball)
Color B: 152AH Pewter, 1 ball
Color C: 153C Licorice, 1 ball
Color D: 123AP Taupe, 1 ball

HOOKS
US F-5 / 3.75 mm, *or size needed to obtain gauge*
US C-2 / 2.75 mm

NOTIONS
Stitch markers • Tapestry needle • Polyester stuffing • 18 mm black safety eyes • 2 chenille stems • Scissors

GAUGE
With larger hook 16 sc and 14 sc rounds = 4 in. / 10 cm; *make sure to check your gauge.*

ABBREVIATIONS
Back loop only (BLO), chain(s) (ch(s)), front loop only (FLO), half double crochet (hdc), single crochet (sc), slip stitch(es) (sl st(s)), stitch(es) (st(s)), two single crochet closed together (sc2tog), yarn over (yo).

SPECIAL ABBREVIATIONS
inv-dec (invisible single crochet decrease): Insert hook in FLO of each of next 2 sts, yo and draw through both sts, yo and draw through 2 loops on hook—1 st decreased.

NOTES

Work in continuous rounds unless otherwise indicated. When instructed to join, join with a slip stitch in first stitch. Most of the pieces are crocheted with yarn held double; take note of when yarn is held single and smaller hook is used.

"He's a gigantic fluffy monster with an arrow on his head! It's kinda hard to miss him!"

–SOKKA (Book 1, Episode 10)

CHIN

With **A** held double and larger hook.
Rnd 1: Ch 2, 8 sc in second ch from hook–8 sc.
Rnd 2: 2 sc in each st around–16 sc.
Rnd 3: [2 sc in next st, sc in next] around–24 sc.
Rnds 4–5: Sc in each st around.
Fasten off, leaving a long tail for sewing. Set aside to join to Head.

HEAD

With **A** held double and larger hook.
Rnd 1: Ch 2, 6 sc in second ch from hook–6 sc.
Rnd 2: 2 sc in each st around–12 sc.
Rnd 3: [2 sc in next st, sc in next] around–18 sc.
Rnd 4: [Sc in next st, 2 sc in next, sc in next] around–24 sc.
Rnd 5: [2 sc in next st, sc in next 3] around–30 sc.
Rnd 6: [Sc in next 2 sts, 2 sc in next, sc in next 2] around–36 sc.
Rnd 7: [2 sc in next st, sc in next 5] around–42 sc.
Rnd 8: [Sc in next 3 sts, 2 sc in next, sc in next 3] around–48 sc.
Rnd 9: [2 sc in next st, sc in next 7] around–54 sc.
Rnd 10: [Sc in next 4 sts, 2 sc in next, sc in next 4] around–60 sc.
Rnds 11–14: Sc in each st around.
Rnd 15 (Join Chin): Sc in next 15 sts, holding Chin in line with Head sts sc in next 12 sts on Chin, leave remaining 12 sts on Chin unworked, skip next 12 sts on Head, sc in next 33–60 sc.
Rnds 16–24: Sc in each st around.
Rnd 25 (Fringe): (Sc, ch 6) in each st around–60 sc, 60 ch-6.
Rnd 26: Working behind ch-6 spaces (Fringe), sc in each sc around–60 sc.
Rnd 27: Sc in each st around.
Rnd 28: [Sc in next 4 sts, sc2tog, sc in next 4] around–54 sc.
Rnd 29: [Sc2tog, sc in next 7 sts] around–48 sc.
Rnd 30: [Sc in next 3 sts, sc2tog, sc in next 3] around–42 sc.
Rnd 31: [Sc2tog, sc in next 5 sts] around–36 sc.
Rnd 32: [Sc in next 2 sts, sc2tog, sc in next 2] around–30 sc.
Rnd 33: [Sc2tog, sc in next 3 sts] around–24 sc.
Stuff and continue stuffing as work progresses.
Rnd 34: [Sc in next st, sc2tog, sc in next] around–18 sc.
Rnd 35: [Sc2tog, sc in next st] around–12 sc.
Rnd 36: [Sc2tog] around–6 sc.
Fasten off, leaving a long tail for sewing. Sew remaining 6 sts closed. Using the tail from the Chin, sew Chin and Head seam closed. Weave in ends.

MUZZLE

With **B** held double and larger hook.
Rnd 1: Ch 18, starting in second ch from hook sc in next 16 chs, 5 hdc in next, rotate to work in underside of starting ch, sc in next 16, 5 hdc in last–42 sts.
Rnd 2: *Sc in next 16 sts, 2 hdc in next 5; repeat from * around–52 sts.
Rnd 3: *Sc in next 16 sts, [2 hdc in next, hdc in next] 5 times; repeat from * around–62 sts.
Rnd 4: *Sc in next 16 sts, [hdc in next, 2 hdc in next, hdc in next] 5 times; repeat from * around–72 sts.
Rnd 5: Sc in each st around–72 sc.
Fasten off, leaving a long tail for sewing. Stuff and pin Muzzle in place between Chin and Rnd 16 of Head. Do not sew.

NOSE

With **C** held double and larger hook.
Rnd 1: Ch 7, starting in second ch from hook sc in next 5, 3 sc in last, rotate to work in underside of starting ch, sc in next 5, 3 sc in last–16 sc.
Rnd 2: *Sc in next 5 sts, 2 sc in next 3; repeat from * around–22 sc.
Rnd 3: Sc in next 2 sts, 3 hdc in next, sc in next 19–24 sts.
Rnd 4: Sc in next 2 sts, 2 hdc in next 3, sc in next 19–27 sts.
Rnd 5: Sc in each st around–27 sc.
Fasten off, leaving a long tail for sewing. Stuff and pin Nose to front of Muzzle. Do not sew.

EYE PLATE

With **B** held double and larger hook.
Row 1: Ch 21, starting in second ch from hook sc in each ch across, turn–20 sc.
Rows 2–3: Ch 1, sc in each st across, turn.
Fasten off, leaving a long tail for sewing. Pin in place, centered above Muzzle. Do not sew.

EYE (MAKE 2)

With **A** held double and larger hook, make a magic loop.
Rnd 1: Ch 1, [3 sc, hdc, dc, hdc] twice in loop, join–12 sts.
Without adding backing, push safety eye to center of loop and tighten Eye loop. Push safety eyes through each side of Eye Plate and add safety backing to eyes.

HEAD FINISHING

Sew Muzzle, Eye Plate, Nose, and Eyes in place and weave in ends. With **A** held double, insert needle into bottom of Head, through Head and out at top center. Send needle back through and cinch bottom of Head in a dimple, ensuring not to dimple top of Head by pulling too tightly. Secure with a knot and weave in ends. With **A** held double, embroider eyelids over safety eyes. Weave in ends. With **A** held double, cut sixty 3 in. / 7.5 cm pieces of yarn and loop them through each of the 60 fringe spaces around Head. Trim fringe to about halfway covering safety eyes.

INNER EAR (MAKE 2)

With **B** held double and larger hook.
Rnd 1: Ch 2, 6 sc in second ch from hook–6 sc.
Rnd 2: 2 sc in each st around–12 sc.
Rnd 3: [2 sc in next st, sc in next] around–18 sc.
Fasten off, weave in ends.

OUTER EAR (MAKE 2)

With **A** held double and larger hook.
Rnds 1–3: Repeat Rnds 1–3 of Inner Ear.
Rnd 4 (Joining): Place Inner Ear and Outer Ear on top of each other with Inner Ear facing, join with a sl st through both thicknesses, ch 1, working through both thicknesses around to join [sc in next, 2 sc in next, sc in next] around, join–24 sc.
Fasten off, leaving a long tail for sewing. Sew Ears to sides of Head under fringe. Weave in ends.

HORN (MAKE 2)

With **C** held single and smaller hook.
Rnd 1: Ch 2, 3 sc in second ch from hook–3 sc.
Rnd 2: 2 sc in next, sc in each st around–4 sc.
Rnds 3–13: Repeat Rnd 2–15 sc at end of Rnd 13.
Rnds 14–18: Sc in each st around.
Rnd 19: Sc-BLO in next 8 sts (mark first FLO with a st marker), now working in both loops sc in next 7–15 sc.
Rnds 20–23: Sc in each st around.
Rnd 24: Sc-FLO in marked st and next 7 from Rnd 19, skip 8 sts on working round, sc in next 7 on working round–15 sc.
Rnds 25–28: Sc in each st around.
Fasten off, leaving a long tail for sewing. Insert a chenille stem into Horn and stuff around chenille stem. With bend of Horn facing outward, sew Horns to either side of Head, above fringe and in line with Ears. Bend tips of Horns using photos as a guide. Weave in ends.

BODY

With **A** held double and larger hook, leave a long tail at start for sewing.
Rnd 1: Ch 60; being careful not to twist, join to first ch with a sl st to form a ring, ch 1, sc in each st around, join–60 sc.
Rnds 2–5: Ch 1, sc in each st around, join.
Rnd 6: Ch 1, sc in next 27 sts, [2 sc in next, sc in next] 3 times, sc in next 27, join–63 sc.
Rnd 7: Ch 1, sc in next 27 sts, [sc in next, 2 sc in next, sc in next] 3 times, sc in next 27, join–66 sc.
Rnd 8: Ch 1, sc in next 27 sts, [2 sc in

next, sc in next 3] 3 times, sc in next 27, join–69 sc.
Rnd 9: Ch 1, sc in next 27 sts, [sc in next 2, 2 sc in next, sc in next 2] 3 times, sc in next 27, join–72 sc.
Rnd 10: Ch 1, sc in next 27 sts, [2 sc in next, sc in next 5] 3 times, sc in next 27, join–75 sc.
Rnd 11: Ch 1, sc in next 27 sts, [sc in next 3, 2 sc in next, sc in next 3] 3 times, sc in next 27, join–78 sc.
Rnds 12–18: Ch 1, sc in each st around, join.
Rnd 19: Ch 1, sc in next 27 sts, [sc in next 3, sc2tog, sc in next 3] 3 times, sc in next 27, join–75 sc.
Rnd 20: Ch 1, sc in next 27 sts, [sc2tog, sc in next 5] 3 times, sc in next 27, join–72 sc.
Rnd 21: Ch 1, sc in next 27 sts, [sc in next 2, sc2tog, sc in next 2] 3 times, sc in next 27, join–69 sc.
Rnd 22: Ch 1, sc in next 27 sts, [sc2tog, sc in next 3] 3 times, sc in next 27, join–66 sc.
Rnd 23: Ch 1, sc in next 27 sts, [sc in next, sc2tog, sc in next] 3 times, sc in next 27, join–63 sc.
Rnd 24: Ch 1, sc in next 27 sts, [sc in next, sc2tog] 3 times, sc in next 27, join–60 sc.
Rnd 25: Ch 1, sc in next 15 sts, [sc in next 4, sc2tog, sc in next 4] 3 times, sc in next 15, join–57 sc.
Rnd 26: Ch 1, sc in next 15 sts, [sc2tog, sc in next 7] 3 times, sc in next 15, join–54 sc.
Rnd 27: Ch 1, sc in next 15 sts, [sc in next 3, sc2tog, sc in next 3] 3 times, sc in next 15, join–51 sc.
Rnd 28: Ch 1, sc in next 15 sts, [sc2tog, sc in next 5] 3 times, sc in next 15, join–48 sc.
Rnd 29: Ch 1, sc in next 15 sts, [sc in next 2, sc2tog, sc in next 2] 3 times, sc in next 15, join–45 sc.
Rnd 30: Ch 1, sc in next 15 sts, [sc2tog, sc in next 3] 3 times, sc in next 15, join–42 sc.
Rnd 31: Ch 1, sc in next 15 sts, [sc in next, sc2tog, sc in next] 3 times, sc in next 15, join–39 sc.
Rnd 32: Ch 1, sc in next 15 sts, [sc in next, sc2tog] 3 times, sc in next 15, join–36 sc.
Rnd 33: Ch 1, sc in next 9 sts, [sc in next 2, sc2tog, sc in next 2] 3 times, sc in next 9, join–33 sc.
Rnd 34: Ch 1, sc in next 9 sts, [sc2tog, sc in next 3] 3 times, sc in next 9, join–30 sc.
Rnd 35: Ch 1, [sc2tog, sc in next 3] 6 times, join–24 sc.
Rnd 36: Ch 1, [sc in next, sc2tog, sc in next] 6 times, join–18 sc.
Rnd 37: Ch 1, [sc in next, sc2tog] 6 times, join–12 sc.
Rnd 38: Ch 1, [sc2tog] around, join–6 sc.
Fasten off, leaving a long tail for sewing. Sew remaining 6 sts closed and weave in end. Stuff Body firmly. Sew to back of Head just under fringe line and Rnd 1 of Head. Weave in ends.

TAIL

With **A** held double and larger hook.
Rnd 1: Ch 2, working in second ch from hook 6 sc–6 sc.
Rnd 2: 2 sc in each st around–12 sc.
Rnd 3: [2 sc in next st, sc in next] around–18 sc.
Rnd 4: [Sc in next st, 2 sc in next, sc in next] around–24 sc.
Rnd 5: [2 sc in next st, sc in next 3] around–30 sc.
Rnd 6: [Sc in next 2 sts, 2 sc in next, sc in next 2] around–36 sc.
Rnd 7: [2 sc in next st, sc in next 5] around–42 sc.
Rnd 8: [Sc in next 3 sts, 2 sc in next, sc in next 3] around–48 sc.
Rnd 9: [2 sc in next st, sc in next 7] around–54 sc.
Rnds 10–18: Sc in each st around.
Rnd 19: [Sc in next 8 sts, sc2tog, sc in next 8] 3 times–51 sc.
Rnd 20: [Sc2tog, sc in next 15 sts] 3 times–48 sc.
Rnd 21: [Sc in next 7 sts, sc2tog, sc in next 7] 3 times–45 sc.
Rnd 22: [Sc2tog, sc in next 13 sts] 3 times–42 sc.
Rnd 23: [Sc in next 6 sts, sc2tog, sc in next 6] 3 times–39 sc.
Rnd 24: [Sc2tog, sc in next 11 sts] 3 times–36 sc.
Rnd 25: [Sc in next 5 sts, sc2tog, sc in next 5] 3 times–33 sc.
Rnd 26: [Sc2tog, sc in next 9 sts] 3 times–30 sc.
Rnds 27–35: Sc in each st around.
Fasten off, leaving a long tail for sewing. Leave Tail unstuffed. Sew Tail to back of Body. Weave in ends.

BACK PIECE (ARROW)

With **D** held single and smaller hook, leave a long tail at start for sewing.
Row 1: Ch 2, 2 sc in second ch from hook, turn–2 sc.
Row 2: Ch 1, 2 sc in next st, sc in each st across, turn–3 sc.
Rows 3–17: Repeat Row 2–18 sc at the end of Row 17.
Fasten off and skip 6 sts, join to next st.
Row 18: Ch 1, sc in next 6 sts, turn leaving remaining 6 sts unworked–6 sc.
Rows 19–53: Ch 1, sc in each st across, turn.
Row 54: Ch 2 (counts as first hdc here and throughout), 2 hdc in same st, sc in each st across to last st, 3 hdc in last, turn–10 sts.
Rows 55–59: Repeat Row 54–30 sts at end of Row 59.
Row 60: Ch 1, sc in each st across, turn–30 sc.
Row 61: Ch 1, sl st in next 7 sts, ch 1, sc2tog, sc in next 14, sc2tog, turn–16 sc.
Row 62: Ch 1, sc2tog twice, sc in next 8, sc2tog twice, turn–12 sc.

Row 63: Ch 1, sc2tog twice, sc in next 4, sc2tog twice, turn–8 sc.
Row 64: Ch 1, sc2tog, sc in next 4, sc2tog, turn–6 sc.
Rows 65–74: Ch 1, sc in each st across, turn.
Rows 75–85: Repeat Rows 54–64.
Rows 86–95: Repeat Rows 65–74.
Rows 96–106: Repeat Rows 54–64.
Rows 107–116: Repeat Rows 65–74.
Rows 117–127: Repeat Rows 54–64.
Rows 128–137: Repeat Rows 65–74.
Fasten off, leaving a long tail for sewing. Pin Arrow to center of forehead and down entire spine of Body using photos as a guide. End of Back Piece should stop midway down Tail. Do not sew.

TAIL BOTTOM

With **D** held single and smaller hook.
Rnd 1: Ch 2, 6 sc in second ch from hook–6 sc.
Rnd 2: 2 sc in each st around–12 sc.
Rnd 3: [2 sc in next st, sc in next] around–18 sc.

Rnd 4: [Sc in next st, 2 sc in next, sc in next] around–24 sc.
Rnd 5: [2 sc in next st, sc in next 3] around–30 sc.
Rnd 6: [Sc in next 2 sts, 2 sc in next, sc in next 2] around–36 sc.
Rnd 7: [2 sc in next st, sc in next 5] around–42 sc.
Rnd 8: [Sc in next 3 sts, 2 sc in next, sc in next 3] around–48 sc.
Rnd 9: [2 sc in next st, sc in next 7] around–54 sc.
Rnd 10: [Sc in next 4 sts, 2 sc in next, sc in next 4] around–60 sc.
Rnd 11: [2 sc in next st, sc in next 9] around–66 sc.
Rnd 12: [Sc in next 5 sts, 2 sc in next, sc in next 5] around–72 sc.
Rnd 13: [2 sc in next st, sc in next 11] around–78 sc.
Rnd 14: [Sc in next 6 sts, 2 sc in next, sc in next 6] around–84 sc.
Rnds 15–20: Sc in each st around.
Fasten off, leaving a long tail for sewing. Cap bottom of Tail with this piece. Sew end of Back Piece to middle of Tail Bottom. Sew Tail Bottom around bottom of Tail. Weave in ends. Sew Back Piece in place. Weave in ends.

BELLY PATCH

With **B** held double and larger hook.
Row 1: Ch 13, starting in second ch from hook, sc in each ch across, turn–12 sc.
Rows 2–60: Ch 1, sc-BLO in each st across, turn.
Rnd 61 (Border): Ch 1, sc in next 12 sts, rotate to work 60 sc across row ends, rotate to work 12 sc across underside of starting ch, rotate to work 60 sc across opposite edge row ends, join–144 sc.
Fasten off, leaving a long tail for sewing. Pin Belly Patch in place on underside of Body from edge of Tail Bottom to Rnd 1 of Body. Sew in place. Weave in ends.

TOE (MAKE 18)

With **B** held single and smaller hook.
Rnd 1: Ch 2, 6 sc in second ch from hook–6 sc.
Rnd 2: 2 sc in each st around–12 sc.
Rnds 3–4: Sc in each st around.
Fasten off, leaving a long tail for sewing.

LEG (MAKE 6)

With **B** held double and larger hook, make a magic loop.
Rnd 1: Ch 1, 8 sc in loop–8 sc.
Rnd 2: 2 sc in each st around–16 sc.
Rnd 3: [2 sc in next st, sc in next] around–24 sc.
Change to **A** held double.
Rnd 4: Ch 1, sc-BLO in each st around, join–24 sc.
Rnds 5–14: Ch 1, sc in each st around, join.
Pinch top of Leg closed.
Row 15: Ch 1, sc across top of Leg through both thicknesses to close–12 sc.
Fasten off, leaving a long tail for sewing. Pin 3 Legs to either side of Body, starting at Rnd 4 of Body and working back from there. Stuff Legs and stuff top of Leg before sewing each Leg to side of Body. Weave in ends. Sew 3 Toes to front of each foot in line with Rnd 3 of Leg. Weave in ends.

FOOT PAD (MAKE 6)

With **C** held single and smaller hook.
Rnd 1: Ch 1, 8 sc in loop–8 sc.
Rnd 2: 2 sc in each st around–16 sc.
Rnd 3: [2 sc in next st, sc in next] around–24 sc.
Fasten off, leaving a long tail for sewing. Sew to the bottom of each foot. Weave in ends.

TOE PAD (MAKE 18)

With **C** held single and smaller hook.
Rnd 1: Ch 1, 8 sc in loop–8 sc.
Fasten off, leaving a long tail for sewing. Sew to bottom of each Toe. Weave in ends.

MOMO

Designed by
NICOLE ROGOWSKI

Skill Level:
BEGINNER

When Aang and his friends set out to explore the Southern Air Temple for any remaining Airbenders, they stop for a quick bite to eat. And when a quick little hand reaches out and steals a moon peach from Sokka, the friends discover one of the last known flying lemurs living in the isolated Air Temple ruins. Motivated by food and companionship, Momo tags along and joins the gang on their adventures, becoming a loyal, clever, and scrappy member of Team Avatar.

The amigurumi version of Momo is so cute! Just don't ask him to bring you any water—who knows what he will bring you back in return.

"Wait! Someone's missing from your group, someone very important. . . . Where's Momo?"

—KING BUMI (Book 3, Episode 19)

FINISHED MEASUREMENTS
Height: 7 in. / 18 cm • Width: 4½ in. / 11.5 cm

YARN
Worsted weight (#4, Medium) yarn, shown in Lion Brand *Basic Stitch* (100% Acrylic, 185 yd. / 169 m per 3.5 oz. / 100 g ball)
Color A: 100 White, 1 ball
Color B: 129B Cocoa, 1 ball
Color C: 126AL Mahogany, 1 ball
Color D: 123AS Cedarwood, 1 ball
Color E: 153 Black, 1 ball

HOOK
US E-4 / 3.5 mm, *or size needed to obtain gauge*

NOTIONS
Stitch markers • Tapestry needle • Polyester stuffing • 20 mm sinker-style safety eyes • 12 x 10 mm black safety nose • 16-gauge craft wire • Wire cutters • Needle-nosed jewelry pliers • Scissors

GAUGE
20 sc and 24 sc rounds = 4 in. / 10 cm; *make sure to check your gauge.*

ABBREVIATIONS
Back loop only (BLO), chain(s) (ch(s)), fasten off (FO), front loop only (FLO), magic ring (MR), right side (RS), single crochet (sc), skip (sk), slip stitch(es) (sl st(s)), space(s) (sp(s)), stitch(es) (st(s)), three single crochet closed together (sc3tog), two single crochet closed together (sc2tog), wrong side (WS), yarn over (yo).

SPECIAL ABBREVIATIONS
esc (extended single crochet): Insert hook in indicated st, yo and pull up a loop, yo and pull through first loop on hook, yo and pull through all loops on hook.
esc2tog (extended single crochet two together): Insert hook in indicated st, yo and pull up a loop, yo and pull through first loop on hook, insert hook in next st, yo and pull up a loop, yo and pull through first loop on hook, yo and pull through all loops on hook.
inv-dec (invisible single crochet decrease): Insert hook in FLO of each of next 2 sts, yo and draw through both sts, yo and draw through 2 loops on hook–1 st decreased.

NOTES

Use of front loops for Torso, Ears, Thighs, and Head will keep stitches from slanting while working continuously in the round. Work in continuous rounds unless otherwise indicated. When instructed to join, join with a slip stitch in first stitch.

Aang: You, me, and Appa; we're all that's left of this place. We have to stick together. Katara, Sokka, say hello to the newest member of our family.
Katara: What are you going to name him?
Aang: Momo.

(Book 1, Episode 3)

HEAD

With **B**, ch 13.
Row 1 (RS): Working in back bump of chs, sc in second ch from hook, sc in next 10 chs, 2 sc in last ch, ch 1 and turn–14 sc.
Row 2 (WS): 2 sc in first st, sc in next 3, ch 6, sk 6, sc in next 3, 2 sc in last st, ch 1 and turn–10 sc, 1 ch-6 space.
Row 3: 2 sc in first st, sc in next 4, 6 sc across next ch-space, sc in next 4, 2 sc in last st, ch 1 and turn–18 sc.
Row 4: Esc2tog, esc in next 14 sts, esc2tog, ch 1 and turn–16 esc.
Row 5: Esc2tog, esc in next, ch 1, sk 1 (first eyehole), esc in next 8, ch 1, sk 1 (second eyehole), esc in next, esc2tog, ch 1 and turn–12 esc, 2 ch-1 spaces.
Row 6: Esc2tog, esc in ch sp, esc in next 3 sts, sc2tog, esc in next 3, esc in ch sp, esc2tog, ch 1 and turn–11 sts.
Row 7: With **B**, esc2tog, esc in next, esc2tog; with **A**, 3 esc-BLO in next; with **B**, esc2tog, esc in next, esc2tog, ch 1 and rotate piece to work in row ends–9 esc.
Insert safety eyes in Row 5 eyeholes.

Continuing from Row 7, work around Head starting with **B**.
Rnd 1: Sc 8 evenly across row ends, sc 12 under starting ch, sc 8 evenly across row ends; now working across Row 7 sts, sc in next st, sc2tog; with **A**, [2 sc in next] 3 times; with **B**, sc2tog, sc in next, join and change to **A**–38 sc.
Rnd 2: Sl st-BLO in same st as join, sl st-BLO in next 29 sts, sc in next 6, sl st-BLO in next 2.
Begin working in continuous rounds. Use a st marker to keep track of rounds.
Rnd 3: [Sc-BLO in next 3 sts, 2 sc-BLO in next] 7 times, sc-BLO in next 2, sc in next 6, sc-BLO in next, 2 sc-BLO in next–46 sc.
Rnd 4: [Sc in next 4 sts, 2 sc in next] 6 times, sc in next 7, 2 sc in next, sc in next 4, 2 sc in next, sc in next 3–54 sc.
Rnds 5–7: Sc in next 16 sts; with **B**, sc-FLO in next 9; with **A**, sc in next 29.
Rnd 8: Sc in next 15 sts, 2 sc in next; with **B**, inv-dec, sc-FLO in next 5, inv-dec; with **A**, 2 sc in next, sc in next 28.
Rnd 9: Sc in next 3 sts, inv-dec, [sc in next 4, inv-dec] twice; with **B**, sc-FLO in next 4, inv-dec, sc-FLO in next; with **A**, sc in next 3, inv-dec, [sc in next 4, inv-dec] 4 times, sc in next–45 sc.
Rnd 10: Sc in next 2 sts, inv-dec, [sc in next 3, inv-dec] twice; with **B**, sc-FLO in next 3, inv-dec, sc-FLO in next; with **A**, sc in next 2, inv-dec, [sc in next 3, inv-dec] 4 times, sc in next–36 sc.
Rnd 11: Sc in next, inv-dec, [sc in next 2, inv-dec] twice; with **B**, sc-FLO in next 2, inv-dec, sc-FLO in next; with **A**, sc in next, inv-dec, [sc in next 2, inv-dec] 4 times, sc in next–27 sc.
Rnd 12: Sc in next 8 sts; with **B**, sc-FLO in next 4; with **A**, sc in next 15.
Stuff firmly.
Rnd 13: Inv-dec, [sc in next, inv-dec] twice; with **B**, sc-FLO in next, inv-dec, sc-FLO in next; with **A**, inv-dec, [sc in next, inv-dec] 4 times, sc in next–18 sc.
Rnd 14: Sc in next, [inv-dec] twice; with **B**, sc3tog; with **A**, [inv-dec] 5 times–9 sc.
Fasten off and sew closed with **A** tail.

SNOUT

Join with **B** to first skipped st of Row 2 of Head and ch 1.
Rnd 1: Sc in same st as join, sc in next 5 skipped sts, sc2tog in corner, 6 sc across unworked loops of ch-6 sp, sc2tog in corner–14 sc.
The last two rounds will be worked continuously. Use a st marker to keep track of rounds.
Rnd 2: Sc in each st around.
Rnd 3: [Inv-dec] 7 times–7 sc.
Fasten off. Stuff Snout and sew opening closed with tail.

NOSE EMBROIDERY

Using a length of **E**, embroider an upside-down triangle on Snout. Weave ends in. If using a safety nose instead of embroidery, place it into the MR opening of Rnd 1 of Snout.

RIGHT EAR

With **A**, make a MR and ch 1.
Rnd 1: 5 sc in MR and pull tail to close–5 sc.

Begin working in continuous rounds. Use a st marker to keep track of rounds.
Rnd 2: Sc in each st around.
Rnd 3: [2 sc in next st] 5 times–10 sc.
Rnd 4: Sc in each st around.
Rnd 5: Sc in next 4 sts; with **C**, [2 sc-FLO in next] twice; with **A**, sc in next 4–12 sc.
Rnd 6: [Sc in next st, 2 sc in next] twice; with **C**, [sc-FLO in next, 2 sc-FLO in next] twice; with **A**, [sc in next, 2 sc in next] twice–18 sc.
Rnds 7–8: Sc in next 6 sts; with **C**, sc-FLO in next 6; with **A**, sc in next 6.
Rnd 9: [Sc in next 2 sts, 2 sc in next] twice; with **C**, [sc-FLO in next 2, 2 sc-FLO in next] twice; with **A**, [sc in next 2, 2 sc in next] twice–24 sc.
Rnds 10–11: Sc in next 8 sts; with **D**, sc-FLO in next 8; with **A**, sc in next 8.
Rnd 12: [Sc in next 3 sts, 2 sc in next] twice; with **D**, [sc-FLO in next 3, 2 sc-FLO in next] twice; with **A**, [sc in next 3, 2 sc in next] twice–30 sc.
Rnds 13–14: Sc in next 10 sts; with **D**, sc-FLO in next 10; with **A**, sc in next 10.
Rnd 15: [Sc in next 4 sts, 2 sc in next] twice; with **C**, [sc-FLO in next 4, 2 sc-FLO in next] twice; with **A**, [sc in next 4, 2 sc in next] twice–36 sc.
Rnds 16–17: Sc in next 12 sts; with **C**, sc-FLO in next 12; with **A**, sc in next 12.
Rnd 18: [Sc in next 5 sts, 2 sc in next] twice; with **C**, [sc-FLO in next 5, 2 sc-FLO in next] twice; with **A**, [sc in next 5, 2 sc in next] twice–42 sc.
Rnd 19: Sc in next 14 sts; with **C**, sc-FLO in next 14; with **A**, sc in next 14.
Rnd 20: Sc in next 14 sts, with **D**, sc-FLO in next 14; with **A**, sc in next 14.
Rnd 21: [Sc in next 6, 2 sc in next] twice; with **D**, [sc-FLO in next 6, 2 sc-FLO in next] twice; with **A**, [sc in next 6, 2 sc in next] twice–48 sc.
Rnds 22–24: Sc in next 14 sts, sc-BLO in next 2; with **D**, sc-FLO in next 16; with **A**, sc in next 16.
Fasten off **D**.
Rnd 25: Sc in next 14 sts, sc-BLO in next 2; with **C**, sc-FLO in next 16; with **A**, sc in next 16.
Rnd 26: [Sc in next 4 sts, inv-dec] twice, sc in next 2, sc-BLO in next 2; with **C**, inv-dec, [sc-FLO in next 4, inv-dec] twice, sc-FLO in next 2; with **A**, sc in next 2, inv-dec, [sc in next 4, inv-dec] twice–40 sc.
Rnds 27–29: Sc in next 12 sts, sc-BLO in next 2; with **C**, sc-FLO in next 13; with **A**, sc in next 13.
Fasten off **C**.
Rnd 30: Sc in next 40 sts, join.
Fasten off with a long tail. Do not stuff.

LEFT EAR

Begin with **A**.
Rnds 1–21: Repeat Rnds 1–21 of Right Ear.
Rnds 22–24: Sc in next 16 sts; with **D**, sc-FLO in next 16; with **A**, sc-BLO in next 2, sc in next 14.
Rnd 25: Sc in next 16 sts; with **C**, sc-FLO in next 16; with **A**, sc-BLO in next 2, sc in next 14.
Rnd 26: [Sc in next 4 sts, inv-dec] twice, sc in next 4; with **C**, inv-dec, [sc-FLO in next 4, inv-dec] twice, sc-FLO in next 2; with **A**, sc-BLO in next 2, inv-dec, [sc in next 4, inv-dec] twice–40 sc.
Rnds 27–29: Sc in next 14; with **C**, sc-FLO in next 13; with **A**, sc-BLO in next 2, sc in next 11. Fasten off **C**.
Rnd 30: Sc in next 40 sts, join.
Fasten off with a long tail. Do not stuff.

EAR TUFTS

Cut 32 lengths of **A** measuring 3½ in. / 9 cm. Loop 1 length through each unworked front loop of Rnds 22–29 of both Ears, pull ends through loop, and tighten. Trim using pictures as a guide.

Attach Ears to Head over 10 sts at Rnds 5–6:

Flatten Ear and roll vertically so only two **A** sts are visible at the edge. Fold opposite side one third inward. Sew through both thicknesses at bottom of Ear. Sew Ear to Head curving slightly. Weave ends in.

TORSO

With **B**, ch 16, join to first ch and ch 1.
Rnd 1: Sc in same ch as join and in each ch around–16 sc.
Begin working in continuous rounds. Use a st marker to keep track of rounds.
Rnd 2: Sc in each st around.
Rnd 3: [2 sc in next] 16 times–32 sc.
Rnd 4: [Sc in next 3 sts, 2 sc in next] 8 times–40 sc.
Rnd 5: Sc-FLO in next 6 sts; with **A**, sc in next, 2 sc in next, sc in next 2, 2 sc in next, sc in next; with **B**, sc-FLO in next 13; with **A**, sc in next, 2 sc in next, sc in next; with **B**, sc-FLO in next 2; with **A**, sc in next, 2 sc in next, sc in next; with **B**, sc-FLO in next 7–44 sc.
Rnd 6: Sc-FLO in next 4 sts, inv-dec; with **A**, 2 sc in next, sc in next 6, 2 sc in next; with **B**, inv-dec, sc-FLO in next 9, inv-dec; with **A**, 2 sc in next, sc in next 3; with **B**, sc-FLO in next 2; with **A**, sc in next 3, 2 sc in next; with **B**, inv-dec, sc-FLO in next 5.
Rnd 7: Sc-FLO in next 3 sts, inv-dec; with **A**, 2 sc in next, sc in next 8, 2 sc in next; with **B**, inv-dec, sc-FLO in next 7, inv-dec; with **A**, 2 sc in next, sc in next 4; with **B**, sc-FLO in next 2; with **A**, sc in next 4, 2 sc in next; with **B**, inv-dec, sc-FLO in next 4.
Rnd 8: Sc-FLO in next 2 sts, inv-dec; with **A**, 2 sc in next, sc in next 10, 2 sc in next; with **B**, inv-dec, sc-FLO in next 5, inv-dec; with **A**, 2 sc in next, sc in next 5; with **B**, sc-FLO in next 2; with **A**, sc in next 5, 2 sc in next; with **B**, inv-dec, sc-FLO in next 3.
Rnd 9: Sc-FLO in next st, inv-dec; with **A**, 2 sc in next, sc in next 12, 2 sc in next; with **B**, inv-dec, sc-FLO in next 3, inv-dec; with **A**, 2 sc in next, sc in next 6; with **B**, sc-FLO in next 2; with **A**, sc in next 6, 2 sc in next; with **B**, inv-dec, sc-FLO in next 2.
Rnds 10–11: Sc-FLO in next 2 sts; with **A**, sc in next 16; with **B**, sc-FLO in next 5; with **A**, sc in next 8; with **B**, sc-FLO in next 2; with **A**, sc in next 8; with **B**, sc-FLO in next 3.
Begin stuffing Torso firmly.
Rnd 12: Inv-dec; with **A**, 2 sc in next st, sc in next 6, inv-dec, sc in next 6, 2 sc in next; with **B**, inv-dec, sc-FLO in next, inv-dec; with **A**, 2 sc in next, sc in next 7; with **B**, sc-FLO in next, 2 sc in next; with **A**, sc in next 7, 2 sc in next; with **B**, inv-dec, sc-FLO in next.
Rnds 13–16: Sc-FLO in next st; with **A**, sc in next 17; with **B**, sc-FLO in next 3; with **A**, sc in next 9; sc-FLO in next 3; with **A**, sc in next 9; with **B**, sc-FLO in next 2.
Rnd 17: Sc-FLO in next st; with **A**, sc in next 8, inv-dec, sc in next 7; with **B**, sc-FLO in next 3; with **A**, sc in next 9; with **B**, sc-FLO in next 2, 2 sc in next; with **A**, sc in next 9; with **B**, sc-FLO in next 2.
Rnd 18: Sc-FLO in next st; with **A**, sc in next 16; with **B**, sc-FLO in next 3; with **A**, sc in next 9; with **B**, sc-FLO in next 4; with **A**, sc in next 9; with **B**, sc-FLO in next 2.
Rnd 19: 2 sc-FLO in next st; with **A**, inv-dec, sc in next 12, inv-dec; with **B**, 2 sc-FLO in next, sc-FLO in next, 2 sc-FLO in next; with **A**, inv-dec, sc in next 7; with **B**, sc-FLO in next 4; with **A**, sc in next 7, inv-dec; with **B**, 2 sc-FLO in next, sc-FLO in next.
Rnd 20: Sc-FLO in next 2 sts; with **A**, [sc in next, inv-dec] 4 times, sc in next 2; with **B**, sc-FLO in next 5; with **A**, [sc in next, inv-dec] twice, sc in next 2; with **B**, sc-FLO in next 4; with **A**, sc in next 2, [inv-dec, sc in next] twice; with **B**, sc-FLO in next 3–36 sc.
Continue to stuff Torso firmly.
Rnd 21: Sc-FLO in next 2 sts; with **A**, [sc in next 3, inv-dec] twice; with **B**, sc-FLO in next, inv-dec, sc-FLO in next 2; with **A**, [inv-dec, sc in next] twice; with **B**, sc-FLO in next 4; with **A**, [sc in next, inv-dec] twice; with **B**, sc-FLO in next, inv-dec, join, change to **A** and ch 1–28 sc.
Rnd 22: [Sc in next 2 sts, inv-dec] 7 times–21 sc.
Finish stuffing firmly.
Rnd 23: [Sc in next st, inv-dec] 7 times–14 sc.
Rnd 24: [Inv-dec] 7 times–7 sc.
Fasten off and sew closed.

Attach Torso to Head:

Use tail to sew Head to Torso, ensuring Head and **A** section of Torso (sts 2–18 of Rnds 13–16) are facing forward. Stuff neck firmly before completing seam. Weave ends in.

THIGH (MAKE 2)

With **A**.
Rnd 1: Ch 8, sc in second ch from hook, sc in next 2, 2 sc in next, sc in next 2, 2 sc in last, rotate to work under starting ch, sc in next 3, 2 sc in next, sc in next 2, 2 sc in last–18 sc.
Begin working in continuous rounds. Use a st marker to keep track of rounds.
Rnd 2: 2 sc in next st, sc in next 6, [2 sc in next] 3 times, sc in next 6, [2 sc in next] twice–24 sc.
Rnd 3: [Sc in next st, 2 sc in next] 12 times–36 sc.

Rnds 4–6: Sc in next 2 sts; with **B**, sc in next 14; with **A**, sc in next 20.
Fasten off **B**.
Rnd 7: Inv-dec, sc in next 14 sts, inv-dec, sc in next 18–34 sc.
Rnd 8: Sc in next st, [sc in next 2, inv-dec] 8 times, sc in next, join–26 sc.
Fasten off with a long tail.

Attach Thighs to Torso:

Stuff Thigh. Sew Thigh to bottom third of Torso using tail and using pictures as a guide, with **B** section toward back. Weave ends in.

FOOT (MAKE 2)

With **A**, make a MR and ch 1.
Rnd 1: 8 sc in MR and pull tail to close–8 sc.
Begin working in continuous rounds. Use a st marker to keep track of rounds.
Rnd 2: [Sc in next st, 2 sc in next] 4 times–12 sc.
Rnds 3–8: Sc in each st around.
Rnd 9: [Sc in next, inv-dec] 4 times–8 sc.
Rnd 10: Sc in each st around, join.
Fasten off with a long tail. Do not stuff.
Attach Feet to Thighs:
Flatten Foot and sew to bottom of Thigh angling it away from center of Torso. Weave ends in.

ARMS/HANDS (MAKE 2)

With **A**, make a MR and ch 1.
Rnd 1: 6 sc in MR and pull tail to close–6 sc.
Begin working in continuous rounds. Use a st marker to keep track of rounds.
Rnd 2: [Sc in next st, 2 sc in next] 3 times–9 sc.
Rnds 3–6: Sc in each st around.
Rnd 7: [Sc in next, inv-dec] 3 times–6 sc.
Rnds 8–9: Sc-FLO in each st around.
Rnd 10: [Sc in next 2 sts, 2 sc in next] twice–8 sc.
Rnds 11–13: Sc in each st around.
Rnd 14: [Sc in next 3 sts, 2 sc in next] twice–10 sc.
Rnds 15–24: Sc in each st around. After last rnd, join and ch 1.
Create shoulder cap by working in rows as follows:
Row 1: Sc2tog, sc in next 3 sts, sc2tog, ch 1 and turn–5 sc.
Row 2: Sc in each st across, ch 1 and turn.
Row 3: Sc2tog, sc in next, sc2tog, ch 1 and turn–3 sc.
Row 4: Sc3tog–1 sc.
Fasten off with a long tail.

Attach Arms/Hands to Torso:

Sew beginning of Arm to **B** section of Torso approximately 6 rnds from Thigh, lightly stuffing as you go.

TAIL

With **B**, make a MR and ch 1.
Rnd 1: 8 sc in MR and pull tail to close–8 sc.
Begin working in continuous rounds. Use a st marker to keep track of rounds.
Rnds 2–4: Sc in each st around. After last rnd, change to **A**.
Rnd 5: Sl st-BLO in each st around.
Rnd 6: Sc-BLO in each st around.
Rnd 7: Sc in each st around, change to **B**.
Rnd 8: Sl st-BLO in each st around.
Rnd 9: Sc-BLO in each st around.
Rnd 10: Sc in each st around. At the end of Rnd 10, change to **A** and do NOT ch.
Rnds 11–15: Repeat Rnds 5–9.
Rnds 16–45: Sc in each st around. After last rnd, join.
Fasten off with a long tail. Do not stuff.

FINISHING (WITHOUT WIRE)

Attach Tail to Torso:

Sew Tail to bottom of back side of Torso, aligned with last 3 rounds of back-centered **B** section. Weave ends in.

FINISHING (WITH WIRE)

Attaching Tail to Torso:

Cut a 9 in. / 23 cm length of wire. Bend ¼ in. / 0.6 cm of end onto itself to blunt. Insert blunt end almost entirely into hollow center of Tail. Bend other end into a spiral shape over 1 in. / 2.5 cm. Push spiral completely inside Torso between twenty-fifth and twenty-sixth sts of Rnd 20. Sew Tail to Torso. Weave ends in.

TURTLE-DUCK

Designed by
LIZETTE MEJIA

Skill Level:
BEGINNER

Turtle-ducks, the adorable combination of a cute duck face and a strong turtle shell, are often found in ponds in the Earth Kingdom and Fire Nation, including the royal pond at the palace of the Fire Nation. They are very gentle and friendly animals and will readily accept food, such as breadcrumbs. Prince Zuko and his mother, Ursa, would feed the turtle-ducks that inhabited their garden.

The turtle-duck is now a super soft and huggable crochet creation made just for you! Crochet his little face and shell and enjoy lots of cuddles from this cute creature, no water required.

Young Zuko: Stupid turtle-duck.
Why she'd do that?
Ursa: Zuko. That's what moms are like.
If you mess with their babies, they're gonna bite you back!

(Book 2, Episode 7)

FINISHED MEASUREMENTS

Height: 4 in. / 10 cm • Width: 4.5 in. / 11.5 cm • Length: 6.5 in. / 16.5 cm

YARN

Worsted weight (#4, Medium), shown in Lion Brand *Skein Tones* (100% Acrylic, 185 yd. / 170 m per 3.5 oz. / 100 g ball)
Color A: 125AA Truffle, 1 ball
Color B: 122T Hazelnut, 1 ball
Color C: 134U Honey, 1 ball
And worsted weight (#4, Medium), shown in Lion Brand *Color Theory* (100% Acrylic, 246 yd. / 225 m per 3.5 oz. / 100 g ball)
Color D: 158AI Bee Pollen, 1 ball
And worsted weight (#4, Medium), shown in Lion Brand *Basic Stitch* (100% Acrylic, 185 yd. / 169 m per 3.5 oz. / 100 g ball)
Color E: 102W Clay, 1 ball
And worsted weight (#4, Medium), shown in WeCrochet *Swish* (100% Merino Wool, 110 yd. / 101 m per 1.75 oz. / 50 g ball)
Color F: N4136 Shortbread, 1 ball

HOOK

US D-3 / 3.25 mm, *or size needed to obtain gauge*

NOTIONS

Stitch markers • Tapestry needle • Polyester stuffing • 12 mm safety eyes • Scissors

GAUGE

24 dc and 12 dc rows = 4 in. / 10 cm; *make sure to check your gauge.*

ABBREVIATIONS

Back loop only (BLO), chain(s) (ch(s)), double crochet (dc), front loop only (FLO), half double crochet (hdc), single crochet (sc), slip stitch(es) (sl st(s)), stitch(es) (st(s)), two double crochet closed together (dc2tog), yarn over (yo).

SPECIAL ABBREVIATIONS

inv-dec (invisible single crochet decrease): Insert hook in FLO of each of next 2 sts, yo and draw through both sts, yo and draw through 2 loops on hook–1 st decreased.

NOTES

When referring to the "left" or "right," it is from the perspective of the Doll facing you.

FLIPPERS (MAKE 4)

With C.
Rnd 1: Ch 8, sl st to first ch to form a ring, sc in each ch–8 sc.
Rnd 2: Sc in next 7 sts, 2 sc in next–9 sc.
Rnd 3: Sc in next 9 sts.
Row 4: Flatten and work 4 sl sts through both thicknesses–4 sl sts.
Row 5: Turn, ch 4, sl st in first sl st, [ch 4, sl st in next sl st] 3 times–4 toes.
Do not stuff. Fasten off, weave in ends.

BEAK

With E.
Rnd 1: Ch 5, starting in second ch from hook sc in next 3, 3 sc in last, continue on opposite side of ch, sc in next 3–9 sc.
Rnd 2: [2 sc in next st, sc in next] 4 times, sc in next–13 sc.
Rnd 3: Sc in next 6 sts, 2 sc in next, sc in next 5, 2 sc in next–15 sc.
Fasten off with a long tail. Fold Beak flat. Beginning ch-5 is outside front tip of Beak and where you fastened off is left side of Beak.

TAIL

With F, make a magic ring.
Rnd 1: 4 sc in magic ring–4 sc.
Rnd 2: [2 sc in next st] 4 times–8 sc.
Rnd 3: Sc in next 8 sts.
Rnd 4: [2 sc in next st, sc in next] 4 times–12 sc.
Rnd 5: [2 sc in next st] 4 times, sc in next 8–16 sc.
Rnd 6: [2 sc in next st] 5 times, [inv-dec] 5 times, sc in next–16 sc.
Rnd 7: Sc in next 8 sts, dc in next 7, hdc in next–16 sts.
Stuff. Close opening by flattening it and working 8 sl sts through both thicknesses. Tail should curl up when attached to the Duck. Fasten off.

HEAD

With C, make a magic ring.
Rnd 1: 6 sc in magic ring, pull tight to close–6 sc.
Rnd 2: [2 sc in next st] 6 times–12 sc.
Rnd 3: Join with **F**, 2 sc in next st, sc in next; with **C**, sc in next, 2 sc in next, sc in next 2; with **F**, 2 sc in next, sc in next 2; with **C**, 2 sc in next, sc in next 2–16 sc.
Rnd 4: With **F**, [2 sc in next st, sc in next] twice; with **C**, sc in next 4; with **F**, [sc in next, 2 sc in next] twice; with **C**, sc in next 4–20 sc.
Rnd 5: With **F**, 2 sc in next st, sc in next 3, 2 sc in next, sc in next; with **C**, sc in next 2, 2 sc in next, sc in next; with **F**, sc in next 2, 2 sc in next, sc in next 3; with **C**, sc in next 3, 2 sc in next–25 sc.
Rnd 6: 2 sc in next st; with **F**, sc in next 4, 2 sc in next, sc in next 3; with **C**, sc in next, 2 sc in next, sc in next 2; with **F**, sc in next 2, 2 sc in next, sc in next 4; with **C**, 2 sc in next, sc in next 4–30 sc.
Rnd 7: Sc in next st, 2 sc in next; with **F**, sc in next 5, 2 sc in next, sc in next 4; with **C**, sc in next, 2 sc in next, sc in next 2; with **F**, [sc in next 3, 2 sc in next] twice; with **C**, 2 sc in next, sc in next 5–36 sc.
Rnd 8: Sc in next 5 sts; with **F**, sc in next 10; with **C**, sc in next 4; with **F**, sc in next 10; with **C**, sc in next 7.
Rnd 9: Sc in next 8 sts; with **F**, sc in next 8; with **C**, sc in next 2; with **F**, sc in next 8; with **C**, sc in next 10.
Rnd 10: Sc in next 11 sts; with **F**, sc in next 5; with **C**, sc in next 2; with **F**, sc in next 5; with **C**, sc in next 13.
Rnd 11: Sc in next 4 sts; with **F**, [2 sc in next] 7 times, sc in next 5; with **C**, sc in next 2; with **F**, sc in next 5, [2 sc in next] 7 times; with **C**, sc in next 6–50 sc.
Rnds 12–13: Sc in next 4 sts; with **F**, sc in next 42; with **C**, sc in next 4.
Insert safety eyes between Rnds 10–11 with 9 sts between them.
Rnd 14: Sc in next 3 sts, inv-dec; with **F**, [sc in next 3, inv-dec] 8 times, sc in next 2; with **C**, sc in next, inv-dec–40 sc.
Rnd 15: Sc in next 2 sts, inv-dec; with **F**, [sc in next 2, inv-dec] 8 times, sc in next 2; with **C**, inv-dec–30 sc.
Rnd 16: Sc in next 3 sts; with **F**, sc in next 26; with **C**, sc in next.
Stuff.
Rnd 17: Inv-dec, sc in next st; with **F**, [inv-dec, sc in next] 3 times, sc in next 7, [inv-dec, sc in next] 3 times, inv-dec–22 sc.
Rnd 18: [Sc in next 2, inv-dec] 5 times, sc in next 2–17 sc.
Rnd 19: Sc in next 17 sts.

Rnd 20: Sc in next 8 sts, 2 sc in next, sc in next 8–18 sc.
Rnds 21–22: Sc in next 18 sts.
Rnd 23: Sc in next 5 sts.
Do not fasten off. Pin Beak in a curved shape with center lined up between Rnds 11–12, where **C** ends. Pin sides between Rnds 13–14. Sew Beak to Head with long tail.
Set aside while you complete Rnds 1–9 of Shell.

SHELL

Starting with **A**.
Rnd 1: Ch 7, starting in second ch from hook sc in next 5, 4 sc in last, continue on opposite side of ch, sc in next 5, 2 sc in last ch–16 sc.

Rnd 2: 2 sc in next st, dc in next 2, 2 dc in next, dc in next, [2 dc in next] 4 times, dc in next, 2 dc in next, dc in next 2, sc in next, [2 sc in next] twice–25 sts.
Rnd 3: [2 sc in next st] twice, [dc in next, 2 dc in next] 3 times, dc in next, [2 sc in next] 4 times, [dc in next, 2 dc in next] 3 times, dc in next 3, [2 sc in next] 3 times–40 sts.
Rnd 4: Sc in next 5 sts, dc in next 10, sc in next 10, dc in next 10, sc in next 5.
Rnd 5: Sc in next 5 sts, [dc in next 2, 2 dc in next] 3 times, dc in next 11, [2 dc in next, dc in next 2] twice, 2 dc in next, dc in next 3, sc in next 5–46 sts.
Rnd 6: Sc in next 5 sts, dc in next 36, sc in next 5.
Rnd 7: [2 sc in next st, sc in next] twice, 2 hdc in next, [dc in next 3, 2 dc in next] 9 times, 2 hdc in next, [sc in next, 2 sc in next] twice–61 sts.
Rnd 8: [Sc in next st, 2 sc in next] 3 times, hdc in next 2, [dc in next 4, 2 dc in next] 9 times, hdc in next 2, [2 sc in next, sc in next] twice, 2 sc in next, sl st in next (counts as a st here)–76 sts.
With **B**.
Rnd 9: Ch 2, dc-FLO in next 76, sl st to beginning ch 2–76 sts.
Fasten off with a long tail.
Rnd 10 (Join Head): Using back loops from Rnd 9 of Shell and starting 3 sts to the right of where that rnd ended, join with **F**. Insert hook in first st of Head and indicated st on Shell, sc through both thicknesses, repeat 5 more times for a total of 6 sc through both thicknesses.
Continue working into Shell only: sc in next 11 sts; with **D**, sc in next 20; with **F**, sc in next 8; with **D**, sc in next 20; with **F**, sc in next 11–76 sc.
Rnd 11 (Join Tail): Starting in unworked sts of neck, sc in next st, dc in next 10, sc in next; next sts will be made in Shell sts only: sc in next 7; with **C**, sc in next 4; with **D**, [sc in next 2, inv-dec] 3 times; with **C**, sc in next 4; with **D**, sc in next 2, inv-dec; with **F**, join Tail with 8 sc through both thicknesses (last row of Tail and sts on Shell); with **D**, sc in next 2, inv-dec; with **C**, sc in next 4; with **D**, [sc in next 2, inv-dec] 3 times; with **C**, sc in next 4; with **F**, sc in next 7–68 sts.
Continue stuffing neck as you go.
Rnd 12 (Join Flippers): [2 dc in next st, dc in next] 6 times, dc in next 2, hdc in next, [inv-dec] twice; with **C** and bottom of Flipper facing make 4 sc through both thicknesses (first row of Flipper and sts on Shell); with **D**, sc in next 9; with **C**, join next Flipper with 4 sc through both thicknesses as established; with **D**, sc in next 14; with **C**, join next Flipper with 4 sc through both thicknesses as established; with **D**, sc in next 9; with **C**, join last Flipper with 4 sc through both thicknesses as established; with **F**, [inv-dec] twice, hdc in next, dc in next 2–76 sts.
Rnd 13: [Dc in next st, dc2tog] 7 times, sc in next 2; with **D**, sc in next 48; with **F**, sc in next, [inv-dec] twice–67 sts.
Rnd 14: [Dc in next 2 sts, dc2tog] 4 times; with **D**, sc in next 48; with **F**, sc in next, inv-dec–62 sts.
Rnds 15–16: Dc in next 12 sts; with **D**, sc in next 48; with **F**, sc in next 2.
Rnd 17: Hdc in next 2 sts, [dc2tog] 4 times, hdc in next 2; with **D**, [sc in next 4, inv-dec] 8 times, sc in next 2–50 sts.
Rnd 18: [Inv-dec, sc in next 3 sts] 10 times–40 sc.
Rnd 19: [Sc in next 2 sts, inv-dec] 10 times–30 sc.
Rnd 20: [Inv-dec, sc in next st] 10 times–20 sc.
Rnd 21: [Inv-dec] 10 times–10 sc.
Rnd 22: [Inv-dec] 5 times–5 sc.
Fasten off and close opening by sewing through front loops of next 5 sts.
Weave ends in. Sew Head back by going through Rnd 17 of neck, then directly across from it through Shell as many times as needed to secure.

OTTER-PENGUIN

Designed by
NICOLE ROGOWSKI

Skill Level:
BEGINNER

When you live in a world surrounded by ice and water, what do you do for fun? Build a snowman? Have a snowball fight? How about sledding on an otter-penguin? When Aang first emerges from the iceberg, one of his first requests is to catch an otter-penguin and go for a ride down the slopes!

This black-and-white creature is a beginner-friendly crochet pattern, and a great place to start if you have never made an amigurumi before! Although your crocheted otter-penguin is super cute, we don't recommend taking him for a sledding adventure—stick to real otter-penguins for that!

Aang: I need to ask you something . . .
Katara: What?
Aang: Please . . . come closer.
Katara: What is it?
Aang: Will you go penguin sledding with me?

(Book 1, Episode 1)

FINISHED MEASUREMENTS

Height: 5½ in. / 14 cm • Width: 5 in. / 12.5 cm

YARN

Worsted weight (#4, Medium) yarn, shown in Lion Brand *Basic Stitch* (100% Acrylic, 185 yd. / 169 m per 3.5 oz. / 100 g ball)
Color A: 153 Black, 1 ball
Color B: 100 White, 1 ball
Color C: 158I Mustard, 1 ball

HOOK

US E-4 / 3.5 mm, *or size needed to obtain gauge*

NOTIONS

Stitch markers • Tapestry needle • Polyester stuffing • 10 x 8 mm black safety nose • Black thread • 16-gauge craft wire • Wire cutters • Needle-nosed jewelry pliers • Scissors

GAUGE

20 sc and 24 sc rounds = 4 in. / 10 cm; *make sure to check your gauge.*

ABBREVIATIONS

Back loop only (BLO), chain(s) (ch(s)), double crochet (dc), fasten off (FO), front loop only (FLO), half double crochet (hdc), magic ring (MR), right side (RS), single crochet (sc), skip (sk), slip stitch(es) (sl st(s)), stitch(es) (st(s)), two single crochet closed together (sc2tog), wrong side (WS), yarn over (yo).

SPECIAL ABBREVIATIONS

inv-dec (invisible single crochet decrease): Insert hook in FLO of each of next 2 sts, yo and draw through both sts, yo and draw through 2 loops on hook—1 st decreased.

NOTES

Use of front loops in certain sections keeps stitches from slanting while working continuously in the round. Work in continuous rounds unless otherwise indicated. When instructed to join, join with a slip stitch in first stitch.

BODY

With **A**, make a MR and ch 1.
Rnd 1: 8 sc in MR and pull tail to close–8 sc.
Begin working in continuous rounds. Use a st marker to keep track of rounds.
Rnd 2: Sc-FLO in next 2 sts; with **B**, sc in next 4; with **A**, sc-FLO in next 2.
Rnd 3: [2 sc-FLO in next st] twice; [with **B**, 2 sc in next] 4 times; [with **A**, 2 sc-FLO in next] twice–16 sc.
Rnds 4–5: Sc-FLO in next 4 sts; with **B**, sc in next 8; with **A**, sc-FLO in next 4.
Rnd 6: [Sc-FLO in next st, 2 sc-FLO in next] twice; with **B**, [sc in next, 2 sc in next] 4 times; with **A**, [sc-FLO in next, 2 sc-FLO in next] twice–24 sc.
Rnds 7–10: Sc-FLO in next 6 sts; with **B**, sc in next 12; with **A**, sc-FLO in next 6.
Rnd 11: [Sc-FLO in next st, 2 sc-FLO in next] 3 times; with **B**, [sc in next, 2 sc in next] 6 times; with **A**, [sc-FLO in next, 2 sc-FLO in next] 3 times–36 sc.
Rnd 12: Sc-FLO in next 9 sts; with **B**, sc in next 18; with **A**, sc-FLO in next 9.
Rnd 13: [Sc-FLO in next 2 sts, 2 sc-FLO in next] 3 times; with **B**, [sc in next 2, 2 sc in next] 6 times; with **A**, [sc-FLO in next 2, 2 sc-FLO in next] 3 times–48 sc.
Lightly stuff tail.
Rnds 14–22: Sc-FLO in next 12 sts; with **B**, sc in next 24; with **A**, sc-FLO in next 12.
Begin to stuff Body firmly.
Rnd 23: [Sc-FLO in next 4 sts, inv-dec] twice; with **B**, [sc in next 4, inv-dec] 4 times; with **A**, [sc-FLO in next 4, inv-dec] twice–40 sc.
Rnd 24: Sc-FLO in next 10 sts; with **B**, sc in next 20; with **A**, sc-FLO in next 10.
Rnd 25: [Sc-FLO in next 3 sts, inv-dec] twice; with **B**, [sc in next 3, inv-dec] 4 times; with **A**, [sc-FLO in next 3, inv-dec] twice–32 sc.
Rnds 26–27: Sc-FLO in next 8 sts; with **B**, sc in next 16; with **A**, sc-FLO in next 8.
Rnd 28: Sc-FLO in next 6 sts, inv-dec; with **B**, [sc in next 6, inv-dec] twice; with **A**, sc-FLO in next 6, inv-dec–28 sc.
Rnds 29: Sc-FLO in next 7 sts; with **B**, sc in next 14; with **A**, sc-FLO in next 7.
Continue stuffing firmly.
Rnd 30: Sc-FLO in next 3 sts, inv-dec; with **B**, 2 sc in next, sc in next, [2 sc-FLO in next] 14 times, sc in next, 2 sc in next; with **A**, inv-dec, sc-FLO in next 3–42 sc.
Rnds 31–33: Sc-FLO in next 4 sts; with **B**, sc in next 34; with **A**, sc-FLO in next 4.
Place a st marker around post of seventeenth and twenty-fifth sts of Rnd 33 to help with placement of Whiskers.
Rnd 34: Sc-FLO in next 3 sts, 2 sc-FLO in next; with **B**, inv-dec, sc in next 30, inv-dec; with **A**, 2 sc-FLO in next, sc-FLO in next 3.
Rnd 35: Sc-FLO in next 4 sts, 2 sc-FLO in next; with **B**, inv-dec, sc in next 13; with **A**, sc-FLO in next 2; with **B**, sc in next 13, inv-dec; with **A**, 2 sc-FLO in next, sc-FLO in next 4.
Rnd 36: Sc-FLO in next 5 sts, 2 sc-FLO in next; with **B**, inv-dec, [sc in next 2, inv-dec] 3 times; with **A**, sc-FLO in next 2; with **B**, inv-dec, [sc in next 2, inv-dec] 3 times; with A, 2 sc-FLO in next, sc-FLO in next 5–36 sc.
Rnd 37: Sc-FLO in next 2 sts, inv-dec, sc-FLO in next 2, 2 sc-FLO in next; with **B**, [inv-dec] twice, [sc in next, inv-dec] twice; with **A**, [2 sc-FLO in next] twice; with **B**, [inv-dec, sc in next] twice, [inv-dec] twice; with **A**, 2 sc-FLO in next, sc-FLO in next 2, inv-dec, sc-FLO in next 2–30 sc.
Fasten off **B**. Insert safety nose at eighteenth st, between Rnds 31–32.
Rnd 38: [Inv-dec] 3 times, sc in next st, sl st in next 7, inv-dec, sl st in next 7, sc in next, [inv-dec] 3 times–23 sts.
Rnd 39: Inv-dec, sc in next st, [sc2tog-BLO, sc-BLO] twice, sc2tog-BLO, sc in next, [sc2tog-BLO, sc-BLO] twice, sc2tog-BLO, sc in next, inv-dec–15 sc.
Continue stuffing firmly.
Rnd 40: [Sc in next st, inv-dec] 5 times, join–10 sc.
Fasten off. Use tail to close opening and set aside.

EYES

Using **A**, embroider a thin almond shape over 4 sts in Rnds 34–35, 3 sts away from nose and using pictures as a guide.

WHISKERS

Cut four 4 in. / 10 cm lengths of black thread. Fold two lengths in half, creating a loop at the fold. Insert hook around post of first marked st of Rnd 33 and pull loop through. Pull lengths through loop. Trim Whiskers to ½ in. / 1.5 cm. Repeat with remaining lengths and second marked stitch.

WING (MAKE 4)

With **A**, make a MR and ch 1.
Rnd 1: 6 sc in MR and pull tail to close–6 sc.
Begin working in continuous rounds. Use a st marker to keep track of rounds.
Rnd 2: Sc-FLO in next 2 sts; with **B**, sc in next 3; with **A**, sc-FLO in next.
Rnd 3: [2 sc-FLO in next] twice; with **B**, [2 sc in next] 3 times; with **A**, 2 sc-FLO in next–12 sc.
Rnd 4: Sc-FLO in next 4 sts; with **B**, sc in next 6; with **A**, sc-FLO in next 2.
Rnd 5: 2 sc-FLO in next st, sc-FLO in next 2, 2 sc-FLO in next; with **B**, [sc in next 2, 2 sc in next] twice; with **A**, sc-FLO in next 2–16 sc.
Rnds 6–10: Sc-FLO in next 6 sts; with **B**, sc in next 8; with **A**, sc-FLO in next 2.
Rnd 11: Inv-dec, sc-FLO in next 2 sts, inv-dec; with **B**, [sc in next 2, inv-dec] twice; with **A**, sc-FLO in next–12 sc.
Fasten off **B**.
Rnd 12: Sl st-BLO in each st around, join. Fasten off with a long tail. Using pictures as a guide, use tail to sew Wings to Body.

LEG (MAKE 2)

With **B**.
Rnd 1: Leaving a long tail ch 12, join to form a ring and ch 1. Working all sts in back bump of chs, sc in same ch as join and in each ch around–12 sc.
Begin working in continuous rounds. Use a st marker to keep track of rounds.
Rnd 2: [Inv-dec] 6 times, join, change to **C** and ch 1–6 sc.
Rnd 3: Sc-FLO in same st as join, sc in next 3, inv-dec–5 sc.
Rnd 4: Sc-FLO in each st around, join. Fasten off. Set aside.

FOOT (MAKE 2)

With **C** and leaving a long tail, make a MR and ch 1.
Rnd 1: Work following sts in MR: Sc, hdc, dc, *dc, ch 3, sl st in second ch from hook, sc in next ch, hdc in ring, repeat from * twice, sc in ring, join–13 sts. Fasten off with a long tail.

FINISHING (WITHOUT WIRE)

Attach Feet to Legs: Using tail, sew Foot to top of Rnd 4 of Leg. Weave ends in. Repeat for second Foot.
Attach Legs to Body: Using tail, sew Rnd 1 of Leg to bottom of **A** section of Body, lightly stuffing Leg as you sew. Attach second Leg 5 sts away from first Leg.

FINISHING (WITH WIRE)

Cut a 10 in. / 25.5 cm length of wire. Shape one end of wire into a small circle (½ in. / 1.3 cm in diameter) and bend remaining length perpendicular to circle. Insert end between first and last sts of Rnd 1 of Foot, from WS to RS. Using MR tail, sew wire circle to WS of Foot. Continue to insert wire through bottom of Leg (in at **C** and out at **B** sections). Using tail, sew Foot to top of Leg at Rnd 6. With toe facing forward, bend wire at a 90-degree angle at top of Leg. Insert wire into Body between thirteenth and fourteenth sts of Rnd 12 and out between twenty-third and twenty-fourth sts of same rnd. Pull on wire until bend is at first insertion point. Using tail, sew Leg to Rnd 1 of Body lightly stuffing as you go. Bend wire at a 90-degree angle where it exited Body. Insert wire in second Leg, pushing it through **C** section of bottom of Leg. Sew Leg to Rnd 1 of Body. Insert wire in Foot from RS to WS. Sew Foot to Leg, with toe facing forward. Shape end of wire into a small circle (½ in. / 1.3 cm in diameter) and bend perpendicular to Leg. Trim excess wire. Sew wire circle to WS of Foot. Weave all ends in.

TUI AND LA

Designed by
SARAH CSIACSEK

Skill Level:
BEGINNER

Tui and La are connected spirits representing, respectively, the moon and the ocean. Their mortal forms are manifested as a white koi fish (Tui) and a black koi fish (La), embodying the push and pull between the moon and the tides, forever circling each other in the water of the North Pole's Spirit Oasis. On their adventures, Aang and his friends realize the importance of Tui and La, and they vow to protect them at all costs.

These simple little fish are sure to make a good addition to your home, and if you are very lucky, they may just give you some insight or ancient wisdom about the art of crochet with their beginner-friendly stitches and easy shaping!

"Tui and La, your Moon and Ocean, have always circled each other in an eternal dance. They balance each other, push and pull, life and death, good and evil, yin and yang."

—KOH (Book 1, Episode 20)

FINISHED MEASUREMENTS
Height: 7.5 in. / 19 cm · Width: 5 in. / 12.7 cm

YARN
Worsted weight (#4, Medium), shown in Lion Brand *Basic Stitch* (100% Acrylic, 185 yd. / 169 m per 3.5 oz. / 100 g ball)
Color A: 153 Black, 1 ball
Color B: 100 White, 1 ball

HOOK
US G-6 / 4 mm, *or size needed to obtain gauge*

NOTIONS
Stitch markers · Tapestry needle · Polyester stuffing · 12 mm black safety eyes · 12 mm white safety eyes · Scissors

GAUGE
20 sc and 20 sc rounds = 4 in. / 10 cm; *make sure to check your gauge.*

ABBREVIATIONS
Back loop only (BLO), chain(s) (ch(s)), fasten off (FO), front loop only (FLO), single crochet (sc), slip stitch(es) (sl st(s)), stitch(es) (st(s)), yarn over (yo).

SPECIAL ABBREVIATIONS
Bobble (5 double crochet bobble): (Yo and insert hook into indicated st, yo and draw up a loop, yo and draw through 2 loops) 5 times, yo and draw through all loops.
inv-dec (invisible single crochet decrease): Insert hook in FLO of each of next 2 sts, yo and draw through both sts, yo and draw through 2 loops on hook–1 st decreased.

NOTES

Worked in the round unless otherwise specified. When instructed to join, join with a slip stitch in first stitch.

"Our strength comes from the Spirit of the Moon; our life comes from the Spirit of the Ocean. They work together to keep balance."

—PRINCESS YUE
(Book 1, Episode 19)

BODY

Using **A** for La and **B** for Tui.
Note: You may need to lightly pull the tail so that it curves to the left while working or when finished stuffing.
Rnd 1: 8 sc in a magic ring, join–8 sc.
Rnd 2: Ch 1, sc in next 2 sts, 3 sc in next, sc in next 3, 3 sc in next, sc in next, join–12 sc.
Rnd 3: Ch 1, *sc in next st, 2 sc in next, repeat from * around, join–18 sc.
Rnd 4: Ch 1, sc in each st around, join.
Rnd 5: Ch 1, *sc in next 2 sts, 2 sc in next, repeat from * around, join–24 sc.
Rnd 6: Ch 1, *2 sc in next st, sc in next 3, repeat from * around, join–30 sc.
Rnd 7: Ch 1, sc in each st around, join.
Rnd 8: Ch 1, *sc in next 4 sts, 2 sc in next, repeat from * around, join–36 sc.
Rnds 9–16: Ch 1, sc in each st around, join.
Rnd 17: Ch 1, *sc in next 4 sts, inv-dec, repeat from * around, join–30 sc.
Rnd 18: Ch 1, sc in each st around, join.
Rnd 19: Ch 1, *inv-dec, sc in next 3 sts, repeat from * around, join–24 sts.
Add safety eyes between Rnds 7–8, 9 sts apart, and begin stuffing Body. Body has an oblong shape when viewed from the front, with the sides on the shorter curve of the oval. Make sure eyes are where shorter curve starts on each side and positioned on top of Body (tail curves to the left when Body is viewed from above). Join sts will all be on bottom of Body.
Rnd 20: Ch 1, sc in each st around, join.
Rnd 21: Ch 1, sc in next 6 sts, [inv-dec, sc in next] twice, sc in next 12, join–22 sc.
Rnd 22: Ch 1, sc in each st around, join.
Rnd 23: Ch 1, sc in next 6 sts, [inv-dec, sc in next] twice, sc in next 10, join–20 sc.
Rnd 24: Ch 1, sc in each st around, join.
Rnd 25: Ch 1, sc in next 4 sts, [inv-dec, sc in next] 3 times, sc in next 7, join–17 sc.
Rnd 26: Ch 1, sc in next 2 sts, [inv-dec, sc in next] 3 times, sc in next 6, join–14 sc.
Rnd 27: Ch 1, sc in each st around, join.
Rnd 28: Ch 1, sc in next st, [inv-dec, sc in next] 3 times, sc in next 4, join–11 sc.
Rnds 29–30: Ch 1, sc in each st around, join.
Rnd 31: Ch 1, sc in first st, [inv-dec] around, join–6 sts.
Make sure to stuff tail before closing.
Fasten off and close Body.

MOUTH AND WHISKERS

Using **A** for La and **B** for Tui.
Rnd 1: 6 sc in a magic ring, join–6 sc.
Rnd 2: Ch 1, 3 sc in first st, sc in next 2, 3 sc in next, sc in next 2, join–10 sc.
Rnd 3: Ch 1, sc in each st around, join.
Rnd 4: Turn, ch 1, sl st in next 5 sts, ch 15, starting in second ch from hook sl st in next 14 chs, sl st in next 5 sts, ch 15, starting in second ch from hook sl st in next 14 chs, join–38 sl sts.
Fasten off, with a long tail for sewing.

FRONT FINS (MAKE 2)

Using **A** for La and **B** for Tui.
Rnd 1: Ch 8, sc in second ch from hook, hdc in next, dc in next 2, hdc in next, sc in next, (sl st, ch 2, sl st) in last. Now, working on opposite side of starting chain, sc in next, hdc in next, dc in next 2, hdc in next, sc in last–12 sts, 2 sl sts, 1 ch-2 space.
Fasten off, with a long tail for sewing.

BACK FINS (MAKE 2)

Using **A** for La and **B** for Tui.
Rnd 1: Ch 5, sc in second ch from hook, hdc in next, sc in next, (sl st, ch 2, sl st) in last. Now, working on opposite side of starting chain, sc in next, hdc in next, sc in last–6 sts, 2 sl sts, 1 ch-2 space.
Fasten off, with a long tail for sewing.

TAIL FINS (MAKE 2)

Using **A** for La and **B** for Tui.
Rnd 1: Ch 11, sc in second ch from hook, sc in next, hdc in next 2, dc in next 2, hdc in next 2, sc in next, (sl st, ch 2, sl st) in last. Now, working on opposite side of starting chain, sc in next, hdc in next 2, dc in next 2, hdc in next 2, sc in next, sl st in last–17 sts, 3 sl sts, 1 ch-2 space.
Fasten off, with a long tail for sewing.

DORSAL FIN

Using **A** for La and **B** for Tui.
Row 1: Ch 11, sc in third ch from hook, 2 dc in each ch across–17 sts.
Fasten off, with a long tail for sewing.

HEAD MARKING

Using **B** for La and **A** for Tui.
Rnd 1: 6 sc in a magic ring, join–6 sc.
Rnd 2: Ch 1, 3 sc in first st, sc in next 2, 3 sc in next, sc in next 2, join–10 sc.
Fasten off, with a long tail for sewing.

FINISHING

It is helpful to pin everything into place before sewing.
Step 1. Attach Mouth and Whiskers so first 2 rnds are directly on top of first 2 rnds of Body, with FO on top. Sew center of Mouth to Body, leaving sl sts from last rnd of Mouth and Whiskers to curve outward. **Step 2.** Attach Front Fins with their flat sides at Body 5 rnds below and 3–4 sts from safety eyes. **Step 3.** Attach Back Fins 10 rnds below Front Fins, in line with each other. Due to the curve in the Body, it may look like left Fin is higher than right Fin, and that's okay. **Step 4.** Sew flat ends of Tail Fins together forming a V and attach to last 2 rnds of Body. **Step 5.** Attach Head Marking with short curve of oval shape pointing toward Mouth and Whiskers. Marking should be centered between eyes, with its top at Rnd 6 of Body and its bottom at Rnd 11. **Step 6.** Attach Dorsal Fin with its FO as its top. Position top of Dorsal Fin at center top of Body, 1 rnd from Head Marking. End of Dorsal Fin rests at last 1–2 rnds of Body. For a frillier Dorsal Fin, position its end higher on Body, keeping its top in the same position.

KATARA

Designed by
LEE SARTORI

Skill Level:
EASY

One of the last Waterbenders of the Southern Water Tribe, Katara is a dedicated, compassionate young woman who brings hope to her village by caring for all the women and children, putting the needs of others ahead of her own as they live through war-torn times. After Katara and her brother, Sokka, free Aang from his hundred-year ice prison, they decide to join Aang and his sky bison, Appa, on an adventure to bring balance to their world. Along the way, she fights against injustice, rallies others to their cause with inspirational speeches, and becomes a waterbending master alongside the Avatar.

The Southern Water Tribe lives in remote locations surrounded by ice and snow. Dressed in her warm clothes, this amigurumi Katara features her traditional Water Tribe braids ("hair loopies") and bright blue colors. And don't forget to add her mother's necklace, an important keepsake to this beloved character!

"I will never, ever turn my back on people who need me!"

—KATARA (Book 3, Episode 3)

FINISHED MEASUREMENTS
Height: 11 in. / 28 cm • Width: 7 in. / 18 cm

YARN
Worsted weight (#4, Medium) yarn, shown in Lion Brand *Lazy Days* (100% Polyester, 179 yd. / 164 m per 3.5 oz. / 100 g ball)
Color A: 123AP Taupe, 1 ball
Color D: 107N Bluebell, 1 ball
Color E: 152AH Pewter, 1 ball
And worsted weight (#4, Medium) yarn, shown in Lion Brand *Basic Stitch* (100% Acrylic, 185 yd. / 169 m per 3.5 oz. / 100 g ball)
Color B: 109 Steel Blue, 1 ball
And worsted weight (#4, Medium) yarn, shown in Lion Brand *24/7 Cotton* (100% Mercerized Cotton, 185 yd. / 170 m per 3.5 oz. / 100 g ball)
Color C: 151X Cool Grey, 1 ball
Color F: 100 White, 1 ball
Color G: 125AB Coffee Beans, 1 ball

HOOK
US C-2 / 2.75 mm, *or size needed to obtain gauge*

NOTIONS
Stitch markers • Tapestry needle • Polyester stuffing • 10 mm safety eyes • Small amount of plastic mesh • Scissors

GAUGE
28 sc and 28 sc rounds = 4 in. / 10 cm; *make sure to check your gauge.*

ABBREVIATIONS
Back loop only (BLO), chain(s) (ch(s)), double crochet (dc), front loop only (FLO), front post single crochet (FPsc), single crochet (sc), slip stitch(es) (sl st(s)), stitch(es) (st(s)), two single crochet closed together (sc2tog), yarn over (yo).

SPECIAL ABBREVIATIONS
inv-dec (invisible single crochet decrease): Insert hook in FLO of each of next 2 sts, yo and draw through both sts, yo and draw through 2 loops on hook–1 st decreased.
Picot-Sc (picot single crochet): Insert hook into indicated st, yo and draw up a loop, [yo and draw through 1 loop] 3 times (3 chs), yo and draw through 2 loops.
Popcorn (popcorn stitch): Work 5 dc in next st, drop loop on hook, insert hook from front to back in first of 5 dc, place dropped loop on hook and draw it through the back of the first dc.

NOTES

Work in continuous rounds unless otherwise indicated. When instructed to join, join with a slip stitch in first stitch.

"Aang, I know you're upset, and I know how hard it is to lose the people you love. I went through the same thing when I lost my mom. Monk Gyatso and the other Airbenders may be gone, but you still have a family—Sokka and I, we're your family now."

—KATARA (Book 1, Episode 3)

ARM (MAKE 2)

With **A**, make a magic loop.
Rnd 1: 6 sc in loop–6 sc.
Rnd 2: 2 sc in each st around–12 sc.
Rnds 3–4: Sc in each st around.
Rnd 5: Popcorn, sc in next 11 sts–12 sts.
Rnds 6–7: Sc in each st around.
Fasten off **A**, change to **B**.
Rnd 8: Ch 1, sl st in each st around, join.
Rnd 9: Ch 1, sc-BLO in each st around, join.
Rnds 10–14: Ch 1, sc in each st around, join.
Change to **C**.
Rnd 15: Ch 1, sl st in each st around, join.
Rnd 16: Ch 1, sc-BLO in each st around, join.
Rnds 17–18: Ch 1, sc in each st around, join.
Rnd 19: Ch 1, [2 sc in next st, sc in next 3] 3 times, join–15 sc.
Rnds 20–23: Ch 1, sc in each st around, join.
Change to **D**.
Rnd 24: Ch 1, sl st in each st around, join.
Fasten off. Stuff. Set aside to join to Body.

BOOT SOLE (MAKE 4)

With **E**.
Rnd 1: Ch 5, sc in second ch from hook, sc in next 2, 3 sc in last, rotate to work on underside of chs, sc in next 3, 3 sc in last–12 sc.
Rnd 2: *Sc in next 3 sts, [2 sc in next] 3 times; repeat from * around–18 sc.
Rnd 3: *Sc in next 3 sts, [2 sc in next, sc in next] 3 times; repeat from * around–24 sc.
Fasten off first piece, do not fasten off second piece. Trace Sole on a piece of plastic mesh. Place mesh between 2 Soles and continue to joining round.
Rnd 4 (Joining): Working in BLO through both thicknesses with plastic mesh sandwiched in between sc in each st around–24 sc.
Fasten off.

BOOT (MAKE 2)

With **E**, join to center back of heel.
Rnds 1–2: Ch 1, sc in each st around, join–24 sc.
Rnd 3: Ch 1, sc in next 8 sts, [inv-dec, sc in next] 3 times, sc in next 7, join–21 sc.
Rnd 4: Ch 1, sc in next 8 sts, [inv-dec] 3 times, sc in next 7, join–18 sc.
Rnd 5: Ch 1, sc in next 6, [inv-dec] 3 times, sc in next 6, join–15 sc.
Change to **F**.
Rnd 6: Ch 1, sl st in each st around, join.
Rnd 7: Ch 1, sc-BLO in each st around, join.
Rnd 8: Ch 1, sc in each st around, join.
Change to **B**.
Rnd 9: Ch 1, sl st in each st around, join.
Rnd 10: Ch 1, sc-BLO in each st around, join.
Rnds 11–12: Ch 1, sc in each st around, join.
Stuff. Continue to Leg.

LEG (MAKE 2)

Continue with **B**.
Rnd 1: Ch 1, sc in each st around, join–15 sc.
Rnd 2: Ch 1 tightly, sc in each st around, do not join.
Rnds 3–9: Sc in each st around.
Rnd 10: [Sc in next 2 sts, 2 sc in next, sc in next 2] 3 times–18 sc.

Rnds 11–13: Sc in each st around.
Fasten off. Mark center of "inner thigh" of each Leg with a locking st marker. Join to marked st of left Leg.
Rnd 14 (Joining): Ch 1, sc 18 around left Leg, sc in marked st of right Leg, sc in each st around right Leg, do not join–36 sc.
Continue to Body.

BODY

Continue with **B**.
Rnds 1–2: Sc in each st around–36 sc.
Rnd 3: 3 sc in first st, 2 sc in next, sc in each st around to last st, 2 sc in last–40 sc.
Rnds 4–6: Sc in each st around.
Change to **F**.
Rnd 7: Ch 1, sl st in each st around, join.
Rnd 8: Ch 1, sc-BLO in each st around, join.
Rnds 9–10: Ch 1, sc in each st around, join.
Change to **D**.
Rnd 11: Ch 1, sl st in each st around, join.
Rnd 12: Ch 1, sc-BLO in each st around, join.
Rnds 13–14: Ch 1, sc in each st around, join.
Mark each "armpit" with a locking st marker, ensuring there are 19 sts between markers for front of Body and 19 sts between markers for back of Body.
Rnd 15 (Join Arms): Ch 1, sc in each st to first marked st, sc in marked st, holding Arm in line with Body sts and ensuring thumb is facing Body, sc in each st around first Arm, sc in each st to second marked st, sc in marked st, holding second Arm in line with Body sts and ensuring thumb is facing Body, sc in each st around second Arm, sc in each remaining st around, join–70 sc.
Rnds 16–18: Ch 1, sc in each st around, join.
Rnd 19: Ch 1, inv-dec, [sc in next 16 sts, inv-dec] 3 times, sc in next 14–66 sc.
Rnd 20: Ch 1, [inv-dec, sc in next 9 sts] 6 times, join–60 sc.
Rnd 21: Ch 1, with **D** [sc in next 4 sts, inv-dec, sc in next 4] 3 times; with **A**, sc in next; with **D**, sc in next 3, inv-dec, sc in next 4, [sc in next 4, inv-dec, sc in next 4] twice, join–54 sc.
Rnd 22: Ch 1, [inv-dec, sc in next 7 sts] twice, inv-dec, sc in next 6; with **A**, sc in next 3; with **D**, inv-dec, sc in next 5, [inv-dec, sc in next 7] twice, join–48 sc.
Rnd 23: Ch 1, [sc in next 3 sts, inv-dec, sc in next 3] twice, sc in next 3, inv-dec, sc in next; with **A**, sc in next 5; with **D**, inv-dec, sc in next 3, [sc in next 3, inv-dec, sc in next 3] twice, join–42 sc.
Rnd 24: Ch 1, [inv-dec, sc in next 5 sts] twice, inv-dec, sc in next 2; with **A**, sc in next 7; with **D**, sc in next, inv-dec, [inv-dec, sc in next 5] twice, join–36 sc.
Rnd 25: Ch 1, [sc in next 2 sts, inv-dec, sc in next 2] twice, sc in next 2; with **A**, inv-dec, sc in next 4, inv-dec, sc in next; with **D**, sc in next, [sc in next 2, inv-dec, sc in next 2] twice, join–30 sc.
Rnd 26: Ch 1, [inv-dec, sc in next 3 sts] twice; with **A**, [inv-dec, sc in next 3] twice; with **D**, [inv-dec, sc in next 3] twice, join–24 sc.
Rnd 27: [Sc in next st, inv-dec, sc in next] twice; with **A**, [sc in next, inv-dec, sc in next] twice; with **D**, [sc in next, inv-dec, sc in next] twice, join–18 sc.
Fasten off. Stuff Body firmly.

HEAD

With **A**, join to center back of Body.
Rnd 1: Ch 1, sc-BLO in each st around, join–18 sc.
Rnds 2–3: Ch 1, sc in each st around, join.
Rnd 4: Ch 1 tightly, [sc in next st, 2 sc in next, sc in next] 6 times, do not join–24 sc.
Begin working in continuous rounds.
Rnd 5: [2 sc in next st, sc in next 3] around–30 sc.
Rnd 6: [Sc in next 2 sts, 2 sc in next, sc in next 2] around–36 sc.
Rnd 7: [2 sc in next st, sc in next 5] around–42 sc.
Rnd 8: [Sc in next 3 sts, 2 sc in next, sc in next 3] around–48 sc.
Rnd 9: [2 sc in next st, sc in next 7] around–54 sc.
Rnd 10: Sc in each st around.
Place a st marker in center front of head to mark for nose.
Rnd 11 (Nose): Sc in each st to marked

st, Picot-Sc in marked st, sc in each st around.
Rnds 12–19: Sc in each st around. Add eyes between Rnds 13–14. With **G** embroider eyebrows above eyes.
Rnd 20: [Inv-dec, sc in next 7 sts] around–48 sc.
Rnd 21: [Sc in next 3 sts, inv-dec, sc in next 3] around–42 sc.
Rnd 22: [Inv-dec, sc in next 5 sts] around–36 sc.
Rnd 23: [Sc in next 2 sts, inv-dec, sc in next 2] around–30 sc.
Rnd 24: [Inv-dec, sc in next 3 sts] around–24 sc.
Rnd 25: [Sc in next st, inv-dec, sc in next] around–18 sc.
Rnd 26: [Inv-dec, sc in next] around–12 sc. Stuff Head.
Rnd 27: [Inv-dec] around–6 sc.
Fasten off, leaving a long tail for sewing. Sew remaining 6 sts closed. Weave in ends.

COAT LINING

Row 1: With **F**, ch 40.
Fasten off, leaving a long tail for sewing. Sew Lining around opening of Coat from neckline, around neck, and back down front of Coat using photos as a guide. Weave in ends.

NECKLACE

Row 1: With **B**, ch 18.
Fasten off, leaving a long tail for sewing. Sew Necklace around neck. Weave in ends.

NECKLACE DETAIL

With **C**, make a magic loop.
Rnd 1: 4 sc in loop, join–4 sc.
Fasten off, leaving a long tail for sewing. Sew Necklace Detail to front of Necklace. Weave in ends.

COAT BOTTOM (MAKE 2)

With **D**.
Row 1: Ch 19, sc in second ch from hook and in each ch across, turn–18 sc.
Rows 2–14: Ch 1, sc in each st across, turn.
Rnd 15 (Border): Ch 1, sc in each st across, ch 1, rotate to sc 14 across row ends, ch 1, sc 18 across underside of starting ch, ch 1, rotate to sc 14 across row ends, ch 1, join–64 sc.
Fasten off. Join with **F** in ch-1 space at bottom right edge.
Row 16: Ch 1, sl st in each st across to opposite ch-1 space, sl st in ch-1 space, turn–20 sl sts.
Row 17: Ch 1, working in top loop of sl sts (FLO of right side) sc in each st across.
Fasten off leaving a long tail for sewing. Sew Coat Bottom to front and back of Body under Rnd 7. Sew side seams about ⅔ of the way down Coat. Weave in ends.

EAR (MAKE 2)

With **A** and leaving a long tail at start for sewing, make a magic loop.
Row 1: Ch 1, 3 sc in loop, turn–3 sc.
Row 2: Ch 1, 2 sc in each st across, turn–6 sc.
Row 3: Ch 3, sl st in starting loop.
Fasten off, leaving a long tail for sewing. Sew Ears to sides of Head. Weave in ends.

HAIR

With **G**, make a magic ring.
Rnd 1: Ch 1, 6 sc in ring, do not join–6 sc.
Rnd 2: 2 sc in each st around–12 sc.
Rnd 3: [2 sc in next st, sc in next] around–18 sc.
Rnd 4: [Sc in next st, 2 sc in next, sc in next] around–24 sc.
Rnd 5: [2 sc in next st, sc in next 3] around–30 sc.
Rnd 6: [Sc in next 2 sts, 2 sc in next, sc in next 2] around–36 sc.
Rnd 7: [2 sc in next st, sc in next 5] around–42 sc.
Rnd 8: [Sc in next 3 sts, 2 sc in next, sc in next 3] around–48 sc.
Begin working in turned rows.
Row 9: Sc in next 27 sts, turn leaving remaining sts unworked–27 sc.
Row 10: Ch 1, sc2tog-BLO, sc to last 2 sts, sc2tog-BLO, turn–25 sc.
Rows 11–15: Repeat Row 10, do not turn at the end of Row 15–15 sc.
Round 16 (Border): Ch 1, rotate to work 6 sc across row ends, sc-BLO in 21 unworked sts from Row 9, rotate to work 6 sc across row ends, ch 1, rotate to work sc-BLO in 15 sts from Row 15, join–48 sc.
Fasten off, leaving a long tail for sewing. Sew Hair to top of Head. Cut 15 strands of **G** measuring approximately 12 in. / 30.5 cm each. Loop each strand through bottom 15 sts of Hair. Braid lengths together and secure.

FRONT BRAID (MAKE 2)

Row 1: With **G**, ch 20.
Fasten off, leaving a long tail for sewing. Sew to front of Hair above eyebrows and looping behind Ears. Using a length of **B**, embroider a small loop at the top of each Front Braid where it meets Hair. Weave in ends.

"You can't knock me down!"

—KATARA (Book 1, Episode 18)

SOKKA

Designed by
LEE SARTORI

Skill Level:
EASY

Sokka is courageous, resourceful, and protective, and, as a non-bender, he relies on his ingenuity and wits to defend his loved ones. Appointed protector of the Southern Water Tribe while his father and the other men were away, Sokka takes his duties as a powerful warrior *extremely* seriously. He's determined to protect his tribe with everything he has at his disposal, including his trusty boomerang. During his journey with Team Avatar, he undergoes significant personal growth, changing his outdated views and embracing his inner hopeless romantic.

Though he's at first reluctant to join his sister, Katara, when she decides to accompany Aang on his journey to learn waterbending, Sokka steps up to protect his companions, ultimately finding his destiny as an inventor and a leader.

"I'm just a guy with a boomerang!"

—SOKKA (Book 1, Episode 2)

FINISHED MEASUREMENTS
Height: 11½ in. / 29 cm • Width: 7 in. / 18 cm

YARN
Worsted weight (#4, Medium) yarn, shown in Lion Brand *Lazy Days* (100% Polyester, 179 yd. / 164 m per 3.5 oz. / 100 g ball)
Color A: 123AP Taupe, 1 ball
Color D: 107N Bluebell, 1 ball
And worsted weight (#4, Medium) yarn, shown in Lion Brand *Basic Stitch* (100% Acrylic, 185 yd. / 169 m per 3.5 oz. / 100 g ball)
Color B: 109 Steel Blue, 1 ball
And worsted weight (#4, Medium) yarn, shown in Lion Brand *24/7 Cotton* (100% Mercerized Cotton, 185 yd. / 170 m per 3.5 oz. / 100 g ball)
Color C: 100 White, 1 ball
Color E: 125AB Coffee Beans, 1 ball
Color F: 122D Taupe, 1 ball
Color G: 151X Cool Grey, 1 ball

HOOK
US C-2 / 2.75 mm, *or size needed to obtain gauge*

NOTIONS
Stitch markers • Tapestry needle • Polyester stuffing • 8 mm safety eyes • Small amount of plastic mesh • Black thread • White thread • Scissors

GAUGE
28 sc and 28 sc rounds = 4 in. / 10 cm; *make sure to check your gauge.*

ABBREVIATIONS
Back loop only (BLO), chain(s) (ch(s)), double crochet (dc), front loop only (FLO), front post single crochet (FPsc), single crochet (sc), slip stitch(es) (sl st(s)), stitch(es) (st(s)), three single crochet closed together (sc3tog), yarn over (yo).

SPECIAL ABBREVIATIONS
inv-dec (invisible single crochet decrease): Insert hook in FLO of each of next 2 sts, yo and draw through both sts, yo and draw through 2 loops on hook—1 st decreased.
Picot-Sc (picot single crochet): Insert hook into indicated st, yo and draw up a loop, [yo and draw through 1 loop] 3 times (3 chs), yo and draw through 2 loops.
Popcorn (popcorn stitch): Work 5 dc in next st, drop loop on hook, insert hook from front to back in first of 5 dc, place dropped loop on hook and draw it through the back of the first dc.

NOTES

Work in continuous rounds unless otherwise indicated. When instructed to join, join with a slip stitch in first stitch.

"That's all I got. It's pretty much my whole identity. Sokka, the meat and sarcasm guy."

—SOKKA (Book 2, Episode 9)

ARM (MAKE 2)

With **A**, make a magic loop.
Rnd 1: 6 sc in loop–6 sc.
Rnd 2: 2 sc in each st around–12 sc.
Change to **B**.
Rnd 3: Ch 1, sl st in each st around, join.
Rnd 4: Ch 1, sc-BLO in each st around, join.
Rnd 5: Ch 1, sc in each st around, join.
Change to **C**.
Rnd 6: Ch 1, sl st in each st around, join.
Rnd 7: With **A** ch 1, Popcorn; with **C**, sc-BLO in each st around, join.
Fasten off **A**.
Rnds 8–13: Ch 1, sc in each st around, join.
Change to **B**.
Rnd 14: Ch 1, sl st in each st around, join.
Rnd 15: Ch 1, sc-BLO in each st around, join.
Rnds 16–18: Ch 1, sc in each st around, join.
Change to **D**.
Rnd 19: Ch 1, sl st in each st around, join.
Rnd 20: Ch 1, working all sts in BLO [2 sc in next st, sc in next] 3 times, join–15 sc.
Rnds 21–24: Ch 1, sc in each st around, join.
Fasten off. Stuff. Set aside to join to Body.

BOOT SOLE (MAKE 4)

With **E**.
Rnd 1: Ch 5, sc in second ch from hook, sc in next 2, 3 sc in last, rotate to work on underside of chs, sc in next 3, 3 sc in last–12 sc.
Rnd 2: *Sc in next 3 sts, [2 sc in next] 3 times; repeat from * around–18 sc.
Rnd 3: *Sc in next 3 sts, [2 sc in next, sc in next] 3 times; repeat from * around–24 sc.
Fasten off first piece, do not fasten off second piece. Trace Sole on a piece of plastic mesh. Place mesh between 2 Soles and continue to joining round.
Rnd 4 (Joining): Working in BLO through both thicknesses with plastic mesh sandwiched in between sc in each st around–24 sc.
Fasten off.

BOOT (MAKE 2)

With **E**, join to center back of heel.
Rnds 1–2: Ch 1, sc in each st around, join–24 sc.
Rnd 3: Ch 1, sc in next 8 sts, [inv-dec, sc in next] 3 times, sc in next 7, join–21 sc.
Rnd 4: Ch 1, sc in next 8 sts, [inv-dec] 3 times, sc in next 7, join–18 sc.
Rnd 5: Ch 1, sc in next 6, [inv-dec] 3 times, sc in next 6, join–15 sc.
Change to **F**.
Rnd 6: Ch 1, sl st in each st around, join.
Rnd 7: Ch 1, sc-BLO in each st around, join.
Change to **E**.
Rnds 8–9: Repeat Rnds 6–7.
Rnds 10–14: Ch 1, sc in each st around, join.
Change to **F**.
Rnd 15: Ch 1, sl st in each st around, join.
Rnd 16: Ch 1, sc-BLO in each st around, join.

LEG (MAKE 2)

With **B**, join to center back of heel.
Rnd 1: Ch 1, FPsc in each st around, join–15 FPsc.
Rnd 2: Ch 1 tightly, [sc in next 2 sts, 2 sc in next, sc in next 2] 3 times, do not join–18 sc.
Rnd 3: [2 sc in next st, sc in next 5] 3 times–21 sc.

Rnds 4–9: Sc in each st around.
Rnd 10: Inv-dec, sc in each st around–20 sc.
Rnds 11–12: Repeat Rnd 10–18 sc at end of Rnd 12.
Rnd 13: Sc in each st around.
Fasten off. Mark center of "inner thigh" of each Leg with a locking st marker. Join to marked st of left Leg.
Rnd 14 (Joining): Ch 1, sc 18 around left Leg, sc in marked st of right Leg, sc in each st around right Leg, do not join–36 sc.
Continue to Body.

BODY

Continue with **B**.
Rnds 1–2: Sc in each st around–36 sc.
Rnd 3: 3 sc in first st, 2 sc in next, sc in each st around to last st, 2 sc in last–40 sc.
Rnds 4–6: Sc in each st around.
Change to **G**.
Rnd 7: Ch 1, sl st in each st around, join.
Rnd 8: Ch 1, sc-BLO in each st around, join.
Change to **D**.
Rnd 9: Ch 1, sl st in each st around, join.
Rnd 10: Ch 1, sc-BLO in each st around, join.
Rnds 11–14: Ch 1, sc in each st around, join.

Mark each "armpit" with a locking st marker, ensuring there are 19 sts between markers for front of Body and 19 sts between markers for back of Body.
Rnd 15 (Join Arms): Ch 1, sc in each st to first marked st, sc in marked st, holding Arm in line with Body sts and ensuring thumb is facing Body, sc in each st around first Arm, sc in each st to second marked st, sc in marked st, holding second Arm in line with Body sts and ensuring thumb is facing Body, sc in each st around second Arm, sc in each remaining st around, join–70 sc.
Rnds 16–18: Ch 1, sc in each st around, join.
Rnd 19: Ch 1, inv-dec, [sc in next 16 sts, inv-dec] 3 times, sc in next 14–66 sc.
Rnd 20: Ch 1, [inv-dec, sc in next 9 sts] 6 times, join–60 sc.
Rnd 21: Ch 1, with **D**, [sc in next 4 sts, inv-dec, sc in next 4] 3 times; with **A**, sc in next; with **D**, sc in next 3, inv-dec, sc in next 4, [sc in next 4, inv-dec, sc in next 4] twice, join–54 sc.
Rnd 22: Ch 1, [inv-dec, sc in next 7 sts] twice, inv-dec, sc in next 6; with **A**, sc in next 3; with **D**, inv-dec, sc in next 5, [inv-dec, sc in next 7] twice, join–48 sc.
Rnd 23: Ch 1, [sc in next 3 sts, inv-dec, sc in next 3] twice, sc in next 3, inv-dec, sc in next; with **A**, sc in next 5; with **D**, inv-dec, sc in next 3, [sc in next 3, inv-dec, sc in next 3] twice, join–42 sc.
Rnd 24: Ch 1, [inv-dec, sc in next 5 sts] twice, inv-dec, sc in next 2; with **A**, sc in next 7; with **D**, sc in next, inv-dec, [inv-dec, sc in next 5] twice, join–36 sc.
Rnd 25: Ch 1, [sc in next 2 sts, inv-dec, sc in next 2] twice, sc in next 2; with **A**, inv-dec, sc in next 4, inv-dec, sc in next; with **D**, sc in next, [sc in next 2, inv-dec, sc in next 2] twice, join–30 sc.
Rnd 26: Ch 1, [inv-dec, sc in next 3 sts] twice; with **A**, [inv-dec, sc in next 3] twice; with **D**, [inv-dec, sc in next 3] twice, join–24 sc.
Rnd 27: [Sc in next st, inv-dec, sc in next] twice; with **A**, [sc in next, inv-dec, sc in next] twice; with **D**, [sc in next, inv-dec, sc in next] twice, join–18 sc.
Fasten off. Stuff Body firmly.

HEAD

With **A**, join to center back of Body.
Rnd 1: Ch 1, sc-BLO in each st around, join–18 sc.
Rnds 2–3: Ch 1, sc in each st around, join.
Rnd 4: Ch 1 tightly, [sc in next st, 2 sc in next, sc in next] 6 times, do not join–24 sc.
Begin working in continuous rounds.
Rnd 5: [2 sc in next st, sc in next 3] around–30 sc.
Rnd 6: [Sc in next 2 sts, 2 sc in next, sc in next 2] around–36 sc.
Rnd 7: [2 sc in next st, sc in next 5] around–42 sc.
Rnd 8: [Sc in next 3 sts, 2 sc in next, sc in next 3] around–48 sc.
Rnd 9: [2 sc in next st, sc in next 7] around–54 sc.
Rnd 10: Sc in each st around.
Place a st marker in center front of Head to mark for nose.
Rnd 11 (Nose): Sc in each st to marked st, Picot-Sc in marked st, sc in each st around.
Rnds 12–20: Sc in each st around.
Add eyes between Rnds 13–14. With **E**, embroider eyebrows above eyes.
Rnd 21: [Inv-dec, sc in next 7 sts] around–48 sc.
Rnd 22: [Sc in next 3 sts, inv-dec, sc in next 3] around–42 sc.
Rnd 23: [Inv-dec, sc in next 5 sts] around–36 sc.
Rnd 24: [Sc in next 2 sts, inv-dec, sc in next 2] around–30 sc.
Rnd 25: [Inv-dec, sc in next 3 sts] around–24 sc.
Rnd 26: [Sc in next st, inv-dec, sc in next] around–18 sc.
Rnd 27: [Inv-dec, sc in next st] around–12 sc.
Stuff Head.
Rnd 28: [Inv-dec] around–6 sc.
Fasten off, leaving a long tail for sewing. Sew remaining 6 sts closed. Weave in ends.

COAT LINING

Row 1: With **G**, ch 40.
Fasten off, leaving a long tail for sewing. Sew lining around opening of Coat from neckline, around neck, and back down front of Coat using photos as a guide. Weave in ends.

NECKLACE

Row 1: With **C**, ch 18.
Fasten off, leaving a long tail for sewing. Sew Necklace around neck. Weave in ends.

COAT BOTTOM (MAKE 2)

With **D**.
Row 1: Ch 19, sc in second ch from hook and in each ch across, turn–18 sc.
Rows 2–8: Ch 1, sc in each st across, turn.
Rnd 9 (Border): Ch 1, sc in next 18 sts, ch 1, rotate to sc 8 across row ends, ch 1, sc 18 across underside of starting ch, ch 1, rotate to sc 8 across row ends, ch 1, join–52 sc.
Fasten off leaving a long tail for sewing. Sew Coat Bottom to front and back of Body under Rnd 7. Weave in ends.

EAR (MAKE 2)

With **A** and leaving a long tail at start for sewing, make a magic loop.
Row 1: Ch 1, work 3 sc in loop, turn–3 sc.

Row 2: Ch 1, 2 sc in each st across, turn–6 sc.
Row 3: Ch 3, sl st in starting loop. Fasten off, leaving a long tail for sewing. Sew Ears to sides of Head. Weave in ends.

HAIR

With E.
Row 1: Ch 2, 3 sc in second ch from hook, turn–3 sc.
Row 2: Ch 1, 2 sc in next st, sc in next, 2 sc in next, turn–5 sc.
Row 3: Ch 1, sc in each st across, turn.
Row 4: Ch 1, 2 sc in next st, sc in next 3, 2 sc in next, turn–7 sc.
Rows 5–12: Ch 1, sc in each st across, turn.
Fasten off, leaving a long tail for sewing. Sew Hair with Row 1 aligned to Rnd 27 of Head and working back. Weave in ends. Cut 7 strands of **E** measuring 3 in. / 7.5 cm each. Loop a strand at back of Hair in each of the 7 sts of Row 12. Secure strands in a ponytail and trim to a length of about 1 in. / 2.5 cm.

BOOMERANG (MAKE 2)

With G.
Row 1: Ch 18, starting in second ch from hook sc 6, sc3tog, sc in next 8, turn–15 sc.
Row 2: Ch 1, sc in next 8 sts, sc3tog, sc in next 5, turn–14 sc.
Fasten off.
Rnd 3 (Border): Place 2 pieces atop one another and join with **C**, ch 1 and sl st in each st around through both thicknesses to join.
Fasten off, weave in ends. Sew Boomerang to Hand. Weave in ends.

"Boomerang, you *do* always come back!"

—SOKKA (Book 2, Episode 5)

PRINCESS YUE

Designed by
LEE SARTORI

Skill Level:
EASY

Daughter of Chief Arnook, Yue is a loyal, graceful, and kind princess of the Northern Water Tribe. When Aang arrives with his friends at the Northern Water Temple to learn waterbending, Yue immediately stands out to Sokka, who falls head over heels in love with her. Unfortunately, when the Siege of the North results in the death of Tui, the Moon Spirit, Yue's strong sense of duty inspires her to sacrifice herself to restore the life force that had saved her during a difficult infancy.

**"It gave me life.
Maybe I can give it back."**

—PRINCESS YUE
(Book 1, Episode 20)

FINISHED MEASUREMENTS

Height: 13 in. / 33 cm • Width: 7 in. / 18 cm

YARN

Worsted weight (#4, Medium) yarn, shown in Lion Brand *Basic Stitch* (100% Acrylic, 185 yd. / 169 m per 3.5 oz. / 100 g ball)
Color A: 102W Clay, 1 ball
Color C: 409F Blush Heather, 1 ball
Color G: 404J Silver Heather, 1 ball
And worsted weight (#4, Medium) yarn, shown in Lion Brand *24/7 Cotton* (100% Mercerized Cotton, 185 yd. / 170 m per 3.5 oz. / 100 g ball)
Color B: 108G Denim, 1 ball
Color E: 100 White, 1 ball
And worsted weight (#4, Medium) yarn, shown in Lion Brand *Lazy Days* (100% Polyester, 179 yd. / 164 m per 3.5 oz. / 100 g ball)
Color D: 152AH Pewter, 1 ball
And worsted weight (#4, Medium) yarn, shown in Lion Brand *Heartland* (100% Acrylic, 251 yd. / 230 m per 5 oz. / 142 g ball)
Color F: 143T Kobuk Valley, 1 ball

HOOK

US C-2 / 2.75 mm, *or size needed to obtain gauge*

NOTIONS

Stitch markers • Tapestry needle • Polyester stuffing • 10 mm safety eyes • Small amount of plastic mesh • Black thread • Brown thread • White thread • Scissors

GAUGE

28 sc and 28 sc rounds = 4 in. / 10 cm; *make sure to check your gauge.*

ABBREVIATIONS

Back loop only (BLO), chain(s) (ch(s)), double crochet (dc), front loop only (FLO), front post single crochet (FPsc), right side (RS), single crochet (sc), slip stitch(es) (sl st(s)), stitch(es) (st(s)), two single crochet closed together (sc2tog), yarn over (yo).

SPECIAL ABBREVIATIONS

Cluster (5 dc cluster): [Yo, insert hook into indicated st, yo and draw through 2 loops on hook] 5 times, yo and draw through all loops on hook.
inv-dec (invisible single crochet decrease): Insert hook in FLO of each of next 2 sts, yo and draw through both sts, yo and draw through 2 loops on hook–1 st decreased.
Picot-Sc (picot single crochet): Insert hook into indicated st, yo and draw up a loop, [yo and draw through 1 loop] 3 times (3 chs), yo and draw through 2 loops.
Popcorn (popcorn stitch): Work 5 dc in next st, drop loop on hook, insert hook from front to back in first of 5 dc, place dropped loop on hook and draw it through the back of the first dc.

ARM (MAKE 2)

With **A**, make a magic loop.
Rnd 1: 6 sc in loop–6 sc.
Rnd 2: 2 sc in each st around–12 sc.
Rnds 3–4: Sc in each st around.
Rnd 5: Popcorn, sc in next 11–12 sts.
Rnds 6–7: Sc in each st around.
Fasten off **A**, change to **B**.
Rnd 8: Ch 1, sl st in each st around, join.
Rnd 9: Ch 1, sc-BLO in each st around, join.
Rnds 10–14: Ch 1, sc in each st around, join.
Change to **C**.
Rnd 15: Ch 1, sl st in each st around, join.
Rnd 16: Ch 1, sc-BLO in each st around, join.
Rnds 17–18: Ch 1, sc in each st around, join.
Rnd 19: Ch 1, [2 sc in next st, sc in next 3] 3 times, join–15 sc.
Rnds 20–23: Ch 1, sc in each st around, join.
Fasten off. Stuff. Set aside to join to Body.

BOOT SOLE (MAKE 4)

With **D**.
Rnd 1: Ch 5, sc in second ch from hook, sc in next 2, 3 sc in last, rotate to work on underside of chs, sc in next 3, 3 sc in last–12 sc.
Rnd 2: *Sc in next 3 sts, [2 sc in next] 3 times; repeat from * around–18 sc.
Rnd 3: *Sc in next 3 sts, [2 sc in next, sc in next] 3 times; repeat from * around–24 sc.
Fasten off first piece, do not fasten off second piece. Trace Sole on a piece of plastic mesh. Place mesh between 2 Soles and continue to joining round.
Rnd 4 (Joining): Working in BLO through both thicknesses with plastic mesh sandwiched in between sc in each st around–24 sc.
Fasten off.

BOOT (MAKE 2)

With **D**, join to center back of heel.
Rnds 1–2: Ch 1, sc in each st around, join–24 sc.
Rnd 3: Ch 1, sc in next 8 sts, [inv-dec, sc in next] 3 times, sc in next 7, join–21 sc.
Rnd 4: Ch 1, sc in next 8 sts, [inv-dec] 3 times, sc in next 7, join–18 sc.
Rnd 5: Ch 1, sc in next 6 sts, [inv-dec] 3 times, sc in next 6, join–15 sc.
Rnds 6–9: Ch 1, sc in each st around, join.
Change to **E**.
Rnd 10: Ch 1, sl st in each st around, join.
Rnd 11: Ch 1, sc-BLO in each st around, join.
Rnd 12: Ch 1, sc in each st around, join.
Fasten off. Stuff. Continue to Leg.

LEG (MAKE 2)

With **B**, join to center back of heel.
Rnd 1: Ch 1, FPsc in each st around, join–15 FPsc.
Rnd 2: Ch 1 tightly, sc in each st around, do not join.
Rnds 3–9: Sc in each st around.
Rnd 10: [Sc in next 2 sts, 2 sc in next, sc in next 2] 3 times–18 sc.
Rnds 11–13: Sc in each st around.
Fasten off. Mark center of "inner thigh" of each Leg with a locking st marker. Join to marked st of left Leg.
Rnd 14 (Joining): Ch 1, sc 18 around left Leg, sc in marked st of right Leg, sc in each st around right Leg, do not join–36 sc.
Continue to Body.

NOTES

Work in continuous rounds unless otherwise indicated. When instructed to join, join with a slip stitch in first stitch.

"The spirits gave me a vision when Yue was born. I saw a beautiful, brave young woman become the Moon Spirit. I knew this day would come."

—CHIEF ARNOOK
(Book 1, Episode 20)

BODY

Continue with **B**.
Rnds 1–2: Sc in each st around–36 sc.
Rnd 3: 3 sc in first st, 2 sc in next, sc in each st around to last st, 2 sc in last–40 sc.
Rnds 4–6: Sc in each st around.
Rnd 7: Ch 1, sl st in each st around, join.
Rnd 8: Ch 1, sc-BLO in each st around, join.
Rnds 9–14: Ch 1, sc in each st around, join.
Mark each "armpit" with a locking st marker ensuring there are 19 sts between markers for front of Body and 19 sts between markers for back of Body.
Rnd 15 (Join Arms): Ch 1, sc in each st to first marked st, sc in marked st, holding Arm in line with Body sts and ensuring thumb is facing Body, sc in each st around first Arm, sc in each st to second marked st, sc in marked st, holding second Arm in line with Body sts and ensuring thumb is facing Body, sc in each st around second Arm, sc in each remaining st around, join–70 sc.
Rnds 16–18: Ch 1, sc in each st around, join.
Rnd 19: Ch 1, inv-dec, [sc in next 16 sts, inv-dec] 3 times, sc in next 14–66 sc.
Rnd 20: Ch 1, [inv-dec, sc in next 9 sts] 6 times, join–60 sc.
Rnd 21: Ch 1, [sc in next 4 sts, inv-dec, sc in next 4] 6 times, join–54 sc.
Rnd 22: Ch 1, [inv-dec, sc in next 7 sts] 6 times, join–48 sc.
Rnd 23: Ch 1, [sc in next 3 sts, inv-dec, sc in next 3] 6 times, join–42 sc.
Rnd 24: Ch 1, [inv-dec, sc in next 5 sts] 6 times, join–36 sc.
Rnd 25: Ch 1, [sc in next 2 sts, inv-dec, sc in next 2] 6 times, join–30 sc.
Rnd 26: Ch 1, [inv-dec, sc in next 3 sts] 6 times, join–24 sc.
Rnd 27: Ch 1, [sc in next st, inv-dec, sc in next] 6 times, join–18 sc.
Fasten off. Stuff Body firmly.

HEAD

With **A**, join to center back of Body.
Rnd 1: Ch 1, sc-BLO in each st around, join–18 sc.
Rnds 2–3: Ch 1, sc in each st around, join.
Rnd 4: Ch 1 tightly, [sc in next st, 2 sc in next, sc in next] 6 times, do not join–24 sc.
Begin working in continuous rounds.
Rnd 5: [2 sc in next st, sc in next 3] around–30 sc.
Rnd 6: [Sc in next 2 sts, 2 sc in next, sc in next 2] around–36 sc.
Rnd 7: [2 sc in next st, sc in next 5] around–42 sc.
Rnd 8: [Sc in next 3 sts, 2 sc in next, sc in next 3] around–48 sc.
Rnd 9: [2 sc in next st, sc in next 7] around–54 sc.
Rnd 10: Sc in each st around.
Place a st marker in center front of Head to mark for nose.
Rnd 11 (Nose): Sc in each st to marked st, Picot-Sc in marked st, sc in each st around.
Rnds 12–19: Sc in each st around.
Add eyes between Rnds 13–14. Using white and black thread, add eye details above and below eyes using photos as a guide. With brown thread, embroider eyebrows above eyes.
Rnd 20: [Inv-dec, sc in next 7 sts] around–48 sc.
Rnd 21: [Sc in next 3 sts, inv-dec, sc in next 3] around–42 sc.
Rnd 22: [Inv-dec, sc in next 5 sts] around–36 sc.
Rnd 23: [Sc in next 2 sts, inv-dec, sc in next 2] around–30 sc.
Rnd 24: [Inv-dec, sc in next 3 sts] around–24 sc.
Rnd 25: [Sc in next st, inv-dec, sc in next] around–18 sc.
Rnd 26: [Inv-dec, sc in next] around–12 sc.
Stuff Head.
Rnd 27: [Inv-dec] around–6 sc.
Fasten off, leaving a long tail for sewing. Sew remaining 6 sts closed. Weave in ends.

EAR (MAKE 2)

With **A** and leaving a long tail at start for sewing, make a magic loop.
Row 1: Ch 1, work 3 sc in loop, turn–3 sc.
Row 2: Ch 1, 2 sc in each st across, turn–6 sc.

Row 3: Ch 3, sl st in starting loop.
Fasten off, leaving a long tail for sewing. Sew Ears to sides of Head. Weave in ends.

HAIR

With **E**, make a magic loop.
Rnd 1: Ch 1, 6 sc in loop, do not join–6 sc.
Rnd 2: 2 sc in each st around–12 sc.
Rnd 3: [2 sc in next st, sc in next] around–18 sc.
Rnd 4: [Sc in next st, 2 sc in next, sc in next] around–24 sc.
Rnd 5: [2 sc in next st, sc in next 5] around–30 sc.
Rnd 6: [Sc in next 2 sts, 2 sc in next, sc in next 2] around–36 sc.
Rnd 7: [2 sc in next st, sc in next 7] around–42 sc.
Rnd 8: [Sc in next 3 sts, 2 sc in next, sc in next 3] around–48 sc.
Begin working in turned rows.
Row 9: Sc in next 27 sts, turn leaving remaining sts unworked–27 sc.
Row 10: Ch 1, working in BLO in all sts sc2tog, sc to last 2, sc2tog, turn–25 sc.
Rows 11–15: Repeat Row 10, do not turn at the end of Row 15–15 sc.
Round 16 (Border): Ch 1, rotate to work 6 sc across row ends, sc-BLO in 21 unworked sts from Row 9, rotate to work 6 sc across row ends, ch 1, rotate to work sc-BLO in 15 sts from Row 15, join–48 sc.
Fasten off, leaving a long tail for sewing. Sew Hair to top of Head. Cut 32 strands of **E** 16 in. / 40.5 cm long. Mark 8 sts at side of Hair on each side, between the edge of the eyebrow and the Ear for strands of hair. Loop 2 strands in each of these 16 marked sts. Bring top half of strands to a tall ponytail at top of Head and secure. Divide top ponytail into 4 sections. Twist each section tightly. Twist 2 sections together to create a twisted braid. Fold each twist in half and secure to base of ponytail. Divide bottom half of strands into 2 sections and twist each section tightly. Twist 2 sections together to create a twisted braid and secure with a knot.

TOP HAIR DETAIL

With **B**.
Row 1: Ch 13, sc in second ch from hook and in each ch across, turn–12 sc.
Rows 2–4: Ch 1, sc in each st across, turn.
Fasten off, leaving a long tail for sewing. Sew Detail around top ponytail and weave in ends.

SIDE HAIR DETAIL (MAKE 2)

With **B**.
Row 1: Ch 6, sc in second ch from hook and in each ch across, turn–5 sc.
Rows 2–4: Ch 1, sc in each st across, turn.
Fasten off, leaving a long tail for sewing. Sew Detail around top of each side twist braid. Weave in ends.

CENTER HAIR DETAIL (MAKE 3)

With **G**, make a magic loop.
Rnd 1: 6 sc in loop–6 sc.
Rnd 2: 2 sc in each st around–12 sc.
Fasten off, leaving a long tail for sewing. Sew to the center of each Hair Detail.

COAT

With **F**, make a magic ring.
Rnd 1: 8 sc in ring–8 sc.
Rnd 2: 2 sc in each st around–16 sc.
Rnd 3: [2 sc in next st, sc in next] around–24 sc.
Rnd 4: [Sc in next st, 2 sc in next, sc in next] around–32 sc.
Rnd 5: [2 sc in next st, sc in next 3] around–40 sc.
Rnd 6: [Sc in next 2 sts, 2 sc in next, sc in next 2] around–48 sc.
Rnd 7: [2 sc in next st, sc in next 5] around–56 sc.
Rnd 8: [Sc in next 3 sts, 2 sc in next, sc in next 3] around–64 sc.
Rnd 9: [2 sc in next st, sc in next 7] around–72 sc.
Rnd 10: [Sc in next 4 sts, 2 sc in next, sc in next 4] around–80 sc.
Rnd 11: [2 sc in next st, sc in next 9] around–88 sc.
Rnd 12: Sc in next 28 sts, ch 12, skip 10 sts (Armhole made), sc in next 12, ch 12, skip 10 sts (Armhole made), sc in next 28–68 sc.
Rnd 13: Sc in each st and ch around–92 sc.

Rnd 14: Sc in each st around.
Rnd 15: [Sc in next 11 sts, 2 sc in next, sc in next 11] 4 times–96 sc.
Rnd 16: [2 sc in next st, sc in next 11] 8 times–104 sc.
Rnd 17: [Sc in next 6 sts, 2 sc in next, sc in next 6] around–112 sc.
Rnd 18: [2 sc in next st, sc in next 13] around–120 sc.
Rnd 19: [Sc in next 7 sts, 2 sc in next, sc in next 7] around–128 sc.
Rnd 20: [2 sc in next st, sc in next 15] around–136 sc.
Rnd 21: [Sc in next 8 sts, 2 sc in next, sc in next 8] around–144 sc.
Fasten off. Place Coat on Doll. Using 2 locking st markers, mark 36 sts around collar that will remain unworked. Remove

Coat from Doll. With RS facing, join to next st after marked st. Begin working in turned rows.
Row 22: Ch 1, [2 sc in next st, sc in next 17] 6 times, turn leaving marked 36 sts of collar unworked–114 sc.
Row 23: Ch 1, [sc in next 9 sts, 2 sc in next, sc in next 9] 6 times, turn–120 sc.
Row 24: Ch 1, [2 sc in next st, sc in next 19] 6 times, turn–126 sc.
Row 25: Ch 1, [sc in next 10 sts, 2 sc in next, sc in next 10] 6 times, turn–132 sc.
Row 26: Ch 1, [2 sc in next st, sc in next 21] 6 times, turn–138 sc.
Rnd 27 (Border): Ch 1, [sc in next 11 sts, 2 sc in next, sc in next 11] 6 times, ch 2, working across row ends sc in next 6, sc in marked 36 sts of collar, working in row ends sc in next 6, ch 2, join–192 sc. Fasten off. Join with **E** in ch-2 space before Rnd 27 join.
Rnd 28: Ch 3 (counts as first dc), (dc, ch 2, 2 dc) in same space, dc in next 144 sc, (2 dc, ch 2, 2 dc) in next ch-2 space, dc in next 48 sc, join–200 dc.
Weave in ends.

ARMHOLE FINISHING

With **F**, join to underside of first of 12 chs of Rnd 12.
Row 1: Ch 1, sc in each ch across, turn–12 sc.
Row 2: Ch 1, 2 sc in first st, sc across to last st, 2 sc in last, turn–14 sc.
Change to **E**.
Row 3: Ch 2, dc in each st across–14 dc.
Fasten off, weave in ends. Repeat for opposite Armhole. Add Coat to Body.

BELT

With **B**.
Row 1: Ch 31, sc in second ch and in each ch across, turn–30 sc.
Rows 2–3: Ch 1, sc in each st across, turn.
Fasten off. Sew Belt around waist of Coat.

SKIRT

With **C** and leaving a long tail at start for sewing.
Note: In Rnds 3, 5, 7 the first sc is made in third starting chain.
Rnd 1: Ch 42, join with a sl st to form a ring, ch 1, working across ch [sc in next, skip 2 chs, 5 dc in next, skip 2 chs] around, join–7 shells.
Rnd 2: Ch 3 (counts as first dc), 2 dc in same space, [skip 2 dc, sc in next dc, skip 2 dc, 5 dc in sc] around to starting st, 2 dc in same st as starting, join–7 shells.
Rnd 3: Ch 1, [sc in next dc, skip next 2 dc, 5 dc in next sc, skip 2 dc] around, join.
Rnd 4: Repeat Rnd 2.
Rnd 5: Ch 1, [sc in next dc, skip 2 dc, 7 dc in next sc, skip next 2 dc] around, join–7 shells.
Rnd 6: Ch 3, 3 dc in same st, [skip 3 dc, sc in next dc, skip 3 dc, 7 dc in next sc] around to first st, 3 dc in first st, join.
Rnd 7: Ch 1, [sc in next dc, skip 3 dc, 7 dc in next, skip 3 dc] around, join.
Rnds 8–12: Repeat Rnds 6–7.
Rnd 13: Repeat Rnd 6.
Fasten off, weave in end. Use starting tail to sew to Body in FLO of Rnd 8.
Weave in ends.

THE CABBAGE MERCHANT

Designed by
LEE SARTORI

Skill Level:
EASY

The Cabbage Merchant just wants a normal life. He'll wake up, go out with his cart, and set his delicious cabbages out in his stall for sale. But something always happens to topple his cart, and one of those things became Team Avatar. No matter where he traveled, there they were! How this continues to happen to the poor Cabbage Merchant over and over is a bit of a mystery. But each time it does, he cleans up the mess, relocates, and tries to have a better day of cabbage vending the next day.

The Cabbage Merchant would be nothing without his cabbages, so although we have only made one for him in this crochet pattern, feel free to make him a whole load of beautiful cabbages that he can admire. He would really appreciate it.

"MY CABBAGES!"

—CABBAGE MERCHANT
(Book 1, Episode 5)

FINISHED MEASUREMENTS
Height: 12 in. / 30.5 cm · Width: 5 in. / 12.5 cm

YARN
Worsted weight (#4, Medium) yarn, shown in Lion Brand *Basic Stitch* (100% Acrylic, 185 yd. / 169 m per 3.5 oz. / 100 g ball)
Color A: 122T Hazelnut, 1 ball
Color C: 128E Ebony, 1 ball
Color D: 407K Pine Heather, 1 ball
Color F: 404J Silver Heather, 1 ball
And worsted weight (#4, Medium) yarn, shown in Lion Brand *Heartland* (100% Acrylic, 251 yd. / 230 m per 5 oz. / 142 g ball)
Color B: 175H Haleakala, 1 ball
And DK weight (#3, Light) yarn, shown in Lion Brand *Coboo* (51% Cotton, 49% Rayon from Bamboo, 232 yd. / 212 m per 3.5 oz. / 100 g ball)
Color E: 132 Olive, 1 ball
And worsted weight (#4, Medium) yarn, shown in Lion Brand *Lazy Days* (100% Polyester, 179 yd. / 164 m per 3.5 oz. / 100 g ball)
Color G: 172AJ Matcha, 1 ball

HOOK
US C-2 / 2.75 mm, *or size needed to obtain gauge*

NOTIONS
Stitch markers · Tapestry needle · Polyester stuffing · 9 mm safety eyes · Small amount of plastic mesh · Black thread · White thread · Scissors

GAUGE
28 sc and 28 sc rounds = 4 in. / 10 cm; *make sure to check your gauge.*

ABBREVIATIONS
Back loop only (BLO), chain(s) (ch(s)), double crochet (dc), front loop only (FLO), front post single crochet (FPsc), half double crochet (hdc), single crochet (sc), slip stitch(es) (sl st(s)), stitch(es) (st(s)), two single crochet closed together (sc2tog), yarn over (yo).

SPECIAL ABBREVIATIONS
Cluster (5 dc cluster): [Yo, insert hook into indicated st, yo and draw through 2 loops on hook] 5 times, yo and draw through all loops on hook.
inv-dec (invisible single crochet decrease): Insert hook in FLO of each of next 2 sts, yo and draw through both sts, yo and draw through 2 loops on hook–1 st decreased.
Picot-Sc (picot single crochet): Insert hook into indicated st, yo and draw up a loop, [yo and draw through 1 loop] 3 times (3 chs), yo and draw through 2 loops.
Popcorn (popcorn stitch): Work 5 dc in next st, drop loop on hook, insert hook from front to back in first of 5 dc, place dropped loop on hook and draw it through the back of the first dc.
Reverse Sc (reverse single crochet/crab stitch): Working in opposite direction of a regular single crochet, insert hook into st before working stitch, yo and draw up a loop, yo and draw through 2 loops.

NOTES

Work in continuous rounds unless otherwise indicated. When instructed to join, join with a slip stitch in first stitch.

"Off with their heads! One for each head of cabbage!"

—CABBAGE MERCHANT
(Book 1, Episode 5)

ARM (MAKE 2)

With **A**, make a magic loop.
Rnd 1: 6 sc in loop–6 sc.
Rnd 2: 2 sc in each st around–12 sc.
Rnds 3–4: Sc in each st around.
Rnd 5: Popcorn, sc in each st around, sl st in next st.
Rnds 6–7: Sc in each st around.
Fasten off, change to **B**.
Rnd 8: Ch 1, sl st in each st around, join.
Rnd 9: Ch 1, sc-BLO in each st around, join.
Rnds 10–17: Ch 1, sc in each st around, join.
Rnd 18: Ch 1, [2 sc in next st, sc in next 3] around, join–15 sc.
Rnds 19–22: Ch 1, sc in each st around, join.
Fasten off, leaving a long tail for sewing. Stuff Arm. Set aside to join to Body.

SOLE (MAKE 4)

With **C**.
Rnd 1: Ch 5, sc in second ch from hook, sc in next 2, 3 sc in last, rotate to work on underside of chs, sc in next 3, 3 sc in last–12 sc.
Rnd 2: *Sc in next 3 sts, [2 sc in next] 3 times; repeat from * around–18 sc.
Rnd 3: *Sc in next 3 sts, [2 sc in next, sc in next] 3 times; repeat from * around–24 sc.
Fasten off first piece, do not fasten off second piece. Trace Sole on a piece of plastic mesh. Place mesh between 2 Soles and continue to joining round.
Rnd 4 (Joining): Working through both thicknesses with plastic mesh sandwiched in between sc in each st around–24 sc.
Fasten off. Continue to Shoe.

SHOE (MAKE 2)

With **C**, join to center back of heel.
Rnds 1–2: Ch 1, sc in each st around, join–24 sc.
Rnd 3: Ch 1, with **C**, sc in next 8 sts; with **B**, [sc in next, inv-dec] 3 times; with **C**, sc in next 7, join–21 sc.
Rnd 4: Ch 1, sc in next 8 sts; with **B**, [inv-dec] 3 times; with **C**, sc in next 7, join–18 sc.
Fasten off **B**.
Rnd 5: Ch 1, sc in next 6 sts, [inv-dec] 3 times, sc in next 6, join–15 sc.
Rnds 6–11: Ch 1, sc in each st around, join.
Fasten off. Continue to Leg.

LEG (MAKE 2)

With **B** join to center back of heel.
Rnd 1: Ch 1, FPsc in each st around, join–15 FPsc.
Rnd 2: Ch 1 tightly, [sc in next 2 sts, 2 sc in next, sc in next 2] 3 times, do not join–18 sc.
Rnd 3: [2 sc in next st, sc in next 5] 3 times–21 sc.
Rnds 4–9: Sc in each st around.
Rnd 10: Inv-dec, sc in each st around–20 sc.
Rnds 11–12: Repeat Rnd 10–18 sc at end of Rnd 12.
Rnd 13: Ch 1, sl st in each st around, join.
Rnd 14: Ch 1, sc-BLO in each st around, join.
Fasten off.

PANT LEG (MAKE 2)

With **B** and leaving a long tail at start for sewing.
Rnd 1: Ch 18, join with a sl st to form a ring, ch 1, [2 sc in next ch, sc in next 5]

3 times, join–21 sc.
Rnd 2: Ch 1 tightly, sc in each st around, do not join.
Begin working in continuous rounds.
Rnds 3–6: Sc in each st around.
Rnd 7: [Sc in next 3 sts, 2 sc in next, sc in next 3] 3 times–24 sc.
Rnds 8–10: Sc in each st around.
Rnd 11: [2 sc in next st, sc in next 3] 6 times–30 sc.
Rnds 12–14: Sc in each st around.
Rnd 15: [Sc in next 2 sts, 2 sc in next, sc in next 2] 6 times–36 sc.
Rnds 16–17: Sc in each st around.
Rnd 18: Sc in each st around, join.
Rnd 19: Ch 1, Reverse Sc in each st around, join.
Fasten off, weave in finishing end.
Using starting tail sew Pant Leg to front loops of Rnd 13 of Leg. Weave in ends.
Continue to Body.

BODY

Continue with **B**.
Mark center of "inner thigh" of each Leg with a locking st marker. Join to marked st of left Leg.
Rnd 1 (Join Legs): Ch 1, sc 18 around left Leg, sc in marked st of right Leg, sc in each st around right Leg, do not join–36 sc.
Rnds 2–3: Sc in each st around.
Rnd 4: 3 sc in first st, 2 sc in next, sc in each st around to last st, 2 sc in last–40 sc.
Rnds 5–7: Sc in each st around, sl st in next.
Change to **D**.
Rnd 8: Ch 1, sl st in each st around, join.
Rnd 9: Ch 1, sc-BLO in each st around, join.
Rnds 10–11: Ch 1, sc in each st around, join.
Change to **E**.
Rnd 12: Ch 1, sl st in each st around, join.
Rnd 13: Ch 1, sc-BLO in each st around, join.
Rnds 14–16: Ch 1, sc in each st around, join.
Fasten off and join to center back of Body.
Mark each "armpit" with a locking st marker ensuring there are 19 sts between markers for front of Body and 19 sts between markers for back of Body.
Rnd 17 (Join Arms): Ch 1, sc in each st to first marked st, sc in marked st, holding first Arm in line with Body and ensuring thumb is facing Body sl st in 15 sts of first Arm to join, sc in each st to next marked st, sc in marked st, holding second Arm in line with Body and ensuring thumb is facing Body sl st in 15 sts of second Arm to join, sc in remaining Body sts, join–40 sc, 30 sl sts.
Rnd 18: Ch 1, sc in each st to first sl st, sc-BLO in next 15 sl sts, sc in each st to next sl st, sc-BLO in next 15 sl sts, sc in remaining sts, join–70 sc.
Rnds 19–20: Ch 1, sc in each st around, join.
Rnd 21: Ch 1, inv-dec, [sc in next 16 sts, inv-dec] 3 times, sc in next 14–66 sc.
Rnd 22: Ch 1, [inv-dec, sc in next 9 sts] 6 times, join–60 sc.
Rnd 23: Ch 1, [sc in next 4 sts, inv-dec, sc in next 4] 6 times, join–54 sc.
Rnd 24: Ch 1, [inv-dec, sc in next 7 sts] 6 times, join–48 sc.
Rnd 25: Ch 1, [sc in next 3 sts, inv-dec, sc in next 3] 6 times, join–42 sc.
Rnd 26: Ch 1, [inv-dec, sc in next 5 sts] 6 times, join–36 sc.
Rnd 27: Ch 1, [sc in next 2 sts, inv-dec, sc in next 2] 6 times, join–30 sc.
Rnd 28: Ch 1, [inv-dec, sc in next 3 sts] 6 times, join–24 sc.
Rnd 29: Ch 1, [sc in next st, inv-dec, sc in next] 6 times, join–18 sc.
Fasten off. Stuff Body firmly.

SHIRT HEM

With **E** and leaving a long tail at the start for sewing.
Rnd 1: Ch 40, sl st to form a ring, ch 1, sc in each ch around, join–40 sc.
Rnd 2: Ch 1, [2 sc in next st, sc in next 19] twice, join–42 sc.
Rnd 3: Ch 1, [sc in next 3 sts, 2 sc in next, sc in next 3] 6 times, join–48 sc.
Rnd 4: Ch 1, [2 sc in next st, sc in next 7] 6 times, join–54 sc.
Rnd 5: Ch 1, [sc in next 4 sts, 2 sc in next, sc in next 4] 6 times, join–60 sc.
Rnds 6–8: Ch 1, sc in each st around, join.
Fasten off, weave in finishing end. Using starting tail sew Shirt Hem to front loops of Rnd 8 of Body. Weave in end.

HEAD

With **A**, join to the center back of Body in BLO.
Rnd 1: Ch 1, sc-BLO in each st around, join–18 sc.
Rnd 2: Ch 1, sc in each st around, join.
Rnd 3: Ch 1, tightly, [sc in next st, 2 sc in next, sc in next] around, do not join–24 sc.
Begin working in continuous rounds.
Rnd 4: [2 sc in next st, sc in next 3] around–30 sc.
Rnd 5: [Sc in next 2 sts, 2 sc in next, sc in next 2] around–36 sc.
Rnd 6: [2 sc in next st, sc in next 5] around–42 sc.
Rnd 7: [Sc in next 3 sts, 2 sc in next, sc in next 3] around–48 sc.
Rnd 8: [2 sc in next st, sc in next 7] around–54 sc.
Rnds 9–10: Sc in each st around.
Place a st marker in center front of Head to mark for nose.
Rnd 11 (Nose): Sc in each st to marked st, Picot-Sc in marked st, sc in each st around.
Rnds 12–19: Sc in each st around.
Fasten off **A**. Join with **E** at back of Head in BLO.
Rnd 20: Ch 1, sl st-BLO in each st around, join.
Rnd 21: Ch 1 tightly, sc-BLO in each st around, do not join.
Place safety eyes between Rnds 13–14.
Using white and black thread, embroider details above and below eyes. Using a length of **F**, embroider eyebrows above eyes. Weave in ends. Stuff and continue stuffing as work progresses.
Rnds 22–25: Sc in each st around.
Rnd 26: [Inv-dec, sc in next 7 sts] around–48 sc.
Rnd 27: [Sc in next 2 sts, inv-dec, sc in next 2] 8 times–40 sc.
Rnd 28: [Inv-dec, sc in next 3 sts] 8 times–32 sc.
Rnd 29: [Sc in next st, inv-dec, sc in next] 8 times–24 sc.
Rnd 30: [Inv-dec, sc in next st] 8 times–16 sc.
Rnd 31: [Inv-dec] around–8 sc.
Fasten off, leaving a long tail for sewing. Sew remaining 8 sts closed. Weave in ends.

EAR (MAKE 2)

With **A** and leaving a long tail at start for sewing, make a magic loop.
Row 1: Ch 1, work 3 sc in loop, turn–3 sc.
Row 2: Ch 1, 2 sc in each st across, turn–6 sc.
Row 3: Ch 3, sl st in starting loop.
Fasten off, leaving a long tail for sewing. Sew Ears to sides of Head. Weave in ends.

HAIR

With **F**, make a magic ring.
Row 1: Ch 35, sc in second ch from hook and in each ch across, turn–34 sc.
Row 2: Ch 1, sc2tog, sc in each st across to last 2 sts, sc2tog, turn–32 sc.
Rows 3–8: Repeat Row 2–20 sc at end of Row 8.
Fasten off, leaving a long tail for sewing. Wrap Hair around back of Head and sew to front loops of Rnd 21. Weave in ends.

JACKET STRIPE

With **D**.
Row 1: Ch 3, sc in second ch from hook and in next ch, turn–2 sc.
Rows 2–3: Ch 1, sc in each st across, turn.
Row 4: Ch 7, sc in second ch from hook and in next 5 chs, sc in next 2 sc, turn–8 sc.
Row 5: Ch 1, sc in next 8 sts, turn.
Row 6: Ch 1, sc in next 2 sts, turn leaving remaining sts unworked–2 sc.
Rows 7–20: Ch 1, sc in each st across, turn.
Row 21: Ch 19, sc in second ch from hook, sc in next 17 chs, sc in next 2 sc, turn–20 sc.
Row 22: Ch 1, sc in each st across.
Fasten off, leaving a long tail for sewing. Using photos as a guide sew to front of Jacket from collar to hem. Weave in ends.

SASH

With **D**.
Row 1: Ch 61, sc in second ch from hook and in each ch across–60 sc.
Row 2: Ch 1, sc in each st across, turn.
Fasten off, weave in ends.
Tie around waist.

CABBAGE

With **G**, make a magic ring.
Rnd 1: Ch 1, 6 sc in ring–6 sc.
Rnd 2: 2 sc in each st around–12 sc.
Rnd 3: [2 sc in next st, sc in next] around–18 sc.
Rnd 4: [Sc in next st, 2 sc in next, sc in next] around–24 sc.
Rnds 5–7: Sc in each st around.
Stuff and continue stuffing as work progresses.
Rnd 8: [Sc in next st, inv-dec, sc in next] around–18 sc.
Rnd 9: [Inv-dec, sc in next st] around–12 sc.
Rnd 10: [Inv-dec] around–6 sc.
Fasten off, leaving a long tail for sewing. Sew remaining 6 sts closed. Weave in ends.

CABBAGE LEAF (MAKE 4)

With **G**.
Rnd 1: Ch 7, sc in second ch from hook, hdc in next, dc in next 3, 5 dc in last, rotate to work across underside of starting ch, dc in next 3 chs, hdc in next, sc in next, sl st in last–16 sts.
Fasten off, leaving a long tail for sewing. Sew Leaves to Cabbage.
Weave in ends.
Sew Cabbage to hands. Weave in ends.

GOATEE

Cut approximately 12 strands of **F**, each measuring 4 in. / 10 cm. Loop strands and secure middle of loop with a long length of **F**. Tie loop to chin area. Using a second length of **F**, tie a knot around bottom of Goatee to secure yarn ends. Trim.

AZULA

Designed by
LEE SARTORI

Skill Level:
EASY

Daughter of Fire Lord Ozai and younger sister of Prince Zuko, Azula strives for perfection and praise. Her troubled upbringing and constant longing for her mother's love and father's approval have created a demanding, cruel force to be reckoned with. A born leader, she intimidates and arouses fear in all who cross her path. As a firebending prodigy, Azula has taken her intense power to new levels, mastering the skill of lightning generation. With her friends Ty Lee and Mai, Azula sets out to capture the Avatar before Zuko can do so and thus secure what she views as her rightful spot on the Fire Nation throne.

Sibling rivalry is never an easy topic to navigate. We recommend keeping the two siblings far away from each other. Things might get heated.

"My own mother thought I was a monster. . . . She was right, of course, but it still hurt."

—AZULA (Book 3, Episode 5)

FINISHED MEASUREMENTS
Height: 13 in. / 33 cm • Width: 7 in. / 18 cm

YARN
DK weight (#3, Light) yarn, shown in Lion Brand *Coboo* (51% Cotton, 49% Rayon from Bamboo, 232 yd. / 212 m per 3.5 oz. / 100 g ball)
Color A: 123Q Tan, 1 ball
And worsted weight (#4, Medium) yarn, shown in Lion Brand *24/7 Cotton* (100% Mercerized Cotton, 185 yd. / 170 m per 3.5 oz. / 100 g ball)
Color B: 148AI Burgundy, 1 ball
And worsted weight (#4, Medium) yarn, shown in Lion Brand *Basic Stitch* (100% Acrylic, 185 yd. / 169 m per 3.5 oz. / 100 g ball)
Color C: 138L Pomegranate, 1 ball
Color E: 158I Mustard, 1 ball
Color F: 153 Black, 1 ball
And worsted weight (#4, Medium) yarn, shown in Lion Brand *Color Theory* (100% Acrylic, 246 yd. / 225 m per 3.5 oz. / 100 g ball)
Color D: 124AD Nutmeg, 1 ball

HOOK
US C-2 / 2.75 mm, *or size needed to obtain gauge*

NOTIONS
Stitch markers • Tapestry needle • Polyester stuffing • 8 mm safety eyes • Small amount of plastic mesh • Black thread • White thread • Scissors

GAUGE
28 sc and 28 sc rounds = 4 in. / 10 cm; *make sure to check your gauge.*

ABBREVIATIONS
Back loop only (BLO), chain(s) (ch(s)), double crochet (dc), front loop only (FLO), front post single crochet (FPsc), half double crochet (hdc), single crochet (sc), slip stitch(es) (sl st(s)), stitch(es) (st(s)), two single crochet closed together (sc2tog), yarn over (yo).

SPECIAL ABBREVIATIONS
inv-dec (invisible single crochet decrease): Insert hook in FLO of each of next 2 sts, yo and draw through both sts, yo and draw through 2 loops on hook–1 st decreased.
Large Picot: Ch 5, sl st in fifth ch from hook.
Picot-Sc (picot single crochet): Insert hook into indicated st, yo and draw up a loop, [yo and draw through 1 loop] 3 times (3 chs), yo and draw through 2 loops.
Popcorn (popcorn stitch): Work 5 dc in next st, drop loop on hook, insert hook from front to back in first of 5 dc, place dropped loop on hook and draw it through the back of the first dc.
Small Picot: Ch 3, sl st in third ch from hook.

NOTES

Work in continuous rounds unless otherwise indicated. When instructed to join, join with a slip stitch in first stitch.

"What choice do I have? Trust is for fools! Fear is the only reliable way. Even you fear me."

—AZULA (Book 3, Episode 20)

ARM (MAKE 2)

With **A**, make a magic loop.
Rnd 1: 6 sc in loop–6 sc.
Rnd 2: 2 sc in each st around–12 sc.
Rnds 3–4: Sc in each st around.
Rnd 5: Popcorn, sc in next 11 sts–12 sts.
Rnd 6: Sc in each st around, join.
Fasten off **A**, change to **B**.
Rnd 7: Ch 1, sl st in each st around, join.
Rnd 8: Ch 1, sc-BLO in each st around, join.
Fasten off **B**, change to **C**.
Rnd 9: Ch 1, sl st in each st around, join.
Rnd 10: Ch 1, sc-BLO in each st around, join.
Rnds 11–15: Ch 1, sc in each st around, join.
Change to **D**.
Rnd 16: Ch 1, FPsc in each st around, join.
Rnd 17: Ch 1, [2 sc in next st, sc in next 3] 3 times, join–15 sc.
Rnds 18–21: Ch 1, sc in each st around, join.
Fasten off **D**, join **B**.
Rnd 22: Ch 1, sl st in each st around, join.
Rnd 23: Ch 1, sc-BLO in each st around, join.
Fasten off. Stuff. Set aside to join to Body.

BOOT SOLE (MAKE 4)

With **E**.
Rnd 1: Ch 5, sc in second ch from hook, sc in next 2, 3 sc in last, rotate to work on underside of chs, sc in next 3, 3 sc in last–12 sc.
Rnd 2: *Sc in next 3 sts, [2 sc in next] 3 times; repeat from * around–18 sc.
Rnd 3: *Sc in next 3 sts, [2 sc in next, sc in next] 3 times; repeat from * around–24 sc.
Fasten off first piece, do not fasten off second piece. Trace Sole on a piece of plastic mesh. Place mesh between 2 Soles and continue to joining round.
Fasten off **E**, join with **C** in BLO.
Rnd 4 (Joining): Working in BLO through both thicknesses, with plastic mesh sandwiched in between, sc in each st around–24 sc.
Fasten off.

BOOT (MAKE 2)

With **C**, join to center back of heel.
Rnds 1–2: Ch 1, sc in each st around, join–24 sc.
Rnd 3: Ch 1, sc in next 8 sts, [inv-dec, sc in next] 3 times, sc in next 7, join–21 sc.
Rnd 4: Ch 1, sc in next 8 sts, [inv-dec] 3 times, sc in next 7, join–18 sc.
Rnd 5: Ch 1, sc in next 6 sts, [inv-dec] 3 times, sc in next 6, join–15 sc.
Change to **B**.
Rnd 6: Ch 1, sl st in each st around, join.
Rnd 7: Ch 1, sc-BLO in each st around, join.
Change to **C**.
Rnds 8–9: Repeat Rnds 6–7.
Rnds 10–13: Ch 1, sc in each st around, join.
Fasten off. Stuff. Continue to Leg.

LEG (MAKE 2)

With **D**, join to center back of Boot.
Rnd 1: Ch 1, FPsc in each st around, join–15 FPsc.
Rnd 2: Ch 1 tightly, [sc in next 2 sts, 2 sc in next, sc in next 2] 3 times, do not join–18 sc.
Rnd 3: [2 sc in next st, sc in next 5] 3 times–21 sc.
Rnds 4–9: Sc in each st around.
Rnd 10: Inv-dec, sc in each st

around–20 sc.
Rnds 11–12: Repeat Rnd 10–18 sc at end of Rnd 12.
Rnd 13: Sc in each st around.
Fasten off. Mark center of "inner thigh" of each Leg with a locking st marker.
Join to marked st of left Leg.
Rnd 14 (Joining): Ch 1, sc 18 around left Leg, sc in marked st of right Leg, sc in each st around right Leg, do not join–36 sc.
Continue to Body.

BODY

Continue with **D**.
Rnds 1–2: Sc in each st around–36 sc.
Rnd 3: 3 sc in first st, 2 sc in next, sc in each st around to last st, 2 sc in last–40 sc.
Rnds 4–6: Sc in each st around.
Fasten off **D**, change to **C**.
Rnd 7: Ch 1, sl st in each st around, join.
Rnd 8: Ch 1, sc-BLO in each st around, join.
Rnds 9–10: Ch 1, sc in each st around, join.
Change to **B**.
Rnds 11–12: Repeat Rnds 7–8.
Rnds 13–15: Ch 1, sc in each st around, join.
Mark each "armpit" with a locking st marker, ensuring there are 19 sts between markers for front of Body and 19 sts between markers for back of Body.
Rnd 16 (Join Arms): Ch 1, sc in each st to first marked st, sc in marked st, holding Arm in line with Body sts and ensuring thumb is facing Body, sc in each st around first Arm, sc in each st to second marked st, sc in marked st, holding second Arm in line with Body sts and ensuring thumb is facing Body, sc in each st around second Arm, sc in each remaining st around, join–70 sc.
Rnd 17: Ch 1, sc in each st around, join.
Rnd 18: Ch 1, inv-dec, [sc in next 16 sts, inv-dec] 3 times, sc in next 14–66 sc.
Rnd 19: Ch 1, sc in each st around, join.
Rnd 20: Ch 1, [inv-dec, sc in next 9 sts] 6 times, join–60 sc.
Rnd 21: Ch 1, sc in each st around, join.
Rnd 22: Ch 1, [sc in next 4 sts, inv-dec, sc in next 4] 6 times, join–54 sc.
Rnd 23: Ch 1, [inv-dec, sc in next 7 sts] 6 times, join–48 sc.
Rnd 24: Ch 1, [sc in next 3 sts, inv-dec, sc in next 3] 6 times, join–42 sc.
Rnd 25: Ch 1, [inv-dec, sc in next 5 sts] 6 times, join–36 sc.
Rnd 26: Ch 1, [sc in next 2 sts, inv-dec, sc in next 2] 6 times, join–30 sc.
Rnd 27: Ch 1, [inv-dec, sc in next 3 sts] 6 times, join–24 sc.
Rnd 28: Ch 1, [sc in next st, inv-dec, sc in next] 6 times, join–18 sc.
Fasten off. Stuff Body firmly.
Continue to Head.

HEAD

With **A**, join to center back of Body in BLO.
Rnd 1: Ch 1, sc-BLO in each st around, join–18 sc.
Rnds 2–3: Ch 1, sc in each st around, join.
Rnd 4: Ch 1 tightly, [sc in next st, 2 sc in next, sc in next] 6 times, do not join–24 sc.
Begin working in continuous rounds.
Rnd 5: [2 sc in next st, sc in next 3] around–30 sc.
Rnd 6: [Sc in next 2 sts, 2 sc in next, sc in next 2] around–36 sc.
Rnd 7: [2 sc in next st, sc in next 5] around–42 sc.
Rnd 8: [Sc in next 3 sts, 2 sc in next, sc in next 3] around–48 sc.
Rnd 9: [2 sc in next st, sc in next 7] around–54 sc.
Rnds 10–11: Sc in each st around.
Place a st marker in center front of Head to mark for nose.
Rnd 12 (Nose): Sc in each st to marked st, Picot-Sc in marked st, sc in each st around.
Rnds 13–20: Sc in each st around.
Add eyes between Rnds 14–15. Using white and black thread, add eye details above and below eyes using photos as a guide. With black thread, embroider eyebrows above eyes.
Rnd 21: [Inv-dec, sc in next 7 sts] around–48 sc.
Rnd 22: [Sc in next 3 sts, inv-dec, sc in next 3] around–42 sc.
Rnd 23: [Inv-dec, sc in next 5 sts] around–36 sc.

Rnd 24: [Sc in next 2 sts, inv-dec, sc in next 2] around–30 sc.
Rnd 25: [Inv-dec, sc in next 3 sts] around–24 sc.
Rnd 26: [Sc in next st, inv-dec, sc in next] around–18 sc.
Rnd 27: [Inv-dec, sc in next st] around–12 sc.
Stuff Head.
Rnd 28: [Inv-dec] around–6 sc.
Fasten off, leaving a long tail for sewing. Sew remaining 6 sts closed. Weave in ends.

EAR (MAKE 2)

With **A** and leaving a long tail at start for sewing, make a magic loop.
Row 1: Ch 1, work 3 sc in loop, turn–3 sc.
Row 2: Ch 1, 2 sc in each st across, turn–6 sc.
Row 3: Ch 3, sl st in starting loop.
Fasten off, leaving a long tail for sewing. Sew Ears to sides of Head. Weave in ends.

SKIRT

With **B**.
Row 1: Ch 3, (2 hdc, ch 2, 2 hdc) in second ch from hook, turn–4 hdc.
Work all rows in the third loop only.
Row 2: Ch 2 (counts as hdc throughout), 2 hdc in same st, hdc in next, (hdc, ch 2, hdc) in ch-2 space, hdc in next, 3 hdc in last, turn–10 sc.
Row 3: Ch 2, 2 hdc in same st, hdc in next 3, skip next st, (hdc, ch 2, hdc) in ch-2 space, skip next st, hdc in next 3, 3 hdc in last, turn–14 hdc.
Row 4: Ch 1, 2 hdc in same st, hdc in next 5, skip next st, (hdc, ch 2, hdc) in ch-2 space, skip next st, hdc in next 5, 3 hdc in last, turn–18 hdc.
Row 5: Ch 2, 2 hdc in same st, hdc in next 7, skip next st, (hdc, ch 2, hdc) in ch-2 space, skip next st, hdc in next 7, 3 hdc in last, turn–22 hdc.
Row 6: Ch 2, 2 hdc in same st, hdc in next 9, skip next st, (hdc, ch 2, hdc) in ch-2 space, skip next st, hdc in next 9, 3 hdc in last, turn–26 hdc.
Row 7: Ch 2, 2 hdc in same st, hdc in next 11, skip next st, (hdc, ch 2, hdc) in ch-2 space, skip next st, hdc in next 11, 3 hdc in last, turn–30 hdc.
Row 8: Ch 2, 2 hdc in same st, hdc in next 13, skip next st, (hdc, ch 2, hdc) in ch-2 space, skip next st, hdc in next 13, 3 hdc in last, turn–34 hdc.
Row 9: Ch 2, 2 hdc in same st, hdc in next 15, skip next st, (hdc, ch 2, hdc) in ch-2 space, skip next st, hdc in next 15, 3 hdc in last, turn–38 hdc.
Row 10: Ch 2, 2 hdc in same st, hdc in next 17, skip next st, (hdc, ch 2, hdc) in ch-2 space, skip next st, hdc in next 17, 3 hdc in last, turn–44 hdc.
Row 11: Ch 2, 2 hdc in same st, hdc in next 19, skip next st, (hdc, ch 2, hdc) in ch-2 space, skip next st, hdc in next 19, 3 hdc in last, turn–48 hdc.
Row 12: Ch 2, 2 hdc in same st, hdc in next 21, skip next st, (hdc, ch 2, hdc) in ch-2 space, skip next st, hdc in next 21, 3 hdc in last, turn–52 hdc.
Row 13: Ch 2, 2 hdc in same st, hdc in next 23, skip next st, (hdc, ch 2, hdc) in ch-2 space, skip next st, hdc in next 23, 3 hdc in last, turn–56 hdc.
Row 14: Ch 1, rotate to work across row ends, sc 54 evenly across row ends (2 sc in each row end and 2 sc in center ch), turn–54 sc.
Fasten off, leaving a long tail for sewing. Sew around Body at Rnd 11. Weave in ends.

UPPER CAPE

With **B**.
Row 1: Ch 19, starting in second ch from hook sc in each ch across, turn–18 sc.
Row 2: Ch 1, [2 sc in next st, sc in next 2] across, turn–24 sc.
Row 3: Ch 1, [2 sc in next st, sc in next 3] across, turn–30 sc.
Row 4: Ch 1, [2 sc in next st, sc in next 4] across, turn–36 sc.
Row 5: Ch 1, [2 sc in next st, sc in next 5] across, turn–42 sc.
Row 6: Ch 1, [2 sc in next st, sc in next 6] across, turn–48 sc.
Row 7: Ch 1, [2 sc in next st, sc in next 7] across, turn–54 sc.
Row 8: Ch 1, working all sts in BLO [2 sc in next st, sc in next 8] across, turn–60 sc.
Rnd 9 (Border): Ch 1, sc in next 60 sts, ch 2, rotate and work 8 sc across row ends, ch 2, rotate and work 18 sc across underside of starting ch, ch 2, rotate and sc 2 in row ends (*mark last sc made with a locking st marker*), sc 8 in row ends, ch 2, join–98 sc.
Fasten off, leaving a long tail for sewing. Continue to Lower Cape.

LOWER CAPE

With **C**.
Row 1: Ch 55, starting in second ch from hook sc in each ch across, turn–54 sc.
Row 2: Ch 1, [2 sc in next st, sc in next 8] across, turn–60 sc.
Row 3: Ch 1, [2 sc in next st, sc in next 9] across, turn–66 sc.
Row 4: Ch 1, [2 sc in next st, sc in next 10] across, turn–72 sc.
Rnd 5 (Border): Ch 1, sc in next 72 sts, ch

2, rotate to work 4 sc across row ends, ch 2, rotate to work 54 sc across underside of starting ch, ch 2, rotate to work 4 sc across opposite edge row ends, ch 2, join–134 sc.
Fasten off, leaving a long tail for sewing. Sew Lower Cape to underside of Upper Cape across Row 8. Weave in ends.

CAPE DETAIL

With **E**, join to marked st of Upper Cape.
Row 1: Ch 1, sc in marked st, sc in next, (sc, ch 2, sc) in ch-2 space, sc in next 18, (sc, ch 2, sc) in ch-2 space, sc in next 2, ch 1, sl st in same st–26 sc.
Fasten off, weave in ends.
Sew completed Cape around collar of Body under Head.

HAIR

With **F**, make a magic ring.
Rnd 1: Ch 1, 6 sc in ring, do not join–6 sc.
Rnd 2: 2 sc in each st around–12 sc.
Rnd 3: [2 sc in next st, sc in next] around–18 sc.
Rnd 4: [Sc in next st, 2 sc in next, sc in next] around–24 sc.
Rnd 5: [2 sc in next st, sc in next 3] around–30 sc.
Rnd 6: [Sc in next 2 sts, 2 sc in next, sc in next 2] around–36 sc.
Rnd 7: [2 sc in next st, sc in next 5] around–42 sc.
Rnd 8: [Sc in next 3 sts, 2 sc in next, sc in next 3] around–48 sc.
Begin working in turned rows.
Row 9: Sc in next 27 sts, turn leaving remaining sts unworked–27 sc.
Row 10: Ch 1, sc2tog-BLO, sc in each st to last 2, sc2tog-BLO, turn–25 sc.
Rows 11–15: Repeat Row 10, do not turn at the end of Row 15–15 sc.
Round 16 (Border): Ch 1, rotate to work 6 sc across row ends, sc-BLO in 21 unworked sts from Row 9, rotate to work 6 sc across row ends, ch 1, rotate to work sc-BLO in 15 sts from Row 15, join–48 sc.
Fasten off, leaving a long tail for sewing. Sew Hair to top of Head.

CENTER BANGS

With **F**.
Row 1: Ch 2, sc in second ch from hook, turn–1 sc.
Row 2: Ch 1, 3 sc in st–3 sc.
Fasten off, leaving a long tail for sewing. Sew to center of Hair at middle of forehead.

HAIR SIDE PIECE (MAKE 2)

With **F**, make a magic loop.
Rnd 1: Ch 1, 3 sc in loop–3 sc.
Rnd 2: 2 sc in next st, sc in each st around–4 sc.
Rnds 3–7: Repeat Rnd 2–9 sc at end of Rnd 7.
Rnds 8–9: Sc in each st around.
Rnd 10: Inv-dec, sc in each st around–8 sc.
Rnds 11–15: Repeat Rnd 10–3 sc at end of Rnd 15.
Fasten off, leaving a long tail for sewing. Sew to sides of Hair, using photos as a guide.

TOPKNOT

With **F**, make a magic loop.
Rnd 1: Ch 1, 8 sc in loop–8 sc.
Rnd 2: 2 sc in each st around–16 sc.
Rnd 3: [2 sc in next st, sc in next] around–24 sc.
Rnd 4: Hdc in each st around.
Rnd 5: [Inv-dec, sc in next st] around–16 sc.
Rnd 6: [Inv-dec] around–8 sc.
Rnd 7: Sc in each st around.
Fasten off, leaving a long tail for sewing. Flatten top of piece. Sew Rnd 7 to top of Hair.

TOP HAIR DETAIL

With **B**.
Row 1: Ch 2, 3 sc in second ch from hook, turn–3 sc.
Row 2: Ch 1, (sc, Small Picot, sc) in first st, (sc, Large Picot, sc) in second, (sc, Small Picot, sc) in last–6 sts, 3 Picots.
Fasten off, leaving a long tail for sewing. Sew Hair Detail at front of Topknot. Weave in ends.

TY LEE

Designed by
LEE SARTORI

Skill Level:
EASY

Ty Lee, one of seven sisters born to a Fire Nation noble, has always wanted to stand out in a crowd. So, when the opportunity to join a Fire Nation circus act presents itself, Ty Lee runs away and becomes a professional acrobat. Equipped with the skills and talents that set her apart from her sisters, Ty Lee is recruited by her old classmate Azula to hunt down and capture Prince Zuko and then, later, the Avatar. With her unique talent for blocking the chi of others, Ty Lee can temporarily halt the bending of her opponents, making her a deadly addition to the team.

A talented member of the Fire Nation, Ty Lee would normally be wearing a similar outfit to that of her partner in crime, Azula. But this circus-loving acrobat marches to her own beat, with an outfit that sets her apart from the crowd.

"I'm really happy here. I mean, my aura has never been pinker!"

—TY LEE (Book 2, Episode 3)

FINISHED MEASUREMENTS
Height: 12½ in. / 32 cm • Width: 7 in. / 18 cm

YARN
Worsted weight (#4, Medium), shown in Lion Brand *Basic Stitch* (100% Acrylic, 185 yd. / 169 m per 3.5 oz. / 100 g ball)
Color A: 122T Hazelnut, 1 ball
Color B: 400G Red Heather, 1 ball
Color C: 112S Deco Rose, 1 ball
Color D: 138L Pomegranate, 1 ball
Color E: 126AL Mahogany, 1 ball

HOOK
US C-2 / 2.75 mm, *or size needed to obtain gauge*

NOTIONS
Tapestry needle • Scissors • Polyester stuffing • Small amount of plastic mesh • Stitch markers • 8 mm safety eyes • White thread • Black thread • Brown thread

GAUGE
28 sc and 28 sc rounds = 4 in. / 10 cm; *make sure to check your gauge.*

ABBREVIATIONS
Back loop only (BLO), chain(s) (ch(s)), front loop only (FLO), front post single crochet (FPsc), single crochet (sc), slip stitch(es) (sl st(s)), stitch(es) (st(s)), two single crochet closed together (sc2tog), yarn over (yo).

SPECIAL ABBREVIATIONS
Cluster (5 dc cluster): [Yo, insert hook into indicated st, yo and draw through 2 loops on hook] 5 times, yo and draw through all loops on hook.
inv-dec (invisible single crochet decrease): Insert hook in FLO of each of next 2 sts, yo and draw through both sts, yo and draw through 2 loops on hook—1 st decreased.
Popcorn (popcorn stitch): Work 5 dc in next st, drop loop on hook, insert hook from front to back in first of 5 dc, place dropped loop on hook, and draw it through the back of the first dc.

NOTES

Work in continuous rounds unless otherwise indicated. When instructed to join, join with a slip stitch in first stitch.

"I joined the circus because I was scared of spending the rest of my life as part of a matched set. At least I'm different now. 'Circus freak' is a compliment!"

—TY LEE (Book 3, Episode 5)

ARMS (MAKE 2)

With **A**, make a magic loop.
Rnd 1: 6 sc in loop–6 sc.
Rnd 2: 2 sc in each st around–12 sc.
Rnds 3–4: Sc in each st around.
Rnd 5: Popcorn, sc in next 11 sts–12 sts.
Rnds 6–7: Sc in each st around.
Fasten off **A**, change to **B**.
Rnd 8: Ch 1, sl st in each st around, join.
Rnd 9: Ch 1, sc-BLO in each st around, join.
Rnd 10: Ch 1, sc in each st around, join.
Change to **A**.
Rnd 11: Ch 1, sl st in each st around, join.
Rnd 12: Ch 1, sc-BLO in each st around, join.
Rnds 13–18: Ch 1, sc in each st around, join.
Rnd 19: Ch 1, [2 sc in next st, sc in next 3] 3 times, join–15 sc.
Rnds 20–22: Ch 1, sc in each st around, join.
Change to **C**.
Rnd 23: Ch 1, sl st in each st around, join.
Rnd 24: Ch 1, sc-BLO in each st around, join.
Fasten off. Stuff. Set aside to join to Body.

BOOT SOLE (MAKE 4)

With **D**.
Rnd 1: Ch 5, sc in second ch from hook, sc in next 2 chs, 3 sc in last, rotate to work on underside of ch, sc in next 3, 3 sc in last–12 sc.
Rnd 2: *Sc in next 3 sts, [2 sc in next] 3 times; repeat from * around–18 sc.
Rnd 3: *Sc in next 3 sts, [2 sc in next, sc in next] 3 times; repeat from * around–24 sc.
Fasten off first piece, but do not fasten off second piece. Trace Sole on a piece of plastic mesh. Place mesh between 2 soles and continue to joining round.
Rnd 4 (Joining): Working in BLO through both thicknesses, with plastic mesh sandwiched in between, sc in each st around–24 sc.
Fasten off.

BOOT (MAKE 2)

With **D**, join to center back of heel.
Rnd 1: Ch 1, sc in each st around, join–24 sc.
Rnd 2: Ch 1, sc in next 8 sts; with **A**, [sc in next, inv-dec] 3 times; with **D**, sc in next 7, join–21 sc.
Fasten off **A**.
Rnd 3: Ch 1, sc in next 8 sts, [inv-dec] 3 times, sc in next 7, join–18 sc.
Fasten off **D**, join with **A** in BLO at back of heel.
Rnd 4: Ch 1, sc-BLO in next 6 sts, [sc2tog-BLO] 3 times, sc-BLO in next 6, join–15 sc.
Rnds 5–10: Ch 1, sc in each st around, join.
Fasten off. Stuff. Continue to Leg.

LEG (MAKE 2)

With **B**, join to center back of heel.
Rnd 1: Ch 1, sl st in each st around, join–15 sts.
Rnd 2: Ch 1, sc-BLO in each st around, join.
Rnd 3: Ch 1, [sc in next 2 sts, 2 sc in next, sc in next 2] 3 times, join–18 sc.
Fasten off **B**, join with **C**.
Rnd 4: Ch 1, sl st in each st around, join.
Rnd 5: Ch 1, [2 sc-BLO in next st, sc-BLO in next 5] 3 times, join–21 sc.
Rnds 6–11: Ch 1, sc in each st around, join.
Rnd 12: Ch 1, inv-dec, sc in each st around–20 sc.

Rnds 13–14: Repeat Rnd 12–18 sc at end of Rnd 14.
Rnd 15: Ch 1, sc in each st around, join. Fasten off. Mark center of "inner thigh" of each Leg with a locking st marker. Join to marked st of left Leg.
Rnd 16 (Joining): Ch 1, sc 18 around left Leg, sc in marked st of right Leg, sc in each st around right Leg, do not join–36 sc.
Continue to Body.

BODY

Continue with **C**.
Rnds 1–2: Sc in each st around–36 sc.
Rnd 3: 3 sc in first st, 2 sc in next, sc in each st around to last st, 2 sc in last–40 sc.
Rnds 4–6: Sc in each st around.
Change to **B**.
Rnd 7: Ch 1, sl st in each st around, join.
Rnd 8: Ch 1, sc-BLO in each st around, join.
Rnd 9: Ch 1, sc in each st around, join.
Change to **A**.
Rnds 10–11: Repeat Rnds 7–8.
Rnds 12–14: Ch 1, sc in each st around, join.
Change to **C**.
Rnds 15–16: Repeat Rnds 7–8.
Mark each "armpit" with a locking st marker, ensuring there are 19 sts between markers for the front of the Body and 19 sts between the markers for the back of the Body.
Rnd 17 (Join Arms): Ch 1, sc in each st to first marked st, sc in marked st; holding Arm in line with Body sts and ensuring thumb is facing the Body, sc in each st around first Arm, sc in each st to second marked st, sc in marked st; holding second Arm in line with Body sts and ensuring thumb is facing the Body, sc in each st around second Arm, sc in each remaining st around, join–70 sc.
Rnds 18–20: Ch 1, sc in each st around, join.
Rnd 21: Ch 1, inv-dec, [sc in next 16 sts, inv-dec] 3 times, sc in next 14–66 sc.
Rnd 22: Ch 1, [inv-dec, sc in next 9 sts] 6 times, join–60 sc.
Rnd 23: Ch 1, [sc in next 4 sts, inv-dec, sc in next 4] 6 times, join–54 sc.
Rnd 24: Ch 1, [inv-dec, sc in next 7 sts] 6 times, join–48 sc.
Rnd 25: Ch 1, [sc in next 3 sts, inv-dec, sc in next 3] 6 times, join–42 sc.
Rnd 26: Ch 1, [inv-dec, sc in next 5 sts] 6 times, join–36 sc.
Rnd 27: Ch 1, [sc in next 2 sts, inv-dec, sc in next 2] 6 times, join–30 sc.
Rnd 28: Ch 1, [inv-dec, sc in next 3 sts] 6 times, join–24 sc.
Rnd 29: Ch 1, [sc in next st, inv-dec, sc in next] 6 times, join–18 sc.
Fasten off. Stuff Body firmly.
Continue to Head.

HEAD

With **A**, join to BLO at center back of Body.
Rnd 1: Ch 1, sc-BLO in each st around, join–18 sc.
Rnds 2–3: Ch 1, sc in each st around, join.
Rnd 4: Ch 1 tightly, [sc in next st, 2 sc in next, sc in next] 6 times, do not join–24 sc.
Begin working in continuous rounds.
Rnd 5: [2 sc in next st, sc in next 3] around–30 sc.
Rnd 6: [Sc in next 2 sts, 2 sc in next, sc in next 2] around–36 sc.
Rnd 7: [2 sc in next st, sc in next 5] around–42 sc.
Rnd 8: [Sc in next 3 sts, 2 sc in next, sc in next 3] around–48 sc.
Rnd 9: [2 sc in next st, sc in next 7] around–54 sc.
Rnds 10–13: Sc in each st around.
Place a st marker in center front of Head to mark for nose.
Rnd 14 (Nose): Sc in each st to marked st, Cluster in marked st, sc in each st around.
Rnds 15–20: Sc in each st around.
Add eyes between Rnds 16–17. Using white and black thread, add eye details above and below eyes using photos as a guide. With brown thread, embroider eyebrows above eyes.
Rnd 21: [Inv-dec, sc in next 7 sts] around–48 sc.
Rnd 22: [Sc in next 3 sts, inv-dec, sc in next 3] around–42 sc.
Rnd 23: [Inv-dec, sc in next 5 sts] around–36 sc.
Rnd 24: [Sc in next 2 sts, inv-dec, sc in next 2] around–30 sc.

Rnd 25: [Inv-dec, sc in next 3 sts] around–24 sc.
Rnd 26: [Sc in next st, inv-dec, sc in next] around–18 sc.
Rnd 27: [Inv-dec, sc in next st] around–12 sc.
Stuff Head.
Rnd 28: [Inv-dec] around–6 sc.
Fasten off, leaving a long tail for sewing. Sew remaining 6 sts closed. Weave in ends.

EAR (MAKE 2)

With **A** and leaving a long tail at start for sewing, make a magic loop.
Row 1: Ch 1, work 3 sc in loop, turn–3 sc.
Row 2: Ch 1, 2 sc in each st across, turn–6 sc.
Row 3: Ch 3, sl st in starting loop.
Fasten off, leaving a long tail for sewing. Sew Ears to sides of Head. Weave in ends.

CAPE

With **B**.
Row 1: Ch 25, sc in second ch from hook and in each ch across, turn–24 sc.
Row 2: Ch 1, *(sc, ch 2, sc) in next st, sc in next 5; repeat from * across, turn–28 sc.
Row 3: Ch 1, *sc in next 6 sts, (sc, ch 2, sc) in ch-2 space, sc in next; repeat from * across, turn–36 sc.
Row 4: Ch 1, *sc in next 2 sts, (sc, ch 2, sc) in ch-2 space, sc in next 7; repeat from * across, turn–44 sc.
Row 5: Ch 1, *sc in next 8 sts, (sc, ch 2, sc) in ch-2 space, sc in next 3; repeat from * across, turn–52 sc.
Row 6: Ch 1, *sc in next 4 sts, (sc, ch 2, sc) in ch-2 space, sc in next 9; repeat from * across, turn–60 sc.
Row 7: Ch 1, *sc in next 10 sts, (sc, ch 2, sc) in ch-2 space, sc in next 5; repeat from * across, turn–68 sc.
Fasten off, leaving a long tail for sewing. Sew around shoulders of Body.

COLLAR

With **C** and leaving a long tail at the start for sewing.
Row 1: Ch 19, sc in second ch from hook and in each ch across, turn–18 sc.
Rows 2–3: Ch 1, sc in each st across, turn.
Fasten off, weave in finishing end. Use starting tail to sew around neck at Collar. Weave in end.

SHIRT SLEEVE (MAKE 2)

With **C** and leaving a long tail for sewing.
Rnd 1: Ch 15, join to first ch to form a ring, ch 1, sc in each ch around, join–15 sc.
Rnd 2: Ch 1, [sc in next 2 sts, 2 sc in next, sc in next 2] around, join—18 sc.
Rnd 3: Ch 1, [2 sc in next st, sc in next 5] around, join–21 sc.
Rnd 4: Ch 1, [2 sc in next st, sc in next 6] around, join–24 sc.
Fasten off, weave in finishing end. Use starting tail to sew to front loops at top of Arm. Weave in end.

SKIRT PANEL (MAKE 10)

With **D**.
Row 1: Ch 2, 2 sc in second ch from hook, turn–2 sc.
Row 2: Ch 1, 2 sc in next st, sc in each st across, turn–3 sc.
Rows 3–5: Repeat Row 2–6 sc at the end of Row 5.
Rows 6–10: Ch 1, sc in each st across, turn–6 sc.

Working in pairs (10 panels become 5), fasten off first piece, do not fasten off second piece. Place 2 pieces atop one another and sc next rnd through both thicknesses to join.
Rnd 11 (Border): Ch 1, working through both thicknesses sc evenly around entire piece, join–21 sc.
Fasten off, leaving a long tail for sewing. Sew Skirt Panels around waist of Body in front loops left from Rnd 7. Weave in ends.

HAIR

With **E**, make a magic loop.
Rnd 1: Ch 1, 6 sc in loop, do not join–6 sc.
Rnd 2: 2 sc in each st around–12 sc.
Rnd 3: [2 sc in next st, sc in next] around–18 sc.
Rnd 4: [Sc in next st, 2 sc in next, sc in next] around–24 sc.
Rnd 5: [2 sc in next st, sc in next 3] around–30 sc.
Rnd 6: [Sc 2 in next st, 2 sc in next, sc in next 2] around–36 sc.
Rnd 7: [2 sc in next st, sc in next 5] around–42 sc.
Rnd 8: [Sc in next 3 sts, 2 sc in next, sc in next 3] around–48 sc.
Begin working in turned rows.
Row 9: Sc in next 27 sts, turn leaving remaining sts unworked–27 sc.
Row 10: Ch 1, sc2tog-BLO, sc-BLO in each st to last 2, sc2tog-BLO, turn–25 sc.
Rows 11–15: Repeat Row 10, do not turn at the end of Row 15–15 sc.
Rnd 16 (Border): Ch 1, rotate to work 6 sc across row ends, sc-BLO in next 21 sts, rotate to work 6 sc across row ends, ch 1, sc-BLO in next 15, join–48 sc.
Fasten off, leaving a long tail for sewing. Sew Hair to top of Head. Cut approximately 40 lengths of Hair measuring roughly 10 in. / 25.5 cm. Using photos as a guide, loop strands of Hair along side part and secure at bottom of Head. Cut approximately 20 strands of Hair measuring 14 in. / 35.5 cm. Loop strands at top back of Hair and braid. Secure bottom of braid.

MAI

Designed by
LEE SARTORI

Skill Level:
EASY

Born to a world of privilege in the Fire Nation, Mai was taught that she could have anything she wanted as long as she was quiet and well behaved. Such an upbringing makes her bored and lonely but also has taught her to conceal her true feelings at all costs. Self-taught in the deadly art of knife throwing, Mai becomes part of Azula's team, dispatched to hunt down Zuko and, later, the Avatar. What Mai didn't expect was how she still feels about Prince Zuko, whom she's known from childhood. Opening up to Zuko is easier than it has been with anyone else, and for that, Mai is willing to sacrifice her position at Azula's side.

How many knives are hidden under Mai's armor? Hopefully zero in this crochet project, but you can never be sure with someone so cunning! Just kidding. You are the captain of this crochet project, so you can decide whether to arm Mai or not. We suggest not.

"I'm sorry I can't be as high-strung and crazy as the rest of you."

—MAI (Book 3, Episode 5)

FINISHED MEASUREMENTS
Height: 12 in. / 30.5 cm • Width: 7 in. / 18 cm

YARN
Worsted weight (#4, Medium), shown in Lion Brand *Lazy Days* (100% Polyester, 179 yd. / 164 m per 3.5 oz. / 100 g ball)
Color A: 123AP Taupe, 1 ball
And worsted weight (#4, Medium), shown in Lion Brand *Basic Stitch* (100% Acrylic, 185 yd. / 169 m per 3.5 oz. / 100 g ball)
Color B: 153 Black, 1 ball
Color C: 138L Pomegranate, 1 ball
Color D: 404J Silver Heather, 1 ball

HOOK
US C-2 / 2.75 mm, *or size needed to obtain gauge*

NOTIONS
Stitch markers • Tapestry needle • Polyester stuffing • 8 mm safety eyes • Small amount of plastic mesh • White thread • Black thread • Scissors

GAUGE
28 sc and 28 sc rounds = 4 in. / 10 cm; *make sure to check your gauge.*

ABBREVIATIONS
Back loop only (BLO), chain(s) (ch(s)), front loop only (FLO), front post single crochet (FPsc), half double crochet (hdc), single crochet (sc), slip stitch(es) (sl st(s)), stitch(es) (st(s)), yarn over (yo).

SPECIAL ABBREVIATIONS
Cluster (5 dc cluster): [Yo, insert hook into indicated st, yo and draw through 2 loops on hook] 5 times, yo and draw through all loops on hook.
inv-dec (invisible single crochet decrease): Insert hook in FLO of each of next 2 sts, yo and draw through both sts, yo and draw through 2 loops on hook—1 st decreased.
Popcorn (popcorn stitch): Work 5 dc in next st, drop loop on hook, insert hook from front to back in first of 5 dc, place dropped loop on hook, and draw it through the back of the first dc.

NOTES

Work in continuous rounds unless otherwise indicated. When instructed to join, join with a slip stitch in first stitch.

Zuko: You're so beautiful when you hate the world.
Mai: I don't hate you.
Zuko: I don't hate you, too.

(Book 3, Episode 2)

ARM (MAKE 2)

With **A**, make a magic loop.
Rnd 1: 6 sc in loop–6 sc.
Rnd 2: 2 sc in each st around–12 sc.
Change to **B**.
Rnd 3: Ch 1, sl st in each st around.
Rnd 4: Ch 1, sc-BLO in each st around, join.
Rnd 5: Ch 1, sc in each st around, join.
Rnd 6: Ch 1, with **A**, Popcorn; with **B**, sc in next 11 sts, join–12 sts.
Fasten off **A**.
Rnds 7–17: Ch 1, sc in each st around, join.
Rnd 18: Ch 1, [2 sc in next st, sc in next 3] around, join–15 sc.
Rnds 19–21: Ch 1, sc in each st around, join.
Change to **C**.
Rnd 22: Ch 1, sl st in each st around, join.
Rnd 23: Ch 1, sc-BLO in each st around, join.
Fasten off. Stuff.

SLEEVE (MAKE 2)

With **C** and leaving a long tail at start for sewing.
Rnd 1: Ch 15, join to first st to form a ring, ch 1, sc in each ch around, join–15 sc.
Rnd 2: Ch 1, sc in next 3 sts, hdc in next 3, dc in next 3, hdc in next 3, sc in next 3, join–15 sts.
Rnd 3: Ch 1, sc in next 3 sts, 2 hdc in next, hdc in next 2, 2 dc in next, dc in next 2, 2 hdc in next, hdc in next 2, sc in next 3, join–18 sts.
Rnd 4: Ch 1, sc in next 3 sts, 2 hdc in next, hdc in next 3, 2 dc in next, dc in next 3, 2 hdc in next, hdc in next 3, sc in next 3, join–21 sts.
Rnd 5: Ch 1, sc in next 3 sts, 2 hdc in next, hdc in next 4, 2 dc in next, dc in next 4, 2 hdc in next, hdc in next 4, sc in next 3, join–24 sts.
Rnd 6: Ch 1, sc in next 3 sts, 2 hdc in next, hdc in next 5, 2 dc in next, dc in next 5, 2 hdc in next, hdc in next 5, sc in next 3, join–27 sts.
Rnd 7: Ch 1, sc in next 3 sts, 2 hdc in next, hdc in next 6, 2 dc in next, dc in next 6, 2 hdc in next, hdc in next 6, sc in next 3, join–30 sts.
Rnd 8: Ch 1, sc in next 3 sts, 2 hdc in next, hdc in next 7, 2 dc in next, dc in next 7, 2 hdc in next, hdc in next 7, sc in next 3, join–33 sts.
Rnd 9: Ch 1, sc in next 3 sts, 2 hdc in next, hdc in next 8, 2 dc in next, dc in next 8, 2 hdc in next, hdc in next 8, sc in next 3, join–36 sts.
Fasten off, weave in finishing end. Sew to front loops of Rnd 22 of Arm. Weave in end. Set Arm aside to join to Body.

BOOT SOLE (MAKE 2 WITH B AND 2 WITH D)

Rnd 1: Ch 5, sc in second ch from hook, sc in next 2, 3 sc in last, rotate to work on underside of ch, sc in next 3, 3 sc in last–12 sc.
Rnd 2: *Sc in next 3 sts, [2 sc in next] 3 times; repeat from * around–18 sc.
Rnd 3: *Sc in next 3 sts, [2 sc in next, sc in next] 3 times; repeat from * around–24 sc.
Fasten off first piece, do not fasten off second piece. Trace Sole on a piece of plastic mesh. Place mesh between 2 Soles and continue to joining round.
Rnd 4 (Joining): Working in BLO through both thicknesses, with plastic mesh sandwiched in between, sc in each st around–24 sc.
Fasten off.

BOOT (MAKE 2)

With **B**, join to center back of heel.
Rnds 1–2: Ch 1, sc in each st around, join–24 sc.
Rnd 3: Ch 1, sc in next 8 sts, [inv-dec, sc in next] 3 times, sc in next 7, join–21 sc.
Rnd 4: Ch 1, sc in next 8 sts, [inv-dec] 3 times, sc in next 7, join–18 sc.
Rnd 5: Ch 1, sc in next 6 sts, [inv-dec] 3 times, sc in next 6, join–15 sc.
Rnds 6–11: Ch 1, sc in each st around, join.
Stuff. Continue to Leg.

LEG (MAKE 2)

Continuing with **B**.
Rnd 1: Ch 1, sc in each st around,

join–15 sc.
Rnd 2: Ch 1, [sc in next 2 sts, 2 sc in next, sc in next 2] around, join–18 sc.
Rnd 3: Ch 1, [2 sc in next st, sc in next 5] around, join–21 sc.
Rnds 4–9: Ch 1, sc in each st around, join.
Rnd 10: Ch 1, inv-dec, sc in each st around, join–20 sc.
Rnd 11: Ch 1, inv-dec, sc in each st around, join–19 sc.
Rnd 12: Ch 1, inv-dec, sc in each st around, join–18 sc.
Rnd 13: Ch 1, sc in each st around, join. Fasten off. Mark center of "inner thigh" of each Leg with a locking st marker. Join to marked st of left Leg.
Rnd 14 (Joining): Ch 1, sc 18 around left Leg, sc in marked st of right Leg, sc in each st around right Leg, do not join–36 sc.
Continue to Body.

BODY

Continue with **B**.
Rnds 1–2: Sc in each st around–36 sc.
Rnd 3: 3 sc in first st, 2 sc in next, sc in each st around to last st, 2 sc in last–40 sc.
Rnds 4–6: Sc in each st around.
Rnd 7: Ch 1, sl st in each st around, join.
Rnd 8: Ch 1, sc-BLO in each st around, join.
Rnd 9: Ch 1, sc in each st around, join. Change to **C**.
Rnd 10: Ch 1, sl st in each st around, join.
Rnd 11: Ch 1, sc-BLO in each st around, join.
Rnds 12–15: Ch 1, sc in each st around, join.
Mark each "armpit" with a locking st marker, ensuring there are 19 sts between markers for the front of the Body and 19 sts between the markers for the back of the Body.
Rnd 16 (Join Arms): Ch 1, sc in each st to first marked st, sc in marked st, holding Arm in line with Body sts and ensuring thumb is facing the Body, sc in each st around first Arm, sc in each st to second marked st, sc in marked st, holding second Arm in line with Body sts and ensuring thumb is facing the Body, sc in each st around second Arm, sc in each remaining st around, join–70 sc.
Rnds 17–19: Ch 1, sc in each st around, join.
Rnd 20: Ch 1, inv-dec, [sc in next 16 sts, inv-dec] 3 times, sc in next 14–66 sc.
Rnd 21: Ch 1, [inv-dec, sc in next 9 sts] 6 times, join–60 sc.
Rnd 22: Ch 1, [sc in next 4 sts, inv-dec, sc in next 4] 6 times, join–54 sc.
Rnd 23: Ch 1, [inv-dec, sc in next 7 sts] 6 times, join–48 sc.
Rnd 24: Ch 1, [sc in next 3 sts, inv-dec, sc in next 3] 6 times, join–42 sc.
Rnd 25: Ch 1, [inv-dec, sc in next 5 sts] 6 times, join–36 sc.
Rnd 26: Ch 1, [sc in next 2 sts, inv-dec, sc in next 2] 6 times, join–30 sc.
Rnd 27: Ch 1, [inv-dec, sc in next 3 sts] 6 times, join–24 sc.
Rnd 28: Ch 1, [sc in next st, inv-dec, sc in next] 6 times, join–18 sc.
Fasten off. Stuff Body firmly.

HEAD

With **C**, join to center back of Body.
Rnd 1: Ch 1, sc-BLO in each st around, join–18 sc.
Rnds 2–3: Ch 1, sc in each st around, join. Change to **A**.
Rnd 4: Ch 1, sl st in each st around, join.
Rnd 5: Ch 1 tightly, [sc in next st, 2 sc in next, sc in next] 6 times, do not join–24 sc.
Begin working in continuous rounds.
Rnd 6: [2 sc in next st, sc in next 3] around–30 sc.
Rnd 7: [Sc in next 2 sts, 2 sc in next, sc in next 2] around–36 sc.
Rnd 8: [2 sc in next st, sc in next 5] around–42 sc.
Rnd 9: [Sc in next 3 sts, 2 sc in next, sc in next 3] around–48 sc.
Rnd 10: [2 sc in next st, sc in next 7] around–54 sc.
Rnds 11–14: Sc in each st around.
Place a st marker in center front of Head to mark for nose.
Rnd 15 (Nose): Sc in each st to marked st, Cluster in marked st, sc in each st around.
Rnds 16–21: Sc in each st around.
Add eyes between Rnds 17–18. Using white and black thread, add eye details

above and below eyes using photos as a guide. With black thread, embroider eyebrows above eyes.
Rnd 22: [Inv-dec, sc in next 7 sts] around–48 sc.
Rnd 23: [Sc in next 3 sts, inv-dec, sc in next 3] around–42 sc.
Rnd 24: [Inv-dec, sc in next 5 sts] around–36 sc.
Rnd 25: [Sc in next 2 sts, inv-dec, sc in next 2] around–30 sc.
Rnd 26: [Inv-dec, sc in next 3 sts] around–24 sc.
Rnd 27: [Sc in next st, inv-dec, sc in next] around–18 sc.
Rnd 28: [Inv-dec, sc in next st] around–12 sc.
Stuff Head.
Rnd 29: [Inv-dec] around–6 sc.
Fasten off, leaving a long tail for sewing. Sew remaining 6 sts closed. Weave in ends.

EAR (MAKE 2)

With **A** and leaving a long tail at start for sewing, make a magic loop.
Row 1: Ch 1, work 3 sc in loop, turn–3 sc.
Row 2: Ch 1, 2 sc in each st across, turn–6 sc.
Row 3: Ch 3, sl st in starting loop.
Fasten off, leaving a long tail for sewing. Sew Ears to sides of Head. Weave in ends.

HAIR

With **B**, make a magic loop.
Rnd 1: Ch 1, 6 sc in loop, do not join–6 sc.
Rnd 2: 2 sc in each st around–12 sc.
Rnd 3: [2 sc in next st, sc in next] around–18 sc.
Rnd 4: [Sc in next st, 2 sc in next, sc in next] around–24 sc.
Rnd 5: [2 sc in next st, sc in next 3] around–30 sc.
Rnd 6: [Sc in next 2 sts, 2 sc in next, sc in next 2] around–36 sc.
Rnd 7: [2 sc in next st, sc in next 5] around–42 sc.
Rnd 8: [Sc in next 3 sts, 2 sc in next, sc in next 3] around–48 sc.
Begin working in turned rows.
Row 9: Sc in next 27 sts, turn leaving remaining sts unworked–27 sc.
Row 10: Ch 1, sc2tog-BLO, sc-BLO in each st to last 2, sc2tog-BLO, turn–25 sc.
Rows 11–15: Repeat Row 10, do not turn at the end of Row 15–15 sc.
Rnd 16 (Border): Ch 1, rotate to work 6 sc across row ends, sc-BLO in next 21 sts, rotate to work 6 sc across row ends, ch 1, sc-BLO in next 15, join–48 sc.
Fasten off, leaving a long tail for sewing. Sew Hair to top of Head. Cut approximately 30 strands of hair measuring roughly 16 in. / 40.5 cm long. Divide strands in half and secure to center top of Head for pigtails. Loop one section up and tie a knot for first bun right above Ears. Secure section with a length of **B** right below Ears. Twist section and secure section again with another strand of **B**. For bangs, cut approximately 15 strands of **B** measuring roughly 3 in. / 7.5 cm long. Loop strands through Hair piece at forehead and trim.

SKIRT

With **C** and leaving a long tail at start for sewing.
Rnd 1: Ch 42, join with a sl st to form a ring, ch 1, working across ch [sc in next, skip 2, 5 dc in next, skip 2] around, join–7 shells.
Rnd 2: Ch 3 (counts as first dc), 2 dc in same space, [skip 2 dc, sc in next dc, skip 2 dc, 5 dc in sc] around to starting st, 2 dc in same st as starting, join–7 shells.
Rnd 3: Ch 1, [sc in next dc, skip next 2 dc, 5 dc in next sc, skip 2 dc] around, join.
Rnd 4: Repeat Rnd 2.

Rnd 5: Ch 1, [sc in next dc, skip 2 dc, 7 dc in next sc, skip next 2 dc] around, join–7 shells.
Rnd 6: Ch 3 (counts as first dc), 3 dc in same st, [skip 3 dc, sc in next dc, skip 3 dc, 7 dc in next sc] around to first st, 3 dc in first st, join.
Rnd 7: Ch 1, [sc in next dc, skip 3 dc, 7 dc in next, skip 3 dc] around, join.
Rnds 8–12: Repeat Rnds 6–7.
Rnd 13: Repeat Rnd 6.
Fasten off, weave in end. Use starting tail to sew to Body in the front loops of Rnd 7. Weave in ends.

ROBE PANEL (MAKE 2)

With **B**.
Row 1: Ch 9, sc in second ch from hook and in each ch across, turn–8 sc.
Rows 2–80: Ch 1, sc in each st across, turn.
Rnd 81 (Border): Ch 1, sc in each st across, ch 2, rotate to sc 80 across row ends, ch 2, rotate to sc 8 across underside of starting ch, ch 2, rotate to sc 80 across row ends, ch 2, join–176 sc.
Fasten off, weave in ends. Place middle of each Panel on shoulder. Pin back seam together so each Panel meets down back of Body. Sew seam shut down approximately 20 sts, leaving last 3 in. / 7.5 cm of seam unsewn. Pin front and back Panels together underneath Arm, leaving last 3 in. / 7.5 cm unpinned. Sew side seam closed. Weave in ends.

COLLAR

With **D**.
Mark 20 sts centered around neck area of Robe for Collar. Join with **D** in first marked st.
Row 1: Ch 1, sc in 20 sts around neckline–20 sc.
Fasten off, weave in ends.

BUTTON

With **D**, make a magic loop.
Rnd 1: Ch 1, 6 sc in loop, join–6 sc.
Fasten off, leaving a long tail for sewing. Sew Button to front of Robe at edges of Collar. Weave in ends.

IROH

Designed by
LEE SARTORI

Skill Level:
EASY

Once known as the Dragon of the West, Iroh was a fierce high-ranking general in the Fire Nation's army who spent his early years pursuing power. In his retirement, though, Iroh has occupied himself with drinking tea, playing pai sho, and learning to respect other nations and their cultures. Despite the hard life lessons he endured, he's developed a good-humored, easygoing demeanor in his old age and has become deeply attuned to the Spirit World. After joining his exiled nephew's journey to restore his honor, Iroh seeks to guide him, imparting wisdom and providing support in the hope of steering Zuko onto a more benevolent path.

Crocheting your own Uncle Iroh is the perfect excuse to also brew up a lovely pot of tea! Always quick with sage advice, Iroh is a great companion for a day of crocheting and relaxing.

"Sharing tea with a fascinating stranger is one of life's true delights."

—IROH (Book 2, Episode 8)

FINISHED MEASUREMENTS

Height: 11 in. / 28 cm • Width: 7 in. / 18 cm

YARN

Worsted weight (#4, Medium) yarn, shown in WeCrochet *Swish* (100% Superwash Merino Wool, 110 yd. / 101 m per 1.75 oz. / 50 g ball)
Color A: 4136 Shortbread, 1 ball
And worsted weight (#4, Medium) yarn, shown in Lion Brand *Color Theory* (100% Acrylic, 246 yd. / 225 m per 3.5 oz. / 100 g ball)
Color B: 124AD Nutmeg, 1 ball
And worsted weight (#4, Medium) yarn, shown in Lion Brand *Basic Stitch* (100% Acrylic, 185 yd. / 169 m per 3.5 oz. / 100 g ball)
Color C: 158I Mustard, 1 ball
Color D: 128E Ebony, 1 ball
Color E: 404J Silver Heather, 1 ball
Color F: 148AI Burgundy, 1 ball
Color G: 138L Pomegranate, 1 ball
And worsted weight (#4, Medium) yarn, shown in Lion Brand *24/7 Cotton* (100% Mercerized Cotton, 185 yd. / 170 m per 3.5 oz. / 100 g ball)

HOOK

US C-2 / 2.75 mm, *or size needed to obtain gauge*

NOTIONS

Stitch markers • Tapestry needle • Polyester stuffing • 8 mm safety eyes • Small amount of plastic mesh • Gray eyeshadow • Scissors

GAUGE

28 sc and 28 sc rounds = 4 in. / 10 cm; *make sure to check your gauge.*

ABBREVIATIONS

Back loop only (BLO), chain(s) (ch(s)), double crochet (dc), front loop only (FLO), front post single crochet (FPsc), half double crochet (hdc), single crochet (sc), slip stitch(es) (sl st(s)), stitch(es) (st(s)), three single crochet closed together (sc3tog), two single crochet closed together (sc2tog), yarn over (yo).

SPECIAL ABBREVIATIONS

Cluster (5 dc cluster): [Yo, insert hook into indicated st, yo and draw through 2 loops on hook] 5 times, yo and draw through all loops on hook.
inv-dec (invisible single crochet decrease): Insert hook in FLO of each of next 2 sts, yo and draw through both sts, yo and draw through 2 loops on hook–1 st decreased.
Popcorn (popcorn stitch): Work 5 dc in next st, drop loop on hook, insert hook from front to back in first of 5 dc, place dropped loop on hook and draw it through the back of the first dc.

NOTES

Work in continuous rounds unless otherwise indicated. When instructed to join, join with a slip stitch in first stitch.

"Perfection and power are overrated. I think you are very wise to choose happiness and love."

—IROH (Book 2, Episode 20)

ARM (MAKE 2)

With **A**, make a magic loop.
Rnd 1: 6 sc in loop–6 sc.
Rnd 2: 2 sc in each st around–12 sc.
Rnds 3–4: Sc in each st around.
Rnd 5: Popcorn, sc in next 11 sts–12 sts.
Rnds 6–7: Sc in each st around.
Rnd 8: [2 sc in next st, sc in next 3] 3 times–15 sc.
Rnds 9–12: Sc in each st around.
Rnd 13: 2 sc in next st, sc in each st around–16 sc.
Rnds 14–15: Repeat Rnd 13–18 sc at the end of Rnd 15.
Rnds 16–19: Sc in each st around.
Change to **B**.
Rnd 20: Ch 1, sl st in each st around, join.
Fasten off. Stuff. Set aside to join to Body.

BOOT SOLE (MAKE 2 EACH WITH C AND D)

Rnd 1: Ch 5, sc in second ch from hook, sc in next 2, 3 sc in last, rotate to work on underside of chs, sc in next 3, 3 sc in last–12 sc.
Rnd 2: *Sc in next 3 sts, [2 sc in next] 3 times; repeat from * around–18 sc.
Rnd 3: *Sc in next 3 sts, [2 sc in next, sc in next] 3 times; repeat from * around–24 sc.
Fasten off first piece, do not fasten off second piece. Trace Sole on a piece of plastic mesh. Place mesh between 2 opposite-color Soles and continue to joining round.
Rnd 4 (Joining): Working in BLO through both thicknesses with plastic mesh sandwiched in between sc in each st around–24 sc.
Fasten off.

BOOT (MAKE 2)

With **D**, join to center back of heel.
Rnds 1–2: Ch 1, sc in each st around, join–24 sc.
Rnd 3: Ch 1, sc in next 8 sts, [inv-dec, sc in next] 3 times, sc in next 7, join–21 sc.
Rnd 4: Ch 1, sc in next 8 sts, [inv-dec] 3 times, sc in next 7, join–18 sc.
Rnds 5–9: Ch 1, sc in each st around, join.
Fasten off. Continue to Leg.

LEG (MAKE 2)

With **E**, join to center back of heel.
Rnd 1: Ch 1, FPsc in each st around, join–18 FPsc.
Rnd 2: Ch 1, [2 sc in next st, sc in next 3] 6 times–24 sc.
Rnds 3–11: Sc in each st around.
Fasten off. Mark center of "inner thigh" of each Leg with a locking st marker.
Join to marked st of left Leg.
Rnd 12 (Joining): Ch 1, sc 24 around left Leg, sc in marked st of right Leg, sc in each st around right Leg, do not join–48 sc.
Continue to Body.

BODY

Continue with **E**.
Rnd 1: Sc in each st around, sl st to join–48 sc.
Rnd 2: Ch 1, sc in each st around, join.
Rnd 3: Ch 1, 3 sc in next st, sc in next, 3 sc in next, sc in each st around to last 2 sts, 3 sc in next, sc in last, join–54 sc.
Rnds 4–6: Ch 1, sc in each st around, join.
Fasten off **E**, join with **B** in center of back.
Rnd 7: Ch 1, working all sts in BLO sc3tog, sc in next st, sc3tog, sc in each st around to last 4 sts, sc3tog, sc in last, join–48 sc.
Rnd 8: Ch 1, sc in next 21 sts, 3 sc in next, sc in next, 3 sc in next, sc in next, 3 sc in next, sc in next 22, join–54 sc.
Rnds 9–15: Ch 1, sc in each st around, join.
Mark each "armpit" with a locking st marker ensuring there are 26 sts between markers for front of Body and 26 sts between markers for back of Body.
Rnd 16 (Join Arms): Ch 1, sc to first marked st, sc in marked st, holding Arm in line with sts and ensuring thumb is facing Body, sc in each st around first Arm, sc to second marked st, sc in marked st, holding second Arm in line with sts and ensuring thumb is facing Body, sc in each st around second Arm, sc in each st around, join–90 sc.
Rnds 17–19: Ch 1, sc in each st around, join.
Rnd 20: Ch 1, [inv-dec, sc in next 13 sts] 6 times, join–84 sc.

Rnd 21: Ch 1, [sc in next 6 sts, inv-dec, sc in next 6] around, join–78 sc.
Rnd 22: Ch 1, [inv-dec, sc in next 11 sts] around, join–72 sc.
Rnd 23: Ch 1, [sc in next 5 sts, inv-dec, sc in next 5] around, join–66 sc.
Rnd 24: Ch 1, [inv-dec, sc in next 9 sts] around, join–60 sc.
Rnd 25: Ch 1, [sc in next 4 sts, inv-dec, sc in next 4] around, join–54 sc.
Rnd 26: Ch 1, [inv-dec, sc in next 7 sts] around, join–48 sc.
Rnd 27: Ch 1, [sc in next 3 sts, inv-dec, sc in next 3] around, join–42 sc.
Change to **C**.
Rnd 28: Ch 1, sl st in each st around, join–42 sts.
Rnd 29: Ch 1, working all sts in BLO sc in next 4 sts, sc3tog, sc in next 3, sc2tog, sc in next 3, sc3tog, sc in next 6, sc3tog, sc in next 3, sc2tog, sc in next 3, sc3tog, sc in next 4, join–32 sc.
Rnd 30: Ch 1, sc in next 3 sts, sc3tog, sc in next 6, sc3tog, sc in next 4, sc3tog, sc in next 6, sc3tog, sc in next, join–24 sc.
Fasten off. Stuff Body firmly.

SKIRT

With **B**.
Rnd 1 (Bottom): Ch 54, being careful not to twist ch, join with a sl st to first ch to form a ring, ch 1, sc in each ch around, join–54 sc.
Rnd 2: Ch 1 tightly, sc in each st around, do not join.
Begin working in continuous rounds.
Rnds 3–17: Sc in each st around.
Fasten off, leaving a long tail for sewing.
Rnd 18 (Hem): Join with **B** in underside of starting ch, ch 1, hdc in each ch around, join–54 hdc.
Fasten off, weave in ends.
Sew Skirt to Body in front loops of Rnd 7. Weave in end.

SLEEVE (MAKE 2)

With **B**.
Rnd 1 (Bottom): Ch 24, being careful not to twist ch, join with a sl st to form a ring, ch 1, sc in each ch around, join–24 sc.
Rnd 2: Ch 1 tightly, sc in each st around, do not join.
Begin working in continuous rounds.
Rnds 3–4: Sc in each st around.
Rnd 5: [Sc in next 3 sts, inv-dec, sc in next 3] around–21 sc.
Rnds 6–8: Sc in each st around.
Rnd 9: [Inv-dec, sc in next 5 sts] around–18 sc.
Rnd 10: Sc in each st around.
Fasten off, leaving a long tail for sewing.
Rnd 11 (Cuff): Join to underside of starting ch, ch 1, hdc around starting ch, join–24 hdc.
Fasten off, weave in end. Sew to top of Arm in FLO of last round.
Weave in ends.

SHOULDER PAD (MAKE 2)

With **D**.
Rnd 1: Ch 2, [sc, ch 2] in second ch from hook, [sc, ch 2] 3 times in same ch, join–4 sc, 4 ch-2 spaces.
Rnd 2: Ch 1, *sc in next st, (sc, ch 2, sc) in ch-2 space; repeat from * around, join–12 sc, 4 ch-2 spaces.
Rnd 3: Ch 1, *sc in next 2 sts, (sc, ch 2, sc) in ch-2 space, sc in next; repeat from * around, join–20 sc, 4 ch-2 spaces.
Rnd 4: Ch 1, *sc in next 3 sts, (sc, ch 2, sc) in ch-2 space, sc in next 2; repeat from * around, join–28 sc, 4 ch-2 spaces.
Rnd 5: Ch 1, *sc in next 4 sts, (sc, ch 2, sc) in ch-2 space, sc in next 3; repeat from * around, join–36 sc, 4 ch-2 spaces.
Fasten off. Join with **F** in st after ch-2 space.
Rnd 6: Ch 1, *sc in next 9 sts, (sc, ch-2, sc) in ch-2 space; repeat from * around, join–44 sc.
Fasten off, leaving a long tail for sewing. Sew a Shoulder Pad to the top of each Arm. Weave in ends.

CAPE

With **G**.
Row 1: Ch 31, sc in second ch from hook and in each ch across, turn–30 sc.
Row 2: Ch 1, [2 sc in next st, sc in next 4] across, turn–36 sc.
Row 3: Ch 1, [2 sc in next st, sc in next 5] across, turn–42 sc.
Row 4: Ch 1, [2 sc in next st, sc in next

6] across, turn–48 sc.
Row 5: Ch 1, [2 sc in next st, sc in next 7] across, turn–54 sc.
Row 6: Ch 1, [2 sc in next st, sc in next 8] across, turn–60 sc.
Row 7: Ch 1, [2 sc in next st, sc in next 9] across, turn–66 sc.
Fasten off, leaving a long tail for sewing. Sew Cape around shoulders, overlapping Shoulder Pads.

UPPER ARMOR PLATE

With **D**.
Rnd 1: Ch 9, starting in second ch from hook sc in next 7 chs, (sc, ch 2, sc, ch 2, sc) in last ch, rotate to work on underside of starting ch, sc in next 7, (sc, ch 2, sc, ch 2, sc) in last ch, join–20 sc, 4 ch-2 corners.
Rnd 2: Ch 1, *sc in next 8 sts, (sc, ch 2, sc) in ch-2 space, sc in next, (sc, ch 2, sc) in ch-2 space, sc in next; repeat from * around, join–28 sc.
Rnd 3: Ch 1, *sc in next 9 sts, (sc, ch 2, sc) in ch-2 space, sc in next 3, (sc, ch 2, sc) in ch-2 space, sc in next 2; repeat from * around, join–36 sc.
Change to **F**.
Rnd 4: Ch 1, *sc in next 10 sts, (sc, ch 2, sc) in ch-2 space, sc in next 5, (sc, ch 2, sc) in ch-2 space, sc in next 3; repeat from * around, join–48 sc.
Fasten off, leaving a long tail for sewing. Sew to front of Body at chest, overlapping Cape. Weave in ends.

LOWER ARMOR PLATE

With **D**.
Rnd 1: Ch 11, starting in second ch from hook sc in next 9 chs, (sc, ch 2, sc, ch 2, sc) in last ch, rotate to work on underside of starting ch, sc in next 9, (sc, ch 2, sc, ch 2, sc) in last ch, join–24 sc, 4 ch-2 corners.
Rnd 2: Ch 1, *sc in next 10 sts, (sc, ch 2, sc) in ch-2 space, sc in next, (sc, ch 2, sc) in ch-2 space, sc in next; repeat from * around, join–32 sc.
Rnd 3: Ch 1, *sc in next 11 sts, (sc, ch 2, sc) in ch-2 space, sc in next 3, (sc, ch 2, sc) in ch-2 space, sc in next 2; repeat from * around, join–40 sc.
Rnd 4: Ch 1, *sc in next 12 sts, (sc, ch 2, sc) in ch-2 space, sc in next 5, (sc, ch 2, sc) in ch-2 space, sc in next 3; repeat from * around, join–48 sc.
Rnd 5: Ch 1, *sc in next 13 sts, (sc, ch 2, sc) in ch-2 space, sc in next 7, (sc, ch 2, sc) in ch-2 space, sc in next 4; repeat from * around, join–54 sc.
Fasten off, leaving a long tail for sewing. Sew Armor Plate to front of Body, overlapping Upper Armor Plate. Weave in ends.

BELT

Row 1: With **G**, ch 100.
Fasten off. Wrap Belt around lower waist and tie a bow in the front that hangs loosely in front of Skirt. Secure back of Belt with a stitch using **F**.

WAISTBAND

With **G**.
Row 1: Ch 49, sc in second ch from hook and in each ch across, turn–48 sc.
Rows 2–3: Ch 1, sc in each st across, turn.
Fasten off, leaving a long tail for sewing. Wrap Waistband around Body above Belt and overlapping Lower Armor Plate. Sew ends of Waistband together at back of Body and secure ends.

HEAD

With **A**, join to center back of Body.
Rnd 1: Ch 1, sc-BLO in each st around, join–24 sc.
Rnd 2: Ch 1 tightly, sc in each st around, do not join.
Begin working in continuous rounds.
Rnd 3: Sc in each st around.
Rnd 4: [2 sc in next st, sc in next 3] around–30 sc.
Rnd 5: [Sc in next 2 sts, 2 sc in next, sc in next 2] around–36 sc.
Rnd 6: [2 sc in next st, sc in next 5] around–42 sc.
Rnd 7: [Sc in next 3 sts, 2 sc in next, sc in next 3] around–48 sc.
Rnd 8: [2 sc in next st, sc in next 7] around–54 sc.
Rnds 9–15: Sc in each st around.
Place a st marker in center front of Head to mark for nose.
Rnd 16 (Nose): Sc in each st to marked st, Cluster in marked st, sc in each st around.
Rnds 17–23: Sc in each st around.
Add eyes between Rnds 17–18. Using a length of **E**, embroider eyebrows above each eye. Weave in ends.
Rnd 24: [Inv-dec, sc in next 7 sts] around–48 sc.
Rnd 25: [Sc in next 3 sts, inv-dec, sc in next 3] around–42 sc.
Rnd 26: [Inv-dec, sc in next 5 sts] around–36 sc.
Rnd 27: [Sc in next 2 sts, inv-dec, sc in next 2] around–30 sc.
Rnd 28: [Inv-dec, sc in next 3 sts] around–24 sc.
Rnd 29: [Sc in next st, inv-dec, sc in next] around–18 sc.
Rnd 30: [Inv-dec, sc in next st] around–12 sc.
Stuff Head.

Rnd 31: [Inv-dec] around–6 sc.
Fasten off, leaving a long tail for sewing. Sew remaining 6 sts closed. Weave in ends.

EAR (MAKE 2)

With **A** and leaving a long tail at start for sewing, make a magic loop.
Row 1: Ch 1, work 3 sc in loop, turn–3 sc.
Row 2: Ch 1, 2 sc in each st across, turn–6 sc.
Row 3: Ch 3, sl st in starting loop.
Fasten off, leaving a long tail for sewing. Sew Ears to sides of Head. Weave in ends.

HAIR

With E.
Row 1: Ch 21, sc in second ch from hook and in each ch across, turn–20 sc.
Row 2: Ch 1, sc-FLO in each st across, turn.
Row 3: Ch 1, sc-BLO in each st across, turn.
Rows 4–9: Repeat Rows 2–3.
Row 10: Ch 1, working all sts in FLO sc3tog, sc across to last 3 sts, sc3tog, turn–16 sc.
Row 11: Ch 1, working all sts in BLO sc3tog, sc across to last 3 sts, sc3tog, turn–12 sc.
Row 12: Repeat Row 10–8 sc.
Fasten off, leaving a long tail for sewing. Sew Hair to Head, wrapping around back and resting behind Ears. Weave in ends.

FINISHING

Cut approximately 60 strands of **E** measuring 10 in. / 25.5 cm. Loop strands through FLO and BLO of Hair around its perimeter. Add 2 lines of strands to loops running in center of Hair. Loop remaining strands into a bun at top of Hair and secure with a length of **C**. Cut approximately 20 strands of **E** measuring 4 in. / 10 cm. Loop 5 strands along face in 5 spots, using photos as a guide. Trim. Use gray eyeshadow to fill in spaces between beard and goatee, using photos as a guide. Add a small amount of gray eyeshadow to eyebrow lines to fill them out, using photos as a guide.

TOPH

Designed by
LEE SARTORI

Skill Level:
INTERMEDIATE

Stubborn, confident, impatient, and uninhibited by formality, Toph Beifong grew up as a very sheltered rich kid. She was blind from birth, and her parents did everything to protect her from the world, causing her to rebel and run from home—only to find herself lost in a cave with reclusive, blind badgermoles, the original Earthbenders. She learns from the animals how to use her other senses and master her own earthbending skill. By both adapting to and using people's misperceptions of her to her advantage, she hones her skills, even learning to sense the slightest changes in people's heartbeats and breathing to become a human lie detector.

After meeting Aang and hearing his wishes to learn earthbending, Toph joins Aang on his journey to escape her sheltered existence and becomes a hero in her own right, eventually discovering how to metalbend.

"I am the greatest Earthbender in the world!"

—TOPH (Book 2, Episode 19)

FINISHED MEASUREMENTS
Height: 11 in. / 28 cm • Width: 7 in. / 18 cm

YARN
DK weight (#3, Light) yarn, shown in Lion Brand *Coboo* (51% Cotton, 49% Rayon from Bamboo, 232 yd. / 212 m per 3.5 oz. / 100 g ball)
Color A: 123Q Tan, 1 ball
Color B: 132 Olive, 1 ball
Color C: 152R Coal, 1 ball
Color D: 158AI Bee Pollen, 1 ball
Color E: 099W Vanilla Blossom, 1 ball
And worsted weight (#4, Medium) yarn, shown in Lion Brand *Color Theory* (100% Acrylic, 246 yd. / 225 m per 3.5 oz. / 100 g ball)

HOOK
US C-2 / 2.75 mm, *or size needed to obtain gauge*

NOTIONS
Stitch markers • Tapestry needle • Polyester stuffing • 12 mm iridescent safety eyes • Small amount of plastic mesh • Scissors

GAUGE
28 sc and 28 sc rounds = 4 in. / 10 cm; *make sure to check your gauge.*

ABBREVIATIONS
Back loop only (BLO), chain(s) (ch(s)), double crochet (dc), front loop only (FLO), front post single crochet (FPsc), right side (RS), single crochet (sc), slip stitch(es) (sl st(s)), stitch(es) (st(s)), two single crochet closed together (sc2tog), wrong side (WS), yarn over (yo).

SPECIAL ABBREVIATIONS
Cluster (5 dc cluster): [Yo, insert hook into indicated st, yo and draw through 2 loops on hook] 5 times, yo and draw through all loops on hook.
inv-dec (invisible single crochet decrease): Insert hook in FLO of each of next 2 sts, yo and draw through both sts, yo and draw through 2 loops on hook—1 st decreased.
Picot Sc (picot single crochet): Insert hook into indicated st, yo and draw up a loop, [yo and draw through 1 loop] 3 times (3 chs), yo and draw through 2 loops.
Popcorn (popcorn stitch): Work 5 dc in next st, drop loop on hook, insert hook from front to back in first of 5 dc, place dropped loop on hook and draw it through the back of the first dc.

NOTES

Work in continuous rounds unless otherwise indicated. When instructed to join, join with a slip stitch in first stitch.

"One of the good things about being blind is that I don't have to waste my time worrying about appearances. I don't care what I look like. I'm not looking for anyone's approval. I know who I am."

—TOPH (Book 2, Episode 15)

ARM (MAKE 2)

With **A**, make a magic loop.
Rnd 1: 6 sc in loop–6 sc.
Rnd 2: 2 sc in each st around–12 sc.
Rnds 3–4: Sc in each st around.
Rnd 5: Popcorn, sc in each st around, sl st in next st.
Rnd 6: Ch 1, sc in each st around, join.
Fasten off **A**, change to **B**.
Rnd 7: Ch 1, sl st in each st around, join, **turn**.
Rnd 8 (WS): Ch 1, working all sts in BLO [2 sc in next st, sc in next 3] around, join, turn–15 sc.
Fasten off **B**. With **C**, join in first front loop of Rnd 7.
Rnd 9 (RS): Ch 1, sc-FLO in each st of Rnd 7, join.
Rnd 10–11: Ch 1, sc in each st around, join.
Change to **D**.
Rnd 12: Ch 1, sl st in each st around, join.
Rnd 13: Ch 1, sc-BLO in each st around, join.
Change to **A**.
Rnd 14: Ch 1, sl st in each st around, join.
Rnd 15: Ch 1, sc-BLO in each st around, join.
Rnd 16: Ch 1, sc in each st around, join.
Rnd 17: Ch 1, 2 sc in next st, sc in each st around, join–13 sc.
Rnd 18: Ch 1, 2 sc in next st, sc in each st around, join–14 sc.
Rnd 19: Ch 1, 2 sc in next st, sc in each st around, join–15 sc.
Rnds 20–22: Ch 1, sc in each st around, join.
Change to **B**.
Rnd 23: Ch 1, sl st in each st around, join.
Fasten off, leaving a long tail for sewing. Stuff Arm. Set aside to join to Body.

SOLE (MAKE 4)

With **A**.
Rnd 1: Ch 5, sc in second ch from hook, sc in next 2, 3 sc in last, rotate to work on underside of chs, sc in next 3, 3 sc in last–12 sc.
Rnd 2: *Sc in next 3 sts, [2 sc in next] 3 times; repeat from * around–18 sc.
Rnd 3: *Sc in next 3 sts, [2 sc in next, sc in next] 3 times; repeat from * around–24 sc.
Fasten off first piece, do not fasten off second piece. Trace Sole on a piece of plastic mesh. Place mesh between 2 Soles and continue to joining round.
Rnd 4 (Joining): Working through both thicknesses with plastic mesh sandwiched in between sc in each st around–24 sc.
Fasten off. Continue to Foot.

RIGHT FOOT

With **A**, join to center back of heel.
Rnd 1: Ch 1, sc in next 9 sts, Popcorn, sc in next, Picot-Sc in next 4 sts, sc in next 9, join–24 sts.
Rnd 2: Ch 1, sc in each st around, join.
Rnd 3: Ch 1, sc in next 8 sts, [sc in next, inv-dec] 3 times, sc in next 7, join–21 sc.
Rnd 4: Ch 1, sc in next 8 sts, [inv-dec] 3 times, sc in next 7, join–18 sc.
Rnd 5: Ch 1, sc in next 6 sts, [inv-dec] 3 times, sc in next 6, join–15 sc.
Rnd 6: Ch 1, sc in each st around, join.
Change to **B**.
Rnd 7: Ch 1, sl st in each st around, join, **turn**.
Rnd 8 (WS): Ch 1, working all sts in BLO [sc in next 2 sts, 2 sc in next, sc in next 2] 3 times, join, do not turn–18 sc.
Rnd 9 (WS): Ch 1, [2 sc in next st, sc in next 5] 3 times, join, **turn**–21 sc.
Fasten off. Join with **C** in front loop of first st from Rnd 7.
Rnd 10 (RS): Ch 1, sc in each st around, join–15 sc.
Rnd 11: Ch 1, sc in each st around, join.
Continue to Leg.

LEFT FOOT

With **A**, join to center back of heel.
Rnd 1: Ch 1, sc in next 9 sts, Picot-Sc in next 4 sts, sc in next, Popcorn in next, sc in next 9, join–24 sts.
Rnds 2–9: Repeat as per Right Foot.
Continue to Leg.

LEG (MAKE 2)

With **A**.
Rnd 1: Ch 1, sc in each st around, join–15 sc.
Change to **C**.
Rnd 2: Ch 1, sl st in each st around, join.
Rnd 3: Ch 1, sc-BLO in each st around, join.
Rnds 4–5: Ch 1, sc in each st around, join.
Change to **D**.
Rnd 6: Ch 1, sl st in each st around, join.
Rnd 7: Ch 1, sc-BLO in each st around, join.
Change to **A**.
Rnd 8: Ch 1, sl st in each st around, join.
Rnd 9: Ch 1, sc-BLO in each st around, join.
Rnds 10–15: Ch 1, sc in each st around, join.
Change to **B**.
Rnd 16: Ch 1, sl st in each st around, join.
Rnd 17: Ch 1, sc-BLO in each st around, join.
Fasten off. Mark center of "inner thigh" of each Leg with a locking st marker. Join to marked st of left Leg.
Rnd 18 (Joining): Ch 1, sc 15 around left Leg, ch 3, sc in marked st of right Leg, sc in each st around right Leg, do not join–30 sc.
Rnd 19: Sc in each of next 3 chs, sc in each st around Leg, sc in underside of next 3 chs, sc in each st around Leg–36 sc.
Continue to Body.

BODY

Continue with **B**.
Rnds 1–2: Sc in each st around–36 sc.
Rnd 3: 3 sc in first st, 2 sc in next, sc in each st around to last st, 2 sc in last–40 sc.
Rnds 4–11: Sc in each st around, sl st in next.
Rnd 12: Ch 1, sl st in each st around, join.
Rnd 13: Ch 1, sc-BLO in each st around, join.
Rnds 14–16: Ch 1, sc in each st around, join.
Mark each "armpit" with a locking st marker ensuring there are 19 sts between markers for front of Body and 19 sts between markers for back of Body.
Rnd 17 (Join Arms): Ch 1, sc in each st to first marked st, sc in marked st, holding Arm in line with Body sts and ensuring thumb is facing Body, sc in each st around first Arm, sc in each st to second marked st, sc in marked st, holding second Arm in line with Body sts and ensuring thumb is facing Body, sc in each st around second Arm, sc in each remaining st around, join–70 sc.
Rnds 18–20: Ch 1, sc in each st around, join.
Rnd 21: Ch 1, inv-dec, [sc in next 16 sts, inv-dec] 3 times, sc in next 14–66 sc.
Rnd 22: Ch 1, [inv-dec, sc in next 9 sts] 6 times, join–60 sc.
Rnd 23: Ch 1, [sc in next 4 sts, inv-dec, sc in next 4] 6 times, join–54 sc.
Rnd 24: Ch 1, [inv-dec, sc in next 7 sts] 6 times, join–48 sc.
Rnd 25: Ch 1, [sc in next 3 sts, inv-dec, sc in next 3] 6 times, join–42 sc.
Rnd 26: Ch 1, [inv-dec, sc in next 5 sts] 6 times, join–36 sc.
Rnd 27: Ch 1, [sc in next 2 sts, inv-dec, sc in next 2] 6 times, join–30 sc.
Rnd 28: Ch 1, [inv-dec, sc in next 3 sts] 6 times, join–24 sc.
Rnd 29: Ch 1, [sc in next st, inv-dec, sc in next] 6 times, join–18 sc.
Fasten off. Stuff Body firmly.

PANT LEG (MAKE 2)

With **B**.
Rnd 1: Ch 30, join to first ch to form a ring, ch 1, sc in each ch around, join–30 sc.
Rnd 2: Ch 1, sc in each st around, join.

Rnd 3: Ch 1, [sc in next 4 sts, inv-dec, sc in next 4] around, join–27 sc.
Rnd 4: Repeat Rnd 2.
Rnd 5: Ch 1, [inv-dec, sc in next 7 sts] around, join–24 sc.
Rnd 6: Repeat Rnd 2.
Rnd 7: Ch 1, [sc in next 3 sts, inv-dec, sc in next 3] around, join–21 sc.
Rnd 8: Repeat Rnd 2.
Fasten off. Mark center of "inner thigh" of each Pant Leg with a locking st marker. Join to marked st of left Pant Leg.
Rnd 9 (Joining): Ch 1, sc 21 around left Pant Leg, sc in marked st of right Pant Leg, sc in each st around right Pant Leg, do not join–42 sc.
Continue to Pants.

PANTS

Continue with **B**.
Rnds 1–5: Ch 1, sc in each st around, join–42 sc.
Rnd 6: Ch 1, [inv-dec, sc in next 19 sts] around, join–40 sc.
Fasten off **B**. Change to **C**.
Rnd 7: Ch 1, sl st in each st around, join.
Rnd 8: Ch 1, [with **C**, sc in next 4 sts; with **D**, Cluster] around, join.
Rnd 9: With **C**, ch 1, sc in each st around, join.
Rnd 10: Repeat Rnd 8.
Fasten off **D**.
Rnd 11: Ch 1, sc in each st around, join.
Fasten off, weave in ends. Add Pants to Body.

SLEEVE (MAKE 2)

With **B** and leaving a long tail at start for sewing.
Rnd 1: Ch 15, sl st to first ch to form a ring, ch 1, [sc in next 2 chs, 2 sc in next, sc in next 2] around, join–18 sc.
Rnd 2: Ch 1, [2 sc in next st, sc in next 5] around, join–21 sc.
Rnd 3: Ch 1, [sc in next 3 sts, 2 sc in next, sc in next 3] around, join–24 sc.
Rnd 4: Ch 1, [2 sc in next st, sc in next 7] around, join–27 sc.
Fasten off, weave in finishing end. Use starting tail to sew to FLO of last rnd of Arm. Weave in ends.

ROBE PANEL (MAKE 6)

With **E**.
Rnd 1: Ch 2, [sc, ch 2, 2 sc, ch 2] twice in second ch from hook, join–6 sc, 4 ch-2 corners.
Rnd 2: Ch 1, *sc in next st, (sc, ch 2, sc) in ch-2 space, sc in next 2, (sc, ch 2, sc) in ch-2 space; repeat from * around, join–14 sc, 4 ch-2 corners.
Rnd 3: Ch 1, *sc in next 2 sts, (sc, ch 2, sc) in ch-2 space, sc in next 4, (sc, ch 2, sc) in ch-2 space, sc in next; repeat from * around, join–22 sc, 4 ch-2 corners.
Rnd 4: Ch 1, *sc in next 3 sts, (sc, ch 2, sc) in ch-2 space, sc in next 6, (sc, ch 2, sc) in ch-2 space, sc in next 2; repeat from around, join–30 sc, 4 ch-2 corners.

Rnd 5: Ch 1, *sc in next 4, (sc, ch 2, sc) in ch-2 space, sc in next 8, (sc, ch 2, sc) in ch-2 space, sc in next 3; repeat from * around, join–38 sc, 4 ch-2 corners.
Rnd 6: Ch 1, *sc in next 5 sts, (sc, ch 2, sc) in ch-2 space, sc in next 10, (sc, ch 2, sc) in ch-2 space, sc in next 4; repeat from * around, join–46 sc, 4 ch-2 corners.
Fasten off, leaving a long tail for sewing. Sew one Panel to center front of Body under belt using FLO from Rnd 7. Panel will drape over Pants. Sew one Panel to center back of Body under belt using FLO from Rnd 7. Panel will drape over Pants. Sew two Panels to front of Body overlapping above belt using FLO from Rnd 12. Sew two Panels to back of Body overlapping above belt using FLO from Rnd 12. Match front and back Panels above shoulders and seam. Using a length of **B**, tack top loose edge of front Panel down. Weave in ends.

COLLAR

With **E**.
Row 1: Ch 21, sc in second ch from hook and in each ch across, turn–20 sc.
Row 2: Ch 1, sc in each st across, turn.
Fasten off, leaving a long tail for sewing. Sew around top of Robe Panels. Weave in ends.

HEAD

With **A**, join to the center back of the body.
Rnd 1: Ch 1, sc in each st around, join–18 sc.
Rnd 2: Ch 1, tightly, sc in each st around, do not join.
Begin working in continuous rounds.
Rnd 3: Sc in each st around.
Rnd 4: [Sc in next st, 2 sc in next, sc in next] around–24 sc.
Rnd 5: [2 sc in next st, sc in next 3] around–30 sc.
Rnd 6: [Sc in next 2 sts, 2 sc in next, sc in next 2] around–36 sc.
Rnd 7: [2 sc in next st, sc in next 5] around–42 sc.
Rnd 8: [Sc in next 3 sts, 2 sc in next, sc in next 3] around–48 sc.
Rnd 9: [2 sc in next st, sc in next 7] around–54 sc.
Rnds 10–11: Sc in each st around.
Place a st marker in center front of Head to mark for nose.
Rnd 12 (Nose): Sc in each st to marked st, Picot-Sc in marked st, sc in each st around.
Rnds 13–20: Sc in each st around.
Insert safety eyes between Rnds 13–14.
Rnd 21: [Inv-dec, sc in next 7 sts] around–48 sc.
Rnd 22: [Sc in next 3 sts, inv-dec, sc in next 3] around–42 sc.
Using **C**, embroider eyebrows above eyes. Weave in ends. Stuff and continue stuffing as work progresses.
Rnd 23: [Inv-dec, sc in next 5 sts] around–36 sc.

Rnd 24: [Sc in next 2 sts, inv-dec, sc in next 2] around–30 sc.
Rnd 25: [Inv-dec, sc in next 3 sts] around–24 sc.
Rnd 26: [Sc in next st, inv-dec, sc in next] around–18 sc.
Rnd 27: [Inv-dec, sc in next st] around–12 sc.
Rnd 28: [Inv-dec] around–6 sc.
Fasten off, leaving a long tail for sewing. Sew remaining 6 sts closed. Weave in ends.

EAR (MAKE 2)

With **A** and leaving a long tail at start for sewing, make a magic loop.
Row 1: Ch 1, work 3 sc in loop, turn–3 sc.
Row 2: Ch 1, 2 sc in each st across, turn–6 sc.
Row 3: Ch 3, sl st in starting loop.
Fasten off, leaving a long tail for sewing. Sew Ears to sides of Head. Weave in ends.

HAIR

With **C**, make a magic ring.
Rnd 1: Ch 1, 8 sc in ring–8 sc.
Rnd 2: 2 sc in each st around–16 sc.
Rnd 3: [2 sc in next st, sc in next] around–24 sc.
Rnd 4: [Sc in next st, 2 sc in next, sc in next] around–32 sc.
Rnd 5: [2 sc in next st, sc in next 3] around–40 sc.
Rnd 6: [Sc in next 2 sts, 2 sc in next, sc in next 2] around–48 sc.
Rnd 7: [2 sc in next st, sc in next 5] around–56 sc.
Rnd 8: [Sc in next 3 sts, 2 sc in next, sc in next 3] around–64 sc.
Rnd 9: [2 sc in next st, sc in next 7] around–72 sc.
Rnd 10: [Sc in next 4 sts, 2 sc in next, sc in next 4] around–80 sc.
Rnd 11: [2 sc in next st, sc in next 9] around–88 sc.
Rnd 12: Sc in each st around.
Rnd 13: [Inv-dec, sc in next 9 sts] around–80 sc.
Rnd 14: [Sc in next 4 sts, inv-dec, sc in next 4] around–72 sc.
Rnd 15: [Inv-dec, sc in next 7 sts] around–64 sc.
Rnd 16: [Sc in next 3 sts, inv-dec, sc in next 3] around–56 sc.
Rnd 17: [Inv-dec, sc in next 5 sts] around–48 sc.
Rnd 18: Sc in each st around.
Rnd 19: [2 sc in next st, sc in next 5] around–56 sc.
Rnd 20: [Sc in next 3 sts, 2 sc in next, sc in next 3] around–64 sc.
Change to **B**.
Rnd 21: Ch 1, sl st in each st around, join.
Rnd 22: Ch 1, sc-BLO in each st around, join.
Rnd 23: Ch 1, sc in next 30 sts, ch 4, skip 4, sc in next 30, join.
Change to **D**.
Rnd 24: Ch 1, sl st in next 30 sts, ch 4, skip ch-4 space, sl st in next 30, join.
Rnd 25: Ch 1, working all sts in BLO [sc in next 3 sts, sc2tog, sc in next 3] 3 times, sc in next 3, sc2tog, sc in next, dc-BLO in 4 skipped sc 3 rnds below, sc in next, sc2tog, sc in next 3, [sc in next 3, sc2tog, sc in next 3] 3 times, join–56 sts.
Change to **C**.
Rnd 26: Ch 1, sl st in each st around, join.
Rnd 27: Ch 1, working all sts in BLO [sc2tog, sc in next 5 sts] around, join–48 sc.
Fasten off, leaving a long tail for sewing. Sew Hair to back of Head.

SIDE BANG (MAKE 4)

With **C**.
Row 1: Ch 2, sc in second ch from hook, turn–1 sc.
Row 2: Ch 1, sc in each st across, turn.
Row 3: Ch 1, 3 sc in st, turn–3 sc.
Row 4: Repeat Row 2.
Row 5: Ch 1, 2 sc in first st, sc in each st across, turn–4 sc.
Rows 6–11: Repeat Row 2.
Fasten off, leaving a long tail for sewing. Place 2 pieces atop one another and sew together around edges. Sew Side Bangs to sides of face inserting top of Bang underneath the lip of the Hair. Weave in ends.

LARGE CENTER BANG (MAKE 2)

With **C**.
Rows 1–9: Repeat Rows 1–9 of Side Bang.
Fasten off, leaving a long tail for sewing. Place 2 pieces atop one another and sew around edges to join. Sew to middle of forehead and down between the left eye and nose. Weave in ends.

SMALL CENTER BANG

With **C**, make a magic loop.
Rnd 1: Ch 1, 3 sc in loop–3 sc.
Rnd 2: 2 sc in next st, sc in next 2–4 sc.
Rnds 3–8: Sc in each st around.
Fasten off, leaving a long tail for sewing. Sew between right eye and Large Center Bang. Weave in ends.

HAIR DETAIL (MAKE 2)

With **E**, make a magic ring.
Rnd 1: Ch 1, 6 sc in ring–6 sc.
Rnd 2: 2 sc in each st around–12 sc.
Rnd 3: [2 sc in next st, sc in next] around–18 sc.
Rnd 4: Sc in each st around.
Rnd 5: [Inv-dec, sc in next st] around–12 sc.
Fasten off, leaving a long tail for sewing. Stuff shape. Sew to sides of Head above Ears. Weave in ends.

SUKI

Designed by
LEE SARTORI

Skill Level:
INTERMEDIATE

Calm, humble, quick-witted, and perceptive, Suki, a non-bending member of the Earthbending Nation of Kyoshi Island, is a skilled leader of the Kyoshi Warriors. When Aang and his friends arrive on Kyoshi Island, Suki mistakes them for Fire Nation adversaries and attempts to drive them away. But when the visitors become friends, Suki teaches Sokka how to fight—and ultimately how to respect a female warrior. Suki takes a brave stand against Azula and joins Team Avatar, eventually falling in love with Sokka and playing a crucial role in ending the war.

The Kyoshi lifestyle is important to the Kyoshi Warriors, and to Suki in particular. She takes her role as a leader very seriously. In her traditional face paint and robes, Suki is always ready for battle!

"I am a warrior . . . but I'm a girl too."

—SUKI (Book 1, Episode 4)

FINISHED MEASUREMENTS
Height: 12 in. / 30.5 cm • Width: 7 in. / 18 cm

YARN
Worsted weight (#4, Medium), shown in Lion Brand *Color Theory* (100% Acrylic, 246 yd. / 225 m per 3.5 oz. / 100 g ball)
Color A: 173AE Caper, 1 ball
Color H: 158AI Bee Pollen, 1 ball
And worsted weight (#4, Medium), shown in Lion Brand *Basic Stitch* (100% Acrylic, 185 yd. / 169 m per 3.5 oz. / 100 g ball)
Color B: 407K Pine Heather, 1 ball
Color C: 174AA Beryl, 1 ball
Color D: 153 Black, 1 ball
Color E: 158I Mustard, 1 ball
Color F: 100 White, 1 ball
Color G: 125AA Truffle, 1 ball

HOOK
US C-2 / 2.75 mm, *or size needed to obtain gauge*

NOTIONS
Stitch markers • Tapestry needle • Polyester stuffing • 8 mm safety eyes • Small amount of plastic mesh • Red thread • Black thread • Scissors

GAUGE
28 sc and 28 sc rounds = 4 in. / 10 cm; *make sure to check your gauge.*

ABBREVIATIONS
Back loop only (BLO), chain(s) (ch(s)), front loop only (FLO), front post single crochet (FPsc), half double crochet (hdc), single crochet (sc), slip stitch(es) (sl st(s)), stitch(es) (st(s)), two half double crochet closed together (hdc2tog), two single crochet closed together (sc2tog), yarn over (yo).

SPECIAL ABBREVIATIONS
Cluster (5 dc cluster): [Yo, insert hook into indicated st, yo and draw through 2 loops on hook] 5 times, yo and draw through all loops on hook.
inv-dec (invisible single crochet decrease): Insert hook in FLO of each of next 2 sts, yo and draw through both sts, yo and draw through 2 loops on hook–1 st decreased.
Popcorn (popcorn stitch): Work 5 dc in next st, drop loop on hook, insert hook from front to back in first of 5 dc, place dropped loop on hook and draw it through the back of the first dc.

NOTES

Work in continuous rounds unless otherwise indicated. When instructed to join, join with a slip stitch in first stitch.

"I'm an elite warrior who has trained for many years in the art of stealth. . . . I think I can get you backstage."

—SUKI (Book 3, Episode 17)

ARMS (MAKE 2)

With **A**, make a magic loop.
Rnd 1: Ch 1, 6 sc in loop, join–6 sc.
Rnd 2: Ch 1, 2 sc in each st around, join–12 sc.
Rnds 3–4: Ch 1, sc in each st around, join.
Rnd 5: Ch 1, Popcorn, sc in next 11 sts, join–12 sts.
Rnds 6–7: Ch 1, sc in each st around, join.
Change to **B**.
Rnd 8: Ch 1, sl st in each st around, join.
Rnd 9: Ch 1, sc-BLO in each st around, join.
Rnds 10–16: Ch 1, sc in each st around, join.
Change to **C**.
Rnd 17: Ch 1, FPsc in each st around, join–12 FPsc.
Rnd 18: Ch 1, [2 sc in next st, sc in next 3] around, join–15 sc.
Rnds 19–22: Ch 1, sc in each st around, join.
Fasten off. Stuff.

CUFF (MAKE 2)

With **C** and leaving a long tail at start for sewing.
Rnd 1: Ch 12, sl st to first ch to form a ring, ch 1, sc in each ch around, join–12 sc.
Rnd 2: Ch 1, [2 sc in next st, sc in next 3] around, join–15 sc.
Fasten off, weave in finishing end. Using starting tail, sew to front loops from Rnd 8 of Arm. Weave in end.

ARM DETAIL (MAKE 2)

With **E**, make a magic loop.
Rnd 1: Ch 1, 6 sc in loop, join–6 sc.
Change to **B**.
Rnd 2: Ch 1, 2 sc-BLO in each st around, join–12 sc.
Fasten off, leaving a long tail for sewing. Sew Arm Detail to upper arm on opposite edge of each thumb. Weave in ends.

BOOT SOLE (MAKE 4)

With **A**.
Rnd 1: Ch 5, sc in second ch from hook, sc in next 2 chs, 3 sc in last, rotate to work on underside of ch, sc in next 3, 3 sc in last–12 sc.
Rnd 2: *Sc in next 3 sts, [2 sc in next] 3 times; repeat from * around–18 sc.
Rnd 3: *Sc in next 3 sts, [2 sc in next, sc in next] 3 times; repeat from * around–24 sc.
Fasten off first piece, do not fasten off second piece. Trace Sole on a piece of plastic mesh. Place mesh between 2 Soles and continue to joining round.
Rnd 4 (Joining): Working in BLO through both thicknesses, with plastic mesh sandwiched in between, sc in each st around–24 sc.
Fasten off. Continue to Boot.

BOOT (MAKE 2)

With **A**, join to center back of heel.
Rnds 1–2: Ch 1, sc in each st around, join–24 sc.
Rnd 3: Ch 1, sc in next 8 sts, [inv-dec, sc in next] 3 times, sc in next 7, join–21 sc.
Rnd 4: Ch 1, sc in next 8 sts, [inv-dec] 3 times, sc in next 7, join–18 sc.
Rnd 5: Ch 1, sc in next 6 sts, [inv-dec] 3 times, sc in next 6, join–15 sc.
Rnds 6–11: Ch 1, sc in each st around, join.
Stuff. Continue to Leg.

LEG (MAKE 2)

Continue with **A**.
Rnd 1: Ch 1, sc in each st around, join–15 sc.
Rnd 2: Ch 1, [sc in next 2 sts, 2 sc in next, sc in next 2] around, join–18 sc.
Rnd 3: Ch 1, [2 sc in next st, sc in next 5] around, join–21 sc.
Rnds 4–9: Ch 1, sc in each st around, join.
Rnd 10: Ch 1, inv-dec, sc in each st around, join–20 sc.
Rnd 11: Ch 1, inv-dec, sc in each st around, join–19 sc.
Rnd 12: Ch 1, inv-dec, sc in each st around, join–18 sc.
Rnd 13: Ch 1, sc in each st around, join.
Fasten off. Mark center of "inner thigh" of each Leg with a locking st marker. Join to marked st of left Leg.
Rnd 14 (Joining): Ch 1, sc 18 around

left Leg, sc in marked st of right Leg, sc in each st around right Leg, do not join–36 sc.
Continue to Body.

BODY

Continue with **A**.
Rnds 1–2: Sc in each st around–36 sc.
Rnd 3: 3 sc in first st, 2 sc in next, sc in each st around to last st, 2 sc in last–40 sc.
Rnds 4–6: Sc in each st around–40 sc.
Change to **C**.
Rnd 7: Ch 1, sl st in each st around, join–40 sts.
Rnd 8: Ch 1, sc-BLO in each st around, join.
Rnds 9–14: Ch 1, sc in each st around, join.
Mark each "armpit" with a locking st marker, ensuring there are 19 sts between markers for the front of the Body and 19 sts between the markers for the back of the Body.
Rnd 15 (Join Arms): Ch 1, sc in each st to first marked st, sc in marked st, holding Arm in line with Body sts and ensuring thumb is facing the Body, sc in each st around first Arm, sc in each st to second marked st, sc in marked st, holding second Arm in line with Body sts and ensuring thumb is facing the Body, sc in each st around second Arm, sc in each remaining st around, join–70 sc.
Rnds 16–18: Ch 1, sc in each st around, join.
Rnd 19: Ch 1, inv-dec, [sc in next 16 sts, inv-dec] 3 times, sc in next 14–66 sc.
Rnd 20: Ch 1, [inv-dec, sc in next 9 sts] 6 times, join–60 sc.
Rnd 21: Ch 1, [sc in next 4 sts, inv-dec, sc in next 4] 6 times, join–54 sc.
Rnd 22: Ch 1, [inv-dec, sc in next 7 sts] 6 times, join–48 sc.
Rnd 23: Ch 1, [sc in next 3 sts, inv-dec, sc in next 3] 6 times, join–42 sc.
Rnd 24: Ch 1, [inv-dec, sc in next 5 sts] 6 times, join–36 sc.
Rnd 25: Ch 1, [sc in next 2 sts, inv-dec, sc in next 2] 6 times, join–30 sc.
Rnd 26: Ch 1, [inv-dec, sc in next 3 sts] 6 times, join–24 sc.
Rnd 27: Ch 1, [sc in next st, inv-dec, sc in next] 6 times, join–18 sc.
Fasten off. Stuff Body firmly.

HEAD

With **F**, join to center back of Body.
Rnd 1: Ch 1, sl st in each st around, join–18 sts.
Rnd 2: Ch 1, sc-BLO in each st around, join.
Rnds 3–4: Ch 1, sc in each st around, join.
Rnd 5: Ch 1 tightly, [sc in next st, 2 sc in next, sc in next] 6 times, do not join–24 sc.
Begin working in continuous rounds.
Rnd 6: [2 sc in next st, sc in next 3] around–30 sc.
Rnd 7: [Sc in next 2 sts, 2 sc in next, sc in next 2] around–36 sc.
Rnd 8: [2 sc in next st, sc in next 5] around–42 sc.
Rnd 9: [Sc in next 3 sts, 2 sc in next, sc in next 3] around–48 sc.
Rnd 10: [2 sc in next st, sc in next 7] around–54 sc.
Rnds 11–14: Sc in each st around.
Place a st marker in center front of Head to mark for nose.
Rnd 15 (Nose): Sc in each st to marked st, Cluster in marked st, sc in each st around.
Rnds 16–21: Sc in each st around.
Add eyes between Rnds 17–18. Using red and black thread, add eye details above eyes using photos as a guide.
Rnd 22: [Inv-dec, sc in next 7 sts] around–48 sc.
Rnd 23: [Sc in next 3 sts, inv-dec, sc in next 3] around–42 sc.
Rnd 24: [Inv-dec, sc in next 5 sts] around–36 sc.
Rnd 25: [Sc in next 2 sts, inv-dec, sc in next 2] around–30 sc.
Rnd 26: [Inv-dec, sc in next 3 sts] around–24 sc.
Rnd 27: [Sc in next st, inv-dec, sc in next] around–18 sc.
Rnd 28: [Inv-dec, sc in next st] around–12 sc.
Stuff Head.
Rnd 29: [Inv-dec] around–6 sc.
Fasten off, leaving a long tail for sewing. Sew remaining 6 sts closed.
Weave in ends.

EAR (MAKE 2)

With **F** and leaving a long tail at start for sewing, make a magic loop.
Row 1: Ch 1, work 3 sc in loop, turn–3 sc.
Row 2: Ch 1, 2 sc in each st across, turn–6 sc.
Row 3: Ch 3, sl st in starting loop.
Fasten off, leaving a long tail for sewing. Sew Ears to sides of Head. Weave in ends.

HAIR

With **G**, make a magic loop.
Rnd 1: Ch 1, 6 sc in loop, do not join–6 sc.
Rnd 2: 2 sc in each st around–12 sc.
Rnd 3: [2 sc in next st, sc in next] around–18 sc.
Rnd 4: [Sc in next st, 2 sc in next, sc in next] around–24 sc.
Rnd 5: [2 sc in next st, sc in next 3] around–30 sc.
Rnd 6: [Sc in next 2 sts, 2 sc in next, sc in next 2] around–36 sc.
Rnd 7: [2 sc in next st, sc in next 5] around–42 sc.
Rnd 8: [Sc in next 3 sts, 2 sc in next, sc in next 3] around–48 sc.
Begin working in turned rows.
Row 9: Sc in next 27 sts, turn leaving remaining sts unworked–27 sc.
Row 10: Ch 1, sc2tog-BLO, sc-BLO in each st to last 2, sc2tog-BLO, turn–25 sc.
Rows 11–15: Repeat Row 10, do not turn at the end of Row 15–15 sc.
Rnd 16 (Border): Ch 1, rotate to work 6 sc across row ends, sc-BLO in next 21, rotate to work 6 sc across row ends, ch 1, sc-BLO in next 15, join–48 sc.
Fasten off, leaving a long tail for sewing. Sew Hair to top of Head. Cut approximately 60 strands of **G** measuring roughly 10 in. / 25.5 cm. Loop strands of hair through Hair piece along side part and trim to rest just above the shoulders.

HEADBAND

With **B**.
Row 1: Ch 54.
Fasten off, leaving a long tail for sewing. Sew Headband around Head, resting at center of forehead. Weave in ends.

HEADPIECE TRIANGLE

With **H**.
Row 1: Ch 2, (2 sc, ch 2, 2 sc) in second ch from hook, turn–4 sc.
Row 2: Ch 1, sc in next 2 sts, (sc, ch 2, sc) in ch-2 space, sc in next 2, turn–6 sc.
Row 3: Ch 1, sc in next 3 sts, (sc, ch 2, sc) in ch-2 space, sc in next 3, turn–8 sc.
Row 4: Ch 1, sc in next 4 sts, (sc, ch 2, sc) in ch-2 space, sc in next 4, turn–10 sc.
Row 5: Ch 1, sc in next 5 sts, (sc, ch 2, sc) in ch-2 space, sc in next 5, do not turn–12 sc.
Row 6 (Bottom Edge): Ch 1, working across row ends sc 11 evenly–11 sc.
Fasten off, leaving a long tail for sewing. Sew to front of Headband. Weave in ends.

HEADPIECE CENTER

With **E**.
Rnd 1: Ch 2, (sc, ch 2) 4 times in second ch from hook, join–4 sc.
Rnd 2: Ch 1, *sc in next st, (sc, ch 2, sc) in ch-2 space; repeat from * around, join–12 sc.
Fasten off, leaving a long tail for sewing.

HEADPIECE SPIKES (MAKE 2)

With **E**.
Row 1: Ch 20 tightly.
Fasten off. Place Spikes in an X on front of Headpiece Triangle. Place Headpiece Center on top, and using tail from Center, sew all pieces down to secure Spikes. Weave in ends. Trim ends of Spikes.

SKIRT

With **B** and leaving a long tail at start for sewing.
Rnd 1: Ch 42, join with a sl st to form a ring, ch 1, working around starting ch [sc in next, skip 2 chs, 5 dc in next, skip 2 chs] around, join–7 shells.
Rnd 2: Ch 3 (counts as first dc), 2 dc in same space, [skip 2 dc, sc in next dc, skip 2 dc, 5 dc in sc] around to starting st, 2 dc in same st as starting, join–7 shells.
Rnd 3: Ch 1, [sc in next dc, skip next 2 dc, 5 dc in next sc, skip 2 dc] around, join.
Rnd 4: Repeat Rnd 2.
Rnd 5: Ch 1, [sc in next dc, skip 2 dc, 7 dc in next sc, skip next 2 dc] around, join–7 shells.
Rnd 6: Ch 3 (counts as first dc), 3 dc in same st, [skip 3 dc, sc in next dc, skip 3 dc, 7 dc in next sc] around to first st, 3 dc in first st, join.
Rnd 7: Ch 1, [sc in next dc, skip 3 dc, 7 dc in next, skip 3 dc] around, join.
Rnds 8–12: Repeat Rnds 6–7.
Rnd 13: Repeat Rnd 6.
Fasten off, weave in end. Use starting tail to sew to Body in front loops of Rnd 7. Weave in ends.

OVERSKIRT

With **C**.
Row 1: Ch 41, sc in second ch from hook and in each ch across, turn–40 sc.
Row 2: Ch 1, [2 sc in next st, sc in next 9] across, turn–44 sc.
Row 3: Ch 1, [2 sc in next st, sc in next 10] across, turn–48 sc.
Rows 4–14: Ch 1, sc in each st across, turn.
Rnd 15 (Border): Ch 1, sc in next 48 sts, ch 2, rotate to sc 14 across row ends, ch 2, rotate to sc 40 across underside of starting ch, ch 2, rotate to sc 14 across row ends, ch 2, join–116 sc.
Fasten off, leaving a long tail for sewing. Sew Overskirt to front of Body in front of Skirt. Weave in ends.

ARMOR PLATE (MAKE 2)

With **A**.
Row 1: Ch 21, hdc in second ch from hook and in each ch across, turn–20 hdc.
Row 2: Ch 2 (does not count as a st here and throughout), hdc-FLO in each st across, turn.
Row 3: Ch 2, hdc in third loop in each st across, turn.
Rows 4–5: Repeat Rows 2–3.
Row 6: Ch 2, hdc2tog-FLO, hdc-FLO in each st across to last 2 sts, hdc2tog-FLO, turn–18 hdc.
Row 7: Working all sts in third loop, hdc2tog, hdc in each st across to last 2 sts, hdc2tog, turn–16 hdc.
Rows 8–9: Repeat Rows 6–7–12 sts at the end of Row 9.
Round 10 (Border): Ch 1, sc evenly around entire piece, join.
Fasten off, leaving a long tail for sewing.

SHOULDER STRAPS (MAKE 2)

With **D**.
Row 1: Ch 10, sc in second ch from hook and in each ch across, turn–9 sc.
Row 2: Ch 1, [sc in next st, 2 sc in next, sc in next] across, turn–12 sc.
Row 3: Ch 1, [2 sc in next st, sc in next 3] across, turn–15 sc.
Fasten off, leaving a long tail for sewing. Pin an Armor Plate on chest and one on back of Body. Pin a Shoulder Strap to each shoulder and sew edges of Straps to each edge of Armor Plates. Weave in Shoulder Strap ends. Pin edges of Armor Plates where they meet underneath each Arm. Sew underarm seam closed on each side of Armor Plate. Weave in ends.

ARMOR SKIRT PLATE (MAKE 5)

With **A**.
Row 1: Ch 10, starting in third ch from hook hdc, hdc in each ch across, turn–8 hdc.
Row 2: Ch 2 (does not count as a st here and throughout), hdc-FLO in each st across, turn.
Row 3: Ch 2, hdc in third loop in each st across, turn.
Rows 4–5: Repeat Rows 2–3, do not turn after Row 3.
Rnd 6 (Border): Ch 1, rotate to sc 5 across row ends, ch 2, sc 8 across underside of starting ch, ch 2, rotate to sc 5 across row ends, ch 2, sc-BLO in each st across, ch 2, join–26 sc.
Fasten off, leaving a long tail for sewing. Sew Armor Skirt Plates to bottom of Armor using photos as a guide. Weave in ends.

BELT

With **D**.
Row 1: Ch 300 tightly.
Fasten off. Wrap Belt around waist several times and tie a knot at front of Body to secure. Trim ends.

KING BUMI

Designed by
LEE SARTORI

Skill Level:
INTERMEDIATE

Before Aang's unplanned century inside an iceberg, he and Bumi were extremely close childhood friends. After returning, Aang runs into Bumi without recognizing him when Team Avatar ventures to Omashu. As an old man, King Bumi does not seem like he has all his wits about him, but rest assured, he's a master Earthbender and actual King of Omashu. When Aang and his friends are brought before King Bumi for destroying the Cabbage Merchant's cart, Bumi hatches a plan to remind Aang of their friendship without revealing his identity. When Aang successfully guesses Bumi's name, the pair delight in their past friendship and how far they've both come in the past hundred years.

Sometimes cackling, sometimes confusing, but always upbeat and adventurous, King Bumi is a vivid character. Over one hundred years old, King Bumi has learned to enjoy life to the fullest and mastered his earthbending skills with ease.

"You thought I was a frail old man, but I'm the most powerful Earthbender you'll ever see."

—KING BUMI (Book 1, Episode 5)

FINISHED MEASUREMENTS
Height: 12 in. / 30.5 cm • Width: 7 in. / 18 cm

YARN
Worsted weight (#4, Medium) yarn, shown in Lion Brand *Color Theory* (100% Acrylic, 246 yd. / 225 m per 3.5 oz. / 100 g ball)
Color A: 124AD Nutmeg, 1 ball
And worsted weight (#4, Medium) yarn, shown in Lion Brand *Basic Stitch* (100% Acrylic, 185 yd. / 169 m per 3.5 oz. / 100 g ball)
Color B: 128E Ebony, 1 ball
Color C: 404J Silver Heather, 1 ball
Color E: 407K Pine Heather, 1 ball
Color F: 098C Ecru, 1 ball
And DK weight (#3, Light) yarn, shown in Lion Brand *Coboo* (51% Cotton, 49% Rayon from Bamboo, 232 yd. / 212 m per 3.5 oz. / 100 g ball)
Color D: 132 Olive, 1 ball

HOOK
US C-2 / 2.75 mm, *or size needed to obtain gauge*

NOTIONS
Stitch markers • Tapestry needle • Polyester stuffing • 6 mm safety eyes • Small amount of plastic mesh • Small amount of white felt • Scissors

GAUGE
28 sc and 28 sc rounds = 4 in. / 10 cm; *make sure to check your gauge.*

ABBREVIATIONS
Back loop only (BLO), chain(s) (ch(s)), double crochet (dc), front loop only (FLO), front post single crochet (FPsc), single crochet (sc), slip stitch(es) (sl st(s)), stitch(es) (st(s)), two single crochet closed together (sc2tog), yarn over (yo).

SPECIAL ABBREVIATIONS
Cluster (5 dc cluster): [Yo, insert hook into indicated st, yo and draw through 2 loops on hook] 5 times, yo and draw through all loops on hook.
inv-dec (invisible single crochet decrease): Insert hook in FLO of each of next 2 sts, yo and draw through both sts, yo and draw through 2 loops on hook–1 st decreased.
Picot-Sc (picot single crochet): Insert hook into indicated st, yo and draw up a loop, [yo and draw through 1 loop] 3 times (3 chs), yo and draw through 2 loops.
Popcorn (popcorn stitch): Work 5 dc in next st, drop loop on hook, insert hook from front to back in first of 5 dc, place dropped loop on hook and draw it through the back of the first dc.

NOTES

Work in continuous rounds unless otherwise indicated. When instructed to join, join with a slip stitch in first stitch.

"Instead of seeing what they want you to see, you gotta open your brain to the possibilities."

—KING BUMI
(Book 1, Episode 5)

ARM (MAKE 2)

With **A**, make a magic loop.
Rnd 1: 6 sc in loop–6 sc.
Rnd 2: 2 sc in each st around–12 sc.
Rnds 3–4: Sc in each st around.
Rnd 5: Popcorn, sc in each st around, sl st in next st–12 sts.
Rnds 6–7: Sc in each st around.
Fasten off, change to **B**.
Rnd 8: Ch 1, sl st in each st around, join.
Rnd 9: Ch 1, sc-BLO in each st around, join.
Rnd 10: Ch 1, [sc in next st; with **C**, Picot-Sc; with **B**, sc in next] 4 times, join–12 sts.
Rnd 11: Ch 1, sc in each st around, join.
Rnds 12–15: Repeat Rnds 10–11.
Change to **A**.
Rnds 16–17: Repeat Rnds 8–9.
Rnd 18: Ch 1 tightly, sc in each st around, do not join.
Begin working in continuous rounds.
Rnd 19: [2 sc in next st, sc in next 3] 3 times–15 sc.
Rnd 20–23: Sc in each st around.
Fasten off, leaving a long tail for sewing. Stuff Arm. Set aside to join to Body.

SOLE (MAKE 4)

With **A**.
Rnd 1: Ch 5, sc in second ch from hook, sc in next 2, 3 sc in last, rotate to work on underside of chs, sc in next 3, 3 sc in last–12 sc.
Rnd 2: *Sc in next 3 sts, [2 sc in next st] 3 times; repeat from * around–18 sc.
Rnd 3: *Sc in next 3 sts, [2 sc in next, sc in next] 3 times; repeat from * around–24 sc.
Fasten off first piece, do not fasten off second piece. Trace Sole on a piece of plastic mesh. Place mesh between 2 Soles and continue to joining round.
Rnd 4 (Joining): Working through both thicknesses, with plastic mesh sandwiched in between, sc in each st around–24 sc.
Fasten off. Continue to Right Foot.

RIGHT FOOT

With **A**, join to center back of heel.
Rnd 1: Ch 1, sc in next 9 sts, Popcorn, sc in next, Picot-Sc in next 4 sts, sc in next 9, join–24 sts.
Rnd 2: Ch 1, sc in each st around, join–24 sc.
Rnd 3: Ch 1, sc in next 8 sts, [sc in next, inv-dec] 3 times, sc in next 7, join–21 sc.
Rnd 4: Ch 1, sc in next 8 sts, [inv-dec] 3 times, sc in next 7, join–18 sc.
Rnd 5: Ch 1, sc in next 6 sts, [inv-dec] 3 times, sc in next 6, join–15 sc.
Rnd 6: Ch 1, sc in each st around, join.
Change to **B**.
Rnd 7: Ch 1, sl st in each st around, join.
Rnd 8: Ch 1, sc-BLO in each st around, join.
Rnd 9: Ch 1, [sc in next st; with **C**, Picot-Sc; with **B**, sc in next] 5 times, join.
Fasten off **C**, continue with **B**.
Rnd 10: Ch 1, sc in each st around, join.
Change to **A**.
Rnd 11: Ch 1, sl st in each st around, join.
Rnd 12: Ch 1, sc-BLO in each st around, join.
Rnd 13: Ch 1, sc in each st around, join.
Continue to Leg.

LEFT FOOT

With **A**, join to center back of heel.
Rnd 1: Ch 1, sc in next 9 sts, Picot-Sc in next 4, sc in next, Popcorn in next, sc in next 9, join–24 sts.
Rnds 2–13: Repeat as per Right Foot.
Continue to Leg.

LEG (MAKE 2)

With **A**, join to center back of heel.
Rnd 1: Ch 1, sc in each st around, join–15 sc.
Rnd 2: Ch 1, [sc in next 2 sts, 2 sc in next, sc in next 2] 3 times, join–18 sc.
Rnd 3: Ch 1, [2 sc in next st, sc in next 5] 3 times, join–21 sc.
Rnds 4–9: Sc in each st around.
Fasten off **A**, join with **D** in back of Leg.
Rnd 10: Ch 1, sl st in each st around, join.
Rnd 11: Ch 1, sc-BLO in each st around, join.
Fasten off **D**, join with **E**.
Rnd 12: Ch 1, sl st in each st around, join.
Rnd 13: Ch 1, sc2tog-BLO, sc in each st around, join–20 sc.
Rnd 14: Ch 1, inv-dec, sc in each st around, join–19 sc.
Rnd 15: Repeat Rnd 14–18 sc.
Rnd 16: Ch 1, sc in each st around, join.
Fasten off. Mark center of "inner thigh" of each Leg with a locking st marker.
Join to marked st of left Leg.
Rnd 17 (Joining): Ch 1, sc in each st around left Leg, ch 3, sc in marked st of right Leg, sc in each st around right Leg, do not join–36 sc, 1 ch-3 space.
Start of rnd will move to first st made in ch-3 of next rnd.

Rnd 18: Sc in next 3 chs, sc in next 18 sts, sc in underside of next 3 chs, sc in next 18–42 sc.
Continue to Body.

BODY

Continue with **E**.
Rnds 1–6: Sc in each st around–42 sc.
Fasten off, change to **B**.
Rnd 7: Ch 1, sl st in each st around, join.
Rnd 8: Ch 1, sc-BLO in each st around, join.
Rnd 9: Ch 1, [sc in next 3 sts; with **C**, Picot-Sc; with **B**, sc in next 2] around, join.
Fasten off **C**.
Rnd 10: Ch 1, sc in each st around, join.
Fasten off **B**, change to **A**.
Rnd 11: Ch 1, sl st in each st around, join.
Rnd 12: Ch 1 tightly, sc-BLO in each st around, do not join.
Begin working in continuous rounds.
Rnds 13–15: Sc in each st around.
Mark each "armpit" with a locking st marker ensuring there are 20 sts between markers for front of Body and 20 sts between markers for back of Body.
Rnd 16 (Join Arms): Ch 1, sc in each st to first marked st, sc in marked st, holding Arm in line with Body sts and ensuring thumb is facing Body, sc in each st around first Arm, sc in each st to second marked st, sc in marked st, holding second Arm in line with Body sts and ensuring thumb is facing Body, sc in each st around second Arm, sc in each remaining st around–72 sc.
Rnds 17–19: Sc in each st around.
Rnd 20: [Sc in next 5 sts, inv-dec, sc in next 5] around–66 sc.
Rnd 21: [Inv-dec, sc in next 9 sts] around–60 sc.
Rnd 22: [Sc in next 4 sts, inv-dec, sc in next 4] around–54 sc.
Rnd 23: [Inv-dec, sc in next 7 sts] around–48 sc.
Rnd 24: [Sc in next 3 sts, inv-dec, sc in next 3] around–42 sc.
Rnd 25: [Inv-dec, sc in next 5 sts] around–36 sc.
Mark center 9 sts at front of Body for Head Opening.

Rnd 26: Sc in each st to st before first marked st, ch 9, skip 9 marked sts (Head Opening made), sc in each st around–27 sc.
Rnd 27: Sc in each st and ch around–36 sc.
Fasten off, leaving a long tail for sewing. Pinch the back shoulder seam behind Head Opening closed and sew seam shut, leaving Head Opening unseamed. Weave in ends.

HEAD

With **A**, join to underside of first ch at back of Body in Head Opening.
Rnd 1: Ch 1, sc 21 evenly around Head Opening–21 sc.
Rnd 2: [Sc in next 3 sts, 2 sc in next, sc in next 3] 3 times–24 sc.
Rnd 3: [2 sc in next, sc in next 3] 6 times–30 sc.
Rnd 4: [Sc in next 2 sts, 2 sc in next, sc in next 2] around–36 sc.
Rnd 5: [2 sc in next st, sc in next 5] around–42 sc.
Rnd 6: [Sc in next 3 sts, 2 sc in next, sc in next 3] around–48 sc.
Rnd 7: [2 sc in next st, sc in next 7] around–54 sc.
Rnds 8–11: Sc in each st around.
Place a st marker in center front of Head to mark for nose.
Rnd 12 (Nose): Sc in each st to marked st, Cluster in marked st, sc in each st around.
Rnds 13–18: Sc in each st around.
Using photos as a guide, cut 2 circles from white felt and place a safety eye in each felt circle. Insert safety eyes between Rnds 14–15. Using **C**, embroider details above and below eyes. Using a length of **F**, embroider eyebrows above eyes. Weave in ends. Stuff and continue stuffing as work progresses.
Rnd 19: [Inv-dec, sc in next 7 sts] around–48 sc.
Rnd 20: [Sc in next 3 sts, inv-dec, sc in next 3] around–42 sc.
Rnd 21: [Inv-dec, sc in next 5 sts] around–36 sc.
Rnd 22: [Sc in next 2 sts, inv-dec, sc in next 2] around–30 sc.
Rnd 23: [Inv-dec, sc in next 3 sts] around–24 sc.
Rnd 24: [Sc in next st, inv-dec, sc in next] around–18 sc.
Rnd 25: [Inv-dec, sc in next st] around–12 sc.
Rnd 26: [Inv-dec] around–6 sc.
Fasten off, leaving a long tail for sewing. Sew remaining 6 sts closed. Weave in ends.

EAR (MAKE 2)

With **A** and leaving a long tail at start for sewing, make a magic loop.
Row 1: Ch 1, 3 sc in loop, turn–3 sc.
Row 2: Ch 1, 2 sc in each st across, turn–6 sc.
Row 3: Ch 3, sl st in starting loop.
Fasten off, leaving a long tail for sewing. Sew Ears to sides of Head. Weave in ends.

SKIRT

With **D** and leaving a long tail at the start for sewing.

Row 1: Ch 43, sc in second ch from hook and in each ch across, turn–42 sc.
Row 2: Ch 1, 2 sc in next st, sc in each st across to last, 2 sc in last, turn–44 sc.
Rows 3–7: Repeat Row 2–54 sc at the end of Row 7.
Fasten off, weave in finishing end. Use starting tail to sew Skirt to front loops of Rnd 7 of Body with seam in front. Sew seam shut at front of Skirt at an angle. Weave in ends.

HAIR CAP

With **F**.
Row 1: Ch 35, sc in second ch from hook and in each ch across, turn–34 sc.
Row 2: Ch 1, sc2tog, sc in each st across to last 2 sts, sc2tog, turn–32 sc.
Rows 3–8: Repeat Row 2–20 sc at the end of Row 8.
Fasten off, leaving a long tail for sewing. Wrap Hair around back of Head and sew to front loops of Rnd 21 of Head. Weave in ends.

FINISHING

Using **F**, cut approximately 80 strands of hair measuring 4 in. / 10 cm each. Loop strands along Hair Cap for 3 rows. Loop 3 strands in front of Ears. Tie a long length of **F** around 3–4 remaining lengths and knot to create a beard. Secure beard to bottom of face.

"You must master the four elements and confront the Fire Lord. And when you do, I hope you will think like a mad genius!"

–KING BUMI
(Book 1, Episode 5)

FIRE LORD OZAI

Designed by
SARAH CSIACSE

Skill Level:
INTERMEDIATE

It's not enough to be Fire Lord of the Fire Nation. For Fire Lord Ozai, the only acceptable goal is to be King of all the nations—the Phoenix King, ruler of the world. After the death of his brother's son, Ozai seizes the throne, killing his father and banishing his wife. Now the King of the Fire Nation, Ozai uses his title to conquer neighboring nations with an iron fist. When Ozai learns of Sozin's Comet, he creates a plan to use its power to destroy or conquer the nations one by one and rule the world. The only one capable of stopping Ozai is the Avatar, and luckily for Ozai, the Avatar hasn't been seen for more than one hundred years.

Wearing royal robes and the crown of the Fire Nation, Lord Ozai may be the most intimidating character in all Four Nations. Enhanced by his cruelty and malice, Ozai's firebending powers are awe-inspiring and ominous. Crochet this powerful Lord with caution!

**"You *will* learn respect.
And suffering will be your teacher."**

—FIRE LORD OZAI
(Book 1, Episode 12)

FINISHED MEASUREMENTS
Height: 10 in. / 25.5 cm

YARN
Worsted weight (#4, Medium), shown in Lion Brand *Lazy Days* (100% Polyester, 179 yd. / 164 m per 3.5 oz. / 100 g ball)
Color A: 123AP Taupe, 1 ball
And worsted weight (#4, Medium), shown in Lion Brand *Basic Stitch* (100% Acrylic, 185 yd. / 169 m per 3.5 oz. / 100 g ball)
Color B: 138L Pomegranate, 1 ball
Color C: 400G Red Heather, 1 ball
Color D: 158I Mustard, 1 ball
Color E: 153 Black, 1 ball

HOOKS
US G-6 / 4 mm, *or size needed to obtain gauge*
US D-3 / 3.25 mm (used only at Bun Wrap)

NOTIONS
Stitch markers · Tapestry needle · Polyester stuffing · 8 mm safety eyes · 14-gauge aluminum wire (optional, for armature) · Small clear elastic hair ties · Wire cat brush · Hair straightener or iron · Scissors

GAUGE
20 sc and 20 sc rounds = 4 in. / 10 cm; *make sure to check your gauge.*

ABBREVIATIONS
Back loop only (BLO), chain(s) (ch(s)), fasten off (FO), front loop only (FLO), increase (inc, 2 sc in same stitch), single crochet (sc), slip stitch(es) (sl st(s)), stitch(es) (st(s)), yarn over (yo).

SPECIAL ABBREVIATIONS
Bobble (3 double crochet bobble): [Yo, insert hook into st, yo and draw up a loop, yo and pull through 2 loops on hook] 3 times in same stitch, yo and draw through all loops on hook.
inv-dec (invisible single crochet decrease): Insert hook in FLO of each of next 2 sts, yo and draw through both sts, yo and draw through 2 loops on hook—1 st decreased.
Surface crochet: Join yarn with a sl st, ch 1, sc in same st by inserting hook between rows, yo and pull up a loop, sc inserting hook between next two rows. Repeat across entire row.
Picot (picot stitch): Ch 3, insert hook into working st, yo and pull through all loops on hook.

NOTES

Worked in the round unless otherwise specified. When instructed to join, join with a slip stitch in first stitch.

"You're weak! Just like the rest of your people! They did not deserve to live in this world. In *my* world. Prepare to join them. Prepare to die."

—FIRE LORD OZAI
(Book 3, Episode 20)

BODY

Worked from the bottom up.
Rnd 1: With **C**, 6 sc in magic ring, join–6 sc.
Rnd 2: Ch 1, inc in each st around, join–12 sc.
Rnd 3: Ch 1, *sc in next st, inc, repeat from * around, join–18 sc.
Rnd 4: Ch 1, *sc in next 2 sts, inc, repeat from * around, join–24 sc.
Rnd 5: Ch 1, *inc, sc in next 3 sts, repeat from * around, join–30 sc.
Rnd 6: Ch 1, sc-BLO in each st around, join.
Rnds 7–24: Ch 1, sc in each st around, join.
Change to **E** before joining on Rnd 24.
Rnd 25: Ch 1, sl st in each st around, join.
Rnd 26: Ch 1, sc in each st around, join.
Rnd 27: Ch 1, *sc in next 3 sts, inv-dec, repeat from * around, change to **B** before joining, join–24 sc.
Rnd 28: Ch 1, sc-BLO in each st around, join.
Rnd 29: Ch 1, sc in next 6 sts, inv-dec, sc in next 7, inv-dec, sc in next 7, join–22 sc. Place a st marker here for Robe.
Rnds 30–31: Ch 1, sc in each st around, join.
Rnd 32: Ch 1, sc in next 5 sts, inv-dec, sc in next 7 sts, inv-dec, sc in next 6, join–20 sc.
Rnds 33–34: Ch 1, sc in each st around, join.
Rnd 35: Ch 1, sc in next 5 sts, inv-dec, sc in next 7, inv-dec, sc in next 4, join–18 sc.
Rnd 36: Ch 1, sc in each st around, join.
Rnd 37: Ch 1, [inv-dec] around, change to **D** before joining, join–9 sc.
Rnd 38: Ch 1, sc in each st around, join.
Fasten off and leave a long tail for sewing.

ROBE

Row 1: With Body upside down and its bottom facing you, join **C** with a sl st into BLO from Row 29 of Body (bottom of black belt) in tenth st from join using st marker as a guide, sc in next 22 sts, ch 1, turn–22 sc.
Rows 2–3: Sc in next 22 sts, ch 1, turn.
Row 4: Sc in next 11 sts, inc, sc in next 10, ch 1, turn–23 sc.

Rows 5–7: Sc in next 23 sts, ch 1, turn.
Row 8: Sc in next 11 sts, inc, sc in next 11, ch 1, turn–24 sc.
Rows 9–11: Sc in next 24 sts, ch 1, turn.
Row 12: Sc in next 11 sts, inc, sc in next 12, ch 1, turn–25 sc.
Rows 13–14: Sc in next 25 sts, ch 1, turn.
Row 15: Sc in next 12 sts, inc, sc in next 12, ch 1, turn–26 sc.
Row 16: Sc in next 26 sts, ch 2, turn.
Row 17: *Dc-FLO in next 2 sts, dc-FLO inc in next, repeat from * until 2 sts remain, dc in last 2 sts–34 sts.
Fasten off.

Create Edging on Robe.

Row 1: Join with **B** to side of first st of Row 1 of Robe, sc in side of each row down front of Robe, (sc, ch 2, sc) in bottom corner, sc in each dc across back, (sc, ch 2, sc) in next corner, sc in side of each row up other side of robe, to the belt, join with a sl st to BLO on belt.
Fasten off and weave in end.

Create Detailing on Robe.

Row 1: With **D**, join to edging, sc-BLO in each st down sides of Robe and (sc-BLO, ch 2, sc-BLO) in each corner.
Fasten off and weave in end.

SASH/TABARD

Row 1: With Body upside down and its bottom facing you, join **E** with a sl st into BLO from Row 29 on Body (bottom of black belt, skipping 1 stitch from where edging ends), sc in next 3 sts, ch 1, turn–3 sc.
Rows 2–10: Sc in each st across, ch 1, turn.
Row 11: Close 3 sc together.
Fasten off and weave in end.

HEAD

Rnd 1: With **E**, 6 sc in a magic ring, join–6 sc.
Rnd 2: Ch 1, inc in each st around, join–12 sc.
Rnd 3: Ch 1, *sc in next st, inc, repeat from * around, join–18 sc.
Rnd 4: Ch 1, *sc in next 2 sts, inc, repeat from * around, join–24 sc.
Rnd 5: Ch 1, inc, sc in next 3 sts, inc, sc in next; with **A**, sc in next 2, inc, sc in next 3, inc, sc in next 3; with **E**, inc, sc in next 3, inc, sc in next 3, join–30 sc.
Rnd 6: Ch 1, sc in next 4 sts, inc, sc in next 3; with **A**, sc in next, inc, [sc in next 4, inc] twice; with **E**, [sc in next 4, inc] twice, join–36 sc.
Rnd 7: Ch 1, sc in next 9 sts; with **A**, sc in next 15; with **E**, sc in next 12, join.
Rnd 8: Ch 1, sc in next 9 sts; with **A**, sc in next 16; with **E**, sc in next 11, join.
Rnd 9: Ch 1, sc in next 9 sts; with **A**, sc in next 16; with **E**, sc in next 11, join.
Rnd 10: Ch 1, sc in next 9 sts; with **A**, sc in next 17; with **E**, sc in next 10, join.
Rnd 11: Ch 1, sc in next 9 sts; with **A**, sc in next 17; with **E**, sc in next 10, join.
Rnd 12: Ch 1, sc in next 9 sts; with **A**, sc in next 18; with **E**, sc in next 9, join.
Rnd 13: Ch 1, sc in next 9 sts; with **A**, sc in next 18; with **E**, sc in next 9, join.
Rnd 14: Ch 1, sc in next 9 sts; with **A**, sc in next 19; with **E**, sc in next 8, join.
Rnd 15: Ch 1, sc in next 4 sts, inv-dec, sc in next 3; with **A**, sc in next, inv-dec, sc in next 4, inv-dec, sc in next 4, inv-dec, sc in next 4; with **E**, inv-dec, sc in next 4, inv-dec; change to **A** before joining, join–30 sc.
Insert safety eyes between Rnds 10–11, approximately 6 sts apart. Stuff.
Rnd 16: With **A**, *sc in next, inv-dec, repeat from * around, join–20 sc.
Rnd 17: Ch 1, [inv-dec] around, join–10 sc.
Fasten off and weave in end.
Finish stuffing.

ARM (MAKE 2)

Rnd 1: With **A**, 6 sc in magic ring, join–6 sc.
Rnd 2: Ch 1, *sc in next 2 sts, inc, repeat from * around, join–8 sc.
Rnd 3: Ch 1, sc in each st around, join.
Rnd 4: Ch 1, Bobble, sc in each st around, join–8 sc, 1 Bobble.
Rnds 5-9: Ch 1, sc in each st around, join–8 sc.
Rnd 10: Ch 1, sc in each st around, change to **B** before joining, join.
Rnd 11: With **B**, ch 1, sl st in each st around, join.
Rnd 12: Ch 1, sc-BLO in each st around.
Rnds 13–15: Ch 1, sc in each st around, join.
Rnd 16 (First Arm): Ch 1, sl st in next 4 sts, hdc in next 4, join–4 hdc.
Fasten off with a long tail.
Rnd 16 (Second Arm): Ch 1, hdc in next 4 sts, sl st in next 4, join–4 hdc.
Fasten off with a long tail.

SLEEVES (MAKE 2)

Rnd 1: With **B** and hand pointing down, join to last FLO from Rnd 12 of Arm with a sl st, sc in each st around, join–8 sc.
Rnd 2: Ch 1, sc in next st, inc, sc in next 6, join–9 sc.
Rnd 3: Ch 1, sc in next 2 sts, [inc] twice, sc in next 5, join–11 sc.
Rnd 4: Ch 1, sc in next 3 sts, [inc] twice, sc in next 6, join–13 sc.
Rnd 5: Ch 1, sc in next 4 sts, inc, sc in next 8, join–14 sc.
Rnd 6: Ch 1, sc in next 5 sts, [inc] twice, sc in next 10, join–16 sc.
Fasten off and weave in end.

COWL

This piece is worked in the round from the neck down. It will be worked in one piece with 3 Tiers.

Tier 1

With **C**, ch 13, join to first st with a sl st to form a loop.
Rnd 1: Ch 1, working in back bump of each ch, sc in each ch around, change to **E** before joining, join–13 sc.
Rnd 2: With **E**, ch 1, sl st in each st around, join.
Rnd 3: Ch 1, sc in next 2 sts, [inc] twice, sc in next 4, [inc] twice, sc in next 3, join–17 sc.
Rnd 4: Ch 1, sc in next 2 sts, [inc] 3 times, sc in next 6, [inc] 3 times, sc in next 3, join–23 sc.
Rnd 5: Ch 1, sc-FLO in next 4 sts (place a st marker in BLO of last st), [inc-FLO] 3 times, sc-FLO in next 8, [inc-FLO] 3 times, sc-FLO in next 5, join–29 sc.
Rnd 6: Ch 1, sc in next 7 sts, (sc, ch 2, sc) in next, sc in next 6, (sc, ch 2, sc) in next, sc in next 6, (sc, ch 2, sc) in next, sc in next 7, change to **D** before joining, join–32 sc, 3 ch-2 spaces.
Rnd 7: With **D**, ch 1, *working all sts in BLO sc in next 8 sts, (sc, ch 2, sc) in ch-2 space; repeat from * 3 times, sc in last 8 sts, join–38 sc, 3 ch-2 spaces.
Fasten off and weave in end.

Tier 2

Rnd 1: With **B**, sl st into BLO from Rnd 5 of Tier 1 (where you placed a st marker; move marker up), sc-BLO in next 6, inc-BLO, sc-BLO in next 12, inc-BLO, sc-BLO in next 3, leave remaining sts unworked, join–26 sc.
Rnd 2: Ch 1, sc in next 6 sts, [inc] 3 times, sc in next 10, [inc] 3 times, sc in next 4, join–32 sc.
Rnd 3: Ch 1, sc-FLO in each st around, join.
Rnd 4: Ch 1, sc in next 7 sts, (sc, ch 2, sc) in next, sc in next 6, (sc, ch 2, sc) in next, sc in next 7, (sc, ch 2, sc) in next, sc in next 6, join.
Fasten off and weave in end.

Tier 3

Rnd 1: With **B**, sl st into BLO from Rnd 3 of Tier 2 (where you placed a st marker), sc-BLO in each st around, join–32 sc.
Rnds 2–3: Ch 1, sc in each st around, join.
Rnd 4: Ch 1, sc in next 8 sts, (sc, ch 2, sc) in next, sc in next 6, (sc, ch 2, sc) in next, sc in next 6, (sc, ch 2, sc) in next, sc in next 6, join.
FO and weave in end.

BUN WRAP

Rnd 1: With **D** and smaller hook, ch 9, sc in second ch from hook, sc in next 3; (first offshoot) ch 5, sl st in second ch from hook, sl st in next 3; (second offshoot) ch 5, sl st in second ch from hook, sc in next, (hdc, ch 3, hdc) in next ch, rotate to join to underside of this "ch-5," sl st in second ch from hook, sl st in next 23, sl st into next unworked starting ch, sc in each remaining starting ch.
Fasten off with a long tail.

FINISHING

Tip: I find it helpful to pin everything into place before sewing to make sure the positioning is right.

Step 1. Attach Arms to Body. Optional: To add armature, cut a length of wire as long as arm span plus 2 in. / 5 cm; approximately 11 in. / 28 cm total. Bend wire at each end for hands and wrap excess around length. Insert through Body between Rnds 28–29. Lightly stuff Arms and place on wire. Sew ends of Arms closed. **Step 2.** Attach Cowl to Head, gently pulling **D** rnd of neck through neck opening of Cowl. Using yarn tail from Head, sew Head to neck. Curve Tier 1 sides up toward Head. **Step 3.** Create Hair. Create first weft by cutting a length of **E** measuring 8.5 in. / 21.5 cm to stretch across center of back of Head. Next, cut twenty-one 7.5 in. / 19 cm strands of **E** for the Hair. Hook Hair strands along length of weft, leaving an inch or so on each side to sew to Head. Repeat for top of Head, cutting a length of **E** measuring 10 in. / 25 cm, and Hair strands measuring 9.5 in. / 24 cm. Once all strands are in place, leave as is or untwist strands and straighten them with a hair straightener on a low-heat setting to make the Hair look straight and silky. Sew wefts to Head, attaching shorter weft on or below Rnd 10 of Head. The longer weft will be sewn on from smaller weft, following hairline over top of Head and down other side. Once secure, take middle of top portion and fold it back over your fingers to create the bun. Tie bun in place tightly with a length of **E**. **Step 4.** Attach Bun Wrap by wrapping it around bun with both sc portions wrapping around the front. Sew sc ends together using yarn tail. **Step 5.** Make goatee by hooking two strands of **E** 2 rnds below eyes and centered between them. Lightly brush strands with wire cat brush. Trim, then twist the ends for a nice, pointed look. **Step 6.** Embroider eyebrows with **E**. **Step 7.** Make Fire by tying lengths of **C** and **D** around a clear hair tie. Brush yarn with wire cat brush, trim, then twist the ends and push down, making the top pointy and the base round.
Weave in any remaining ends.

PRINCE ZUKO

Designed by
LEE SARTORI

Skill Level:
INTERMEDIATE

It's not easy being Prince Zuko. Spurred forward by the need to impress his father and restore his honor after being punished for speaking out against the Fire Nation's brutish war strategy, Zuko stops at nothing to find and capture the Avatar. While proud, impulsive, and intense, Zuko expresses an inclination toward kindness and nobility, but he often struggles with doing the right thing and doesn't always act in his own best interest. And even though the Avatar hasn't been seen in one hundred years, Zuko is sure that his goal of capturing the Avatar is within his reach—his father's approval finally in his grasp.

Zuko may have started out with a chip on his shoulder—or, more accurately, a scar on his face—but he has come a long way! Now, after a journey of self-acceptance, we think Zuko just needs a friend and some compassion. And we are sure you are the one who can help him!

Zuko: I can't believe a year ago my purpose in life was hunting you down. And now . . .
Aang: And now we're friends.

(Book 3, Episode 21)

FINISHED MEASUREMENTS
Height: 12 in. / 30.5 cm · Width: 7 in. / 18 cm

YARN
Worsted weight (#4, Medium) yarn, shown in Lion Brand *Lazy Days* (100% Polyester, 179 yd. / 164 m per 3.5 oz. / 100 g ball)
Color A: 123AP Taupe, 1 ball
And worsted weight (#4, Medium) yarn, shown in Lion Brand *24/7 Cotton* (100% Mercerized Cotton, 185 yd. / 170 m per 3.5 oz. / 100 g ball)
Color B: 148AI Burgundy, 1 ball
And worsted weight (#4, Medium) yarn, shown in Lion Brand *Basic Stitch* (100% Acrylic, 185 yd. / 169 m per 3.5 oz. / 100 g ball)
Color C: 128E Ebony, 1 ball
Color D: 158I Mustard, 1 ball
Color E: 123Q Tan, 1 ball
Color F: 153 Black, 1 ball
And DK weight (#3, Light) yarn, shown in Lion Brand *Coboo* (51% Cotton, 49% Rayon from Bamboo, 232 yd. / 212 m per 3.5 oz. / 100 g ball)

HOOK
US C-2 / 2.75 mm, *or size needed to obtain gauge*

NOTIONS
Stitch markers · Tapestry needle · Polyester stuffing · 12 mm safety eyes · Small amount of plastic mesh · Scissors

GAUGE
28 sc and 28 sc rounds = 4 in. / 10 cm; *make sure to check your gauge.*

ABBREVIATIONS
Back loop only (BLO), chain(s) (ch(s)), double crochet (dc), front loop only (FLO), front post single crochet (FPsc), single crochet (sc), slip stitch(es) (sl st(s)), stitch(es) (st(s)), yarn over (yo).

SPECIAL ABBREVIATIONS
Cluster (5 dc cluster): [Yo, insert hook into indicated st, yo and draw through 2 loops on hook] 5 times, yo and draw through all loops on hook.
Inv-dec (invisible single crochet decrease): Insert hook in FLO of each of next 2 sts, yo and draw through both sts, yo and draw through 2 loops on hook–1 st decreased.
Picot-Sc (picot single crochet): Insert hook into indicated st, yo and draw up a loop, [yo and draw through 1 loop] 3 times (3 chs), yo and draw through 2 loops.
Popcorn (popcorn stitch): Work 5 dc in next st, drop loop on hook, insert hook from front to back in first of 5 dc, place dropped loop on hook and draw it through the back of the first dc.

NOTES

Work in continuous rounds unless otherwise indicated. When instructed to join, join with a slip stitch in first stitch.

"Today, this war is finally over. I promised my uncle that I would restore the honor of the Fire Nation. And I will. The road ahead of us is challenging. A hundred years of fighting has left the world scarred and divided. But with the Avatar's help, we can get it back on the right path and begin a new era of love and peace."

—PRINCE ZUKO
(Book 3, Episode 21)

ARM (MAKE 2)

With **A**, make a magic loop.
Rnd 1: 6 sc in loop–6 sc.
Rnd 2: 2 sc in each st around–12 sc.
Rnds 3–4: Sc in each st around.
Rnd 5: Popcorn, sc in each st around–12 sts.
Rnd 6: Sc in each st around, join.
Fasten off **A**, change to **B**.
Rnd 7: Ch 1, sl st in each st around, join.
Rnd 8: Ch 1, sc-BLO in each st around, join.
Fasten off **B**, change to **C**.
Rnd 9: Ch 1, sl st in each st around, join.
Rnd 10: Ch 1, sc-BLO in each st around, join.
Rnds 11–14: Ch 1, sc in each st around, join.
Fasten off **C**, change to **D**.
Rnd 15: Ch 1, sl st in each st around, join.
Rnd 16: Ch 1, sc-BLO in each st around, join.
Fasten off **D**, change to **E**.
Rnd 17: Ch 1, sl st in each st around, join.
Rnd 18: Ch 1, [2 sc-BLO in next st, sc-BLO in next 3] around, join–15 sc.
Rnds 19–22: Ch 1, sc in each st around, join.
Fasten off, stuff. Set aside to join to Body.

BOOT SOLE (MAKE 4)

With **E**.
Rnd 1: Ch 5, sc in second ch from hook, sc in next 2, 3 sc in last, rotate to work on underside of chs, sc in next 3, 3 sc in last–12 sc.
Rnd 2: *Sc in next 3 sts, [2 sc in next] 3 times; repeat from * around–18 sc.
Rnd 3: *Sc in next 3 sts, [2 sc in next, sc in next] 3 times; repeat from * around–24 sc.
Fasten off first piece, do not fasten off second piece. Trace Sole on a piece of plastic mesh. Place mesh between 2 Soles and continue to joining round.
Rnd 4 (Joining): Working in BLO through both thicknesses, with plastic mesh sandwiched in between, sc in each st around–24 sc.
Fasten off.

BOOT (MAKE 2)

With **C**, join to center back of heel.
Rnds 1–2: Ch 1, sc in each st around, join–24 sc.
Rnd 3: Ch 1, sc in next 8 sts, [inv-dec, sc in next] 3 times, sc in next 7, join–21 sc.
Rnd 4: Ch 1, sc in next 8 sts, [inv-dec] 3 times, sc in next 7, join–18 sc.
Rnd 5: Ch 1, sc in next 6 sts, [inv-dec] 3 times, sc in next 6, join–15 sc.
Change to **B**.
Rnd 6: Ch 1, sl st in each st around, join.
Rnd 7: Ch 1, sc-BLO in each st around, join.
Change to **C**.
Rnds 8–9: Repeat Rnds 6–7.
Rnds 10–13: Ch 1, sc in each st around, join.
Fasten off.

LEG (MAKE 2)

With **E**, join to center back of heel.
Rnd 1: Ch 1, FPsc in each st around, join–15 FPsc.
Rnd 2: Ch 1 tightly, [sc in next 2 sts, 2 sc in next, sc in next 2] 3 times, do not join–18 sc.
Rnd 3: [2 sc in next st, sc in next 5] 3 times–21 sc.
Rnds 4–9: Sc in each st around.
Rnd 10: Inv-dec, sc in each st around–20 sc.
Rnds 11–12: Repeat Rnd 10–18 sc at end of Rnd 12.
Rnd 13: Sc in each st around.
Fasten off. Mark center of "inner thigh" of each Leg with a locking st marker.
Join to marked st of left Leg.
Rnd 14 (Joining): Ch 1, sc 18 around left Leg, sc in marked st of right Leg, sc in each st around right Leg, do not join–36 sc.
Continue to Body.

BODY

Continue with **E**.
Rnds 1–2: Sc in each st around–36 sc.
Rnd 3: 3 sc in first st, 2 sc in next, sc in each st around to last st, 2 sc in last–40 sc.
Rnds 4–6: Sc in each st around–40 sc.
Fasten off **E**. Join with **C**.
Rnd 7: Ch 1, sl st in each st around, join.

Rnd 8: Ch 1, sc-BLO in each st around, join.
Rnds 9–14: Sc in each st around.
Mark each "armpit" with a locking st marker, ensuring there are 19 sts between markers for front of Body and 19 sts between markers for back of Body.
Rnd 15 (Join Arms): Ch 1, sc to first marked st, sc in marked st, holding Arm in line with sts and ensuring thumb is facing Body, sc in each st around first Arm, sc to second marked st, sc in marked st, holding second Arm in line with sts and ensuring thumb is facing Body, sc in each st around second Arm, sc in each st around, join–70 sc.
Rnds 16–18: Ch 1, sc in each st around, join.
Rnd 19: Ch 1, inv-dec, [sc in next 16 sts, inv-dec] 3 times, sc 14–66 sc.
Rnd 20: Ch 1, [inv-dec, sc in next 9 sts] 6 times, join–60 sc.
Rnd 21: Ch 1, [sc in next 4 sts, inv-dec, sc in next 4] 6 times, join–54 sc.
Rnd 22: Ch 1, [inv-dec, sc in next 7 sts] 6 times, join–48 sc.
Rnd 23: Ch 1, [sc in next 3 sts, inv-dec, sc in next 3] 6 times, join–42 sc.
Rnd 24: Ch 1, [inv-dec, sc in next 5 sts] 6 times, join–36 sc.
Rnd 25: Ch 1, [sc in next 2 sts, inv-dec, sc in next 2] 6 times, join–30 sc.
Rnd 26: Ch 1, [inv-dec, sc in next 3 sts] 6 times, join–24 sc.
Rnd 27: Ch 1, [sc in next st, inv-dec, sc in next] 6 times, join–18 sc.
Fasten off. Stuff Body firmly.

SKIRT

With **C**.
Row 1: Ch 31, starting in second ch from hook sc in each ch across, turn–30 sc.
Row 2: Ch 1, 2 sc in next st, sc in each st across, turn–31 sc.
Rows 3–7: Repeat Row 2–36 sc at end of Row 7.
Rows 8–10: Ch 1, sc in each st across, turn.
Rnd 11 (Border): Ch 1, sc in next 36 sts, ch 1, rotate work to sc 10 across row ends, ch 1, rotate work to sc 30 across underside of starting ch, ch 1, rotate work to sc 10 across row ends, ch 1, join–86 sc.
Fasten off **C**, join with **B** in ch-1 corner at top (short side/Row 1).
Rnd 12: Ch 1, sc 10 down side of Skirt, (sc, ch 2, sc) in ch-1 space, sc in next 36 sts, (sc, ch 2, sc) in ch-1 space, sc 10 up side of Skirt–60 sc.
Fasten off, leaving a long tail for sewing.

UNDERSKIRT LAYER

With **F**.
Rnd 1: Ch 2, [sc, ch 2] in second ch from hook, [sc, ch 2] 3 times in same ch, join–4 sc, 4 ch-2 spaces.
Rnd 2: Ch 1, *sc in next st, (sc, ch 2, sc) in ch-2 space; repeat around, join–12 sc.
Rnd 3: Ch 1, *sc in next 2 sts, (sc, ch 2, sc) in ch-2 space, sc in next; repeat from * around, join–20 sc.
Rnd 4: Ch 1, *sc in next 3 sts, (sc, ch 2, sc) in ch-2 space, sc in next 2; repeat from * around, join–28 sc.
Fasten off, leaving a long tail for sewing. Sew in front of pants, sew Skirt overlapping its Under Layer. Weave in ends.

BELT

Row 1: With **F**, ch 37, starting in second ch from hook sc in each ch across–36 sc.
Fasten off, leaving a long tail for sewing. Sew Belt around waist. Weave in ends.

BELT BUCKLE

Rnd 1: With **D**, ch 2, [3 sc, ch 2, sc, ch 2] twice in second ch from hook work, join–8 sc.
Fasten off, leaving a long tail for sewing. Sew Belt Buckle to front of Belt. Weave in ends.

CHEST PLATE/SHOULDER PLATE (MAKE 4)

With **C**.
Rnd 1: Ch 2, [3 sc, ch 2, sc, ch 2] twice in second ch from hook work, join–8 sc.
Rnd 2: Ch 1, *sc in next 3 sts, (sc, ch 2, sc) in ch-2 space, sc in next, (sc, ch 2, sc) in ch-2 space; repeat from * around, join–16 sc.
Change to **B**.

Rnd 3: Ch 1, *sc in next 4 sts, (sc, ch 2, sc) in ch-2 space, sc in next 3, (sc, ch 2, sc) in ch-2 space, sc in next; repeat from * around, join–24 sc.
Fasten off, leaving a long tail for sewing. Sew one Plate to top of each shoulder. Sew short ends of two Plates together and sew resulting Chest Plate to front of chest. Weave in ends.

CHEST STRAP

With **C**.
Row 1: Ch 19, starting in second ch from hook sc in each ch across, turn–18 sc.
Row 2: Ch 1, sc in each st across, turn.
Fasten off, leaving a long tail for sewing. Sew around back and attach to sides of Chest Plates. Weave in ends.

HEAD

With **C**, join to center back of Body.
Rnds 1–3: Ch 1, sc in each st around, join–18 sc.
Fasten off **C**, change to **A**.
Rnd 4: Ch 1, [sc in next st, 2 sc in next, sc in next] around, join–24 sc.
Rnd 5: Ch 1, [2 sc in next st, sc in next 3] around, join–30 sc.
Rnd 6: Ch 1, [sc in next 2 sts, 2 sc in next, sc in next 2], around, join–36 sc.
Rnd 7: Ch 1, [2 sc in next st, sc in next 5] around, join–42 sc.
Rnd 8: Ch 1, [sc in next 3 sts, 2 sc in next, sc in next 3] around, join–48 sc.
Rnd 9: Ch 1, [2 sc in next st, sc in next 7] around, join–54 sc.
Fasten off. Join to center back of Head. Begin colorwork section.
Rnd 10: Ch 1, with **A**, sc in next 13 sts; with **B**, sc in next 9; with **A**, sc in next 32, join.
Rnd 11 (Nose): Ch 1, sc in next 13 sts; with **B**, sc in next 11; with **A**, sc in next 5, Picot-Sc, sc in next 24, join.
Rnd 12: Ch 1, sc in next 13 sts; with **B**, sc in next 13; with **A**, sc in next 28, join.
Rnd 13: Ch 1, sc in next 13 sts; with **B**, sc in next 13; with **A**, sc in next 28, join.
Rnd 14: Ch 1, sc in next 13 sts; with **E**, sc in next 13; with **A**, sc in next 28, join.
Rnd 15: Ch 1, sc in next 13 sts; with **E**, sc in next 13; with **A**, sc in next 28, join.
Rnd 16: Ch 1, sc in next 13 sts; with **E**, sc in next 12; with **A**, sc in next 29, join.
Rnd 17: Ch 1, sc in next 14 sts; with **E**, sc in next 10; with **A**, sc in next 30, join.
Rnd 18: Ch 1, sc in next 15 sts; with **E**, sc in next 8; with **A**, sc in next 31, join.
Rnd 19: Ch 1, sc in next 17 sts; with **E**, sc in next 5; with **A**, sc in next 32, join.
Fasten off **B** and **E**, continue with **A**.
Rnd 20: Ch 1 tightly, [inv-dec, sc in next 7 sts] around, do not join–48 sc.
Begin working in continuous rounds.
Rnd 21: [Sc in next 3 sts, inv-dec, sc in next 3] around–42 sc.
Add safety eyes between Rnds 13–14. Stuff Head and continue stuffing as work progresses.
Rnd 22: [Inv-dec, sc in next 5 sts] around–36 sc.
Rnd 23: [Sc in next 2 sts, inv-dec, sc in next 2] around–30 sc.
Rnd 24: [Inv-dec, sc in next 3 sts] around–24 sc.
Rnd 25: [Sc in next st, inv-dec, sc in next] around–18 sc.
Rnd 26: [Inv-dec, sc in next st] around–12 sc.
Rnd 27: [Inv-dec] around–6 sc.
Fasten off, leaving a long tail for sewing. Sew remaining 6 sts closed. Weave in ends.

EAR (MAKE 1 EACH WITH A AND B)

Leaving a long tail at start for sewing, make a magic loop.
Row 1: Ch 1, work 3 sc in loop, turn–3 sc.
Row 2: Ch 1, 2 sc in each st across, turn–6 sc.
Row 3: Ch 3, sl st in starting loop.
Fasten off, leaving a long tail for sewing. Sew Ears to sides of Head. Weave in ends.

HAIR

With **F**, make a magic ring.
Rnd 1: Ch 1, 8 sc in ring, join–8 sc.
Rnd 2: [Ch 21, starting in second ch from hook sl st 20, sl st in FLO of Rnd 1] 8 times, join–8 strands of Hair.
Fasten off, leaving a long tail for sewing. Using a long length of **F**, sew tip of each strand together to secure bottom ends. Weave in ends.

HAIR WRAP

With **B**.
Rnd 1: Ch 10, join to first ch to form a ring, ch 1, sc in each ch around, join–10 sc.
Rnds 2–4: Ch 1, sc in each st around, join.
Fasten off, leaving a long tail for sewing. Sew to base of Hair. Sew bottom of Hair Wrap to top of Head. Weave in ends.

CAPE

With **C**.

Row 1: Ch 19, starting in second ch from hook sc in each ch across, turn–18 sc.

Row 2: Ch 1, [2 sc in next st, sc in next 2] across, turn–24 sc.

Row 3: Ch 1, [2 sc in next st, sc in next 3] across, turn–30 sc.

Row 4: Ch 1, [2 sc in next st, sc in next 4] across, turn–36 sc.

Rnd 5: Ch 1, [2 sc in next st, sc in next 5] across, ch 2, rotate to work 4 sc down row ends, ch 2, rotate to sc 18 across underside of starting ch, ch 2 (mark this space with a st marker), rotate to sc 4 up row ends, join–68 sc.

Fasten off. With **B**, join to marked ch-2 space.

Rnd 6: Ch 1, (sc, ch 2, sc) in ch-2 space, sc in next 4 sts, (sc, ch 2, sc) in ch-2 space, sc in next 42, (sc, ch 2, sc) in ch-2 space, sc in next 4, (sc, ch 2, sc) in ch-2 space, sc in next 18, join–76 sc.

Row 7: Ch 1, sc in next 20 sts, leave remaining sts unworked.

Fasten off. With **D**, join to ch-2 space of Rnd 6 below last st of Row 7.

Row 8: Ch 1, sc in ch-2 space, sc in side of Row 7, ch 2, sc in next 20 sts, ch 2, sc in side of Row 7, sc in ch-2 space of Rnd 6–24 sc.

Fasten off, weave in ends.

Place Cape on Doll.

"I used to think this scar marked me—the mark of the banished prince, cursed to chase the Avatar forever. But lately I've realized I'm free to determine my own destiny, even if I'll never be free of my mark."

—PRINCE ZUKO
(Book 2, Episode 20)

THE BLUE SPIRIT

Designed by
SARAH CSIACSE

Skill Level:
INTERMEDIATE

The elusive Blue Spirit is hard to spot. He sneaks through facilities in the dead of night wearing a blue mask with white markings and brandishing twin broadswords. He silently carries out his mission, regardless of who is in his way. Although he would never admit to it, because he doesn't talk, the Blue Spirit has been known to help out Avatar Aang and his friends, a fact that goes against everything the Fire Nation is set out to do. And one could remark on the fact that no one has ever seen Prince Zuko and the Blue Spirit in the same room at the same time. Strange, isn't it?

Does a crocheted doll make a sound when you crochet it? Does a stealth assassin make any sound when he moves through a room? It sounds like the crocheted version of the Blue Spirit is the perfect way to embody this elusive character!

"You're the Blue Spirit—an enemy of the Fire Nation! You freed the Avatar!"

—COMMANDER ZHAO (Book 1, Episode 20)

FINISHED MEASUREMENTS
Height: 8.5 in. / 21.5 cm

YARN
Worsted weight (#4, Medium), shown in Lion Brand *Basic Stitch* (100% Acrylic, 185 yd. / 169 m per 3.5 oz. / 100 g ball)
Color A: 153 Black, 1 ball
Color B: 128E Ebony, 1 ball
Color C: 158I Mustard, 1 ball

HOOKS
US G-6 / 4 mm, *or size needed to obtain gauge*
US E-4 / 3.5 mm crochet hook

NOTIONS
Stitch markers • Tapestry needle • Black or brown polyester stuffing • 8 mm safety eyes • 14-gauge aluminum wire (optional, for armature) • White thread • Blue felt • White felt • Glue gun • Scissors

GAUGE
20 sc and 20 sc rounds = 4 in. / 10 cm; *make sure to check your gauge.*

ABBREVIATIONS
Back loop only (BLO), chain(s) (ch(s)), fasten off (FO), front loop only (FLO), single crochet (sc), slip stitch(es) (sl st(s)), stitch(es) (st(s)), three single crochet stitches closed together (sc3tog), yarn over (yo).

SPECIAL ABBREVIATIONS
Bobble (3 double crochet bobble): (Yo, insert hook into st, yo and draw up a loop, yo and pull through 2 loops on hook) 3 times in same stitch, yo and draw through all loops on hook.
inv-dec (invisible single crochet decrease): Insert hook in FLO of each of next 2 sts, yo and draw through both sts, yo and draw through 2 loops on hook—1 st decreased.

NOTES

Worked in the round unless otherwise specified. When instructed to join, join with a slip stitch in first stitch.

"If we knew each other back then, do you think we could've been friends?"

—AANG (Book 1, Episode 13)

LEG (MAKE 2)

Starting at foot with larger hook and **A**.
Rnd 1: Ch 5, sc in second ch from hook, sc in next 3, 3 sc in last. Rotate and work remaining stitches on opposite side of ch, sc in next, 2 sc in last, join–12 sc.
Rnd 2: Ch 1, sc in next 3 sts, 2 sc in next 3, sc in next 3, 2 sc in next 3, join–18 sc.
Rnd 3: Ch 1, sc-BLO in each st around, change to **B** before joining, join.
Rnd 4: With **B**, ch 1, sl st in each st around.
Rnd 5: Ch 1, sc in next 4 sts, inv-dec, sc in next 8, inv-dec, sc in next 2, join–16 sc.
Rnd 6: Ch 1, sc in next 5 sts, sc3tog, sc in next 8, join–14 sc.
Rnd 7: Ch 1, sc in next 3 sts, inv-dec, sc in next 2, inv-dec, sc in next 5, change to **A** before joining, join–12 sc.
Rnd 8: With **A**, ch 1, sl st in each st around, change to **B** before joining, join.
Rnd 9: With **B**, ch 1, sc in top of sts from Rnd 7, join.
Rnds 10–14: Ch 1, sc in each st around, join.
Rnd 15: Ch 1, sl st in each st around.
Rnd 16: Ch 1, sc in top of sts from Rnd 14, join.
Rnd 17: Ch 1, *sc in next st, 2 sc in next, repeat from * around, join–18 sc.
Rnd 18: Ch 1, sc in each st around, join.
Rnd 19: Ch 1, *sc in next, inv-dec, repeat from * around, join–12 sc.
Rnds 20–22: Ch 1, sc in each st around, join.
Fasten off first Leg; do not fasten off second Leg. Instead join Legs and work Body as follows.

BODY

Continued from second Leg.
Rnd 23: Ch 1, sc in each st around second Leg, join to seventh st of first Leg with sc, sc in each st around first Leg, join with a sl st to first st of second Leg–24 sc.
Rnds 24–25: Ch 1, sc in each st around, join. Change to **A** before joining Rnd 25.
Rnd 26: With **A**, ch 1, sl st in each st around, join.
Rnd 27: Ch 1, sc in each st around, join.
Lightly stuff feet and Legs. Keep stuffing Body as work progresses.
Rnd 28: Ch 1, sc in each st around, change to **B** before joining, join.
Rnd 29: With **B**, ch 1, sl st in each st around, join.
Rnd 30: Ch 1, sc in next 5 sts, inv-dec, sc in next 10, inv-dec, sc in next 5, join–22 sc.
Rnds 31–32: Ch 1, sc in each st around, join.
Rnd 33: Ch 1, sc in next 5 sts, inv-dec, sc in next 10, inv-dec, sc in next 3, join–20 sc.
Rnds 34–35: Ch 1, sc in each st around, join.
Rnd 36: Ch 1, sc in next 5 sts, inv-dec, sc in next 9, inv-dec, sc in next 2, join–18 sc.
Rnd 37: Ch 1, sc in each st around, join.
Rnd 38: Ch 1, [inv-dec] around, join–9 sc.
Rnd 39: Ch 1, sc in each st around, join.
Fasten off and weave in ends.

HEAD

With larger hook and **B**.
Rnd 1: 6 sc in magic ring, join–6 sc.
Rnd 2: Ch 1, 2 sc in each st around, join–12 sc.
Rnd 3: Ch 1, *sc in next st, 2 sc in next, repeat from * around, join–18 sc.
Rnd 4: Ch 1, *sc in next 2 sts, 2 sc in

next, repeat from * around, join–24 sc.
Rnd 5: Ch 1, *2 sc in next st, sc in next 3, repeat from * around, join–30 sc.
Rnd 6: Ch 1, *sc in next 4 sts, 2 sc in next, repeat from * around, join–36 sc.
Rnds 7–14: Ch 1, sc in each st around, join.
Attach safety eyes between Rnds 10–11, approximately 4 sts apart.
Rnd 15: Ch 1, *sc in next, inv-dec, repeat from * around, join–24 sc.
Rnd 16: Ch 1, [inv-dec] around, join–12 sc.
Stuff.
Rnd 17: Ch 1, [inv-dec] around, join–6 sc.
Fasten off with a long tail.

ARM (MAKE 2)

With larger hook and **B**.
Rnd 1: 6 sc in magic ring, join–6 sc.
Rnd 2: Ch 1, *sc in next 2 sts, 2 sc in next, repeat from * around, join–8 sc.
Rnd 3: Ch 1, sc in each st around, join.
Rnd 4: Ch 1, Bobble, sc in each st around, join–7 sc, 1 Bobble.
Rnd 5: Ch 1, sc in each st around, change to **A** before joining, join–8 sc.
Rnd 6: With **A**, ch 1, sl st in each st around, change to **B** before joining, join.
Rnd 7: With **B**, ch 1, sc in each st around, join.
Rnds 8–11: Ch 1, sc in each st around, change to **A** before joining, join.
Rnd 12: With **A**, ch 1, sl st in each st around, change to **B** before joining, join.
Rnds 13–15: With **B**, ch 1, sc in each st around, join.
Rnd 16 (First Arm): Ch 1, sl st in next 4 sts, hdc in next 4, join–4 hdc.
Fasten off with a long tail.
Rnd 16 (Second Arm): Ch 1, hdc in next 4 sts, sl st in next 4, join–4 hdc.
Fasten off with a long tail.

SWORD

With smaller hook and **C**.
Rnd 1: 6 sc in magic ring, join–6 sc.
Rnd 2: Ch 1, sc-BLO in each st around, change to **B** before joining, join.
Rnds 3–11: With **B**, ch 1, sc-BLO in each st around, join.
Rnd 12: Ch 1, sc in next st; with **C**, sc in next 5; change to **B** before joining, join.
Rnd 13: With **B**, ch 1, sc in next st; with **C**, sc in next 5, join.
Rnd 14: Ch 1, sl st in each st around, change to **B** before joining, join.
Insert a small length of wire (or stuff) to keep Sword firm.
Rnd 15: With **B**, ch 1, inv-dec, sc in next 2 sts, inv-dec, join–4 sc.
Rnds 16–17: Ch 1, sc in each st around, join. Change to **C** before joining on Rnd 17.
Rnd 18: With **C**, ch 1, sl st in each st around, join.
Fasten off, sew remaining opening shut, and weave in ends.

SWORD STRAP

With smaller hook and **A**, ch 20.
Fasten off with a long tail.

FINISHING

Tip: I find it helpful to pin everything into place before sewing to make sure the positioning is right.

Step 1. Attach Head to Body. **Step 2.** Attach Arms to Body. Optional: To add armature, cut a length of wire as long as arm span plus 2 in. / 5 cm, approximately 11 in. / 28 cm total. Bend wire at each end for hands and wrap excess around length. Insert through Body between Rnds 28–29. Lightly stuff Arms and place on wire. Sew ends of Arms closed. **Step 3.** Using template, cut Mask pieces and glue in position. **Step 4.** Attach Mask to Head using white thread, first vertically by inserting needle between Head and Mask at base of "ears" and cheeks, pulling thread around back of Head to create a strap, and going back and forth a few times to secure. Tie a knot at side of Head and weave ends in. Next, create a vertical strap by inserting needle at top center of back of Mask and pulling it down to meet first strap. Tie a knot at center of first strap and cut thread leaving small tails for decoration. **Step 5.** Attach Sword Strap to Sword as pictured and sling over shoulder.

AANG

Designed by
LEE SARTORI

Skill Level:
INTERMEDIATE

Playful yet respectful, kind, and adventurous, Aang always helps those in need, and is deeply attuned to nature. After the monks at the Southern Air Temple reveal that he is the reincarnated Avatar tasked with keeping balance in the world, he runs away with his lifetime companion, beloved sky bison Appa—and ends up encased in ice for a hundred years. When siblings Katara and Sokka finally release him, and he discovers that the Fire Nation wiped out the Air Nomads and erupted a century-long war against the other nations, he realizes that he can no longer run from his responsibility. Aang embarks on a perilous journey with his new friends, inspiring hope wherever they go, and ultimately restoring balance to the world.

Decked out in Air Nomad attire and his mastery tattoos, amigurumi Aang is ready to become a fully realized Avatar and save the world!

"I laugh at gravity all the time."

–AANG (Season 1, Episode 17)

FINISHED MEASUREMENTS
Height: 10 in. / 25.5 cm • Width: 6 in. / 15 cm

YARN
Worsted weight (#4, Medium) yarn, shown in WeCrochet *Swish* (100% Superwash Merino Wool, 110 yd. / 101 m per 1.75 oz. / 50 g ball)
Color A: N4136 Shortbread, 1 ball
Color C: N4112 Buoy, 1 ball
Color E: N4113 Burnt Umber Heather, 1 ball
And DK weight (#3, Light) yarn, shown in WeCrochet *Cotlin* (70% Cotton / 30% Linen, 185 yd. / 169 m per 3.5 oz. / 100 g ball)
Color B: 24137 Crème Brûlée, 1 ball
Color D: 24138 Coffee, 1 ball
Color F: 25772 Hydrangea, 1 ball

HOOK
US C-2 / 2.75 mm, *or size needed to obtain gauge*

NOTIONS
Stitch markers • Tapestry needle • Polyester stuffing • 12 mm safety eyes • Small amount of plastic mesh • White thread • Black thread • Scissors

GAUGE
28 sc and 28 sc rounds = 4 in. / 10 cm; *make sure to check your gauge.*

ABBREVIATIONS
Back loop only (BLO), chain(s) (ch(s)), double crochet (dc), front loop only (FLO), front post single crochet (FPsc), right side (RS), single crochet (sc), slip stitch(es) (sl st(s)), stitch(es) (st(s)), two single crochet closed together (sc2tog), wrong side (WS), yarn over (yo).

SPECIAL ABBREVIATIONS
inv-dec (invisible single crochet decrease): Insert hook in FLO of each of next 2 sts, yo and draw through both sts, yo and draw through 2 loops on hook–1 st decreased.
Picot-Sc (picot single crochet): Insert hook into indicated st, yo and draw up a loop, [yo and draw through 1 loop] 3 times (3 chs), yo and draw through 2 loops.
Popcorn (popcorn stitch): Work 5 dc in next st, drop loop on hook, insert hook from front to back in first of 5 dc, place dropped loop on hook and draw it through the back of the first dc.

NOTES

Work in continuous rounds unless otherwise indicated. When instructed to join, join with a slip stitch in first stitch.

"It's easy to do nothing, but it's hard to forgive."

—AANG (Book 3, Episode 16)

ARM (MAKE 2)

With **A**, make a magic loop.
Rnd 1: 6 sc in loop–6 sc.
Rnd 2: 2 sc in each st around–12 sc.
Rnds 3–4: Sc in each st around.
Rnd 5: Popcorn, sc in each st around, join–12 sc.
Rnd 6: Ch 1, sc in each st around, join–12 sc.
Fasten off **A**, change to **B**.
Rnd 7: Ch 1, sl st in each st around, join.
Rnd 8: Ch 1, sc-BLO in each st around, join.
Change to **C**.
Rnd 9: Ch 1, sl st-FLO in each st around, join.
Change to **B**.
Rnd 10: Ch 1, working in BLO of Rnd 8, sc in each st around, join.
Rnds 11–14: Ch 1, sc in each st around, join.
Change to **C**.
Rnd 15: Repeat Rnd 9.
Change to **B**.
Rnd 16: Repeat Rnd 10.
Rnd 17: Ch 1 tightly, 2 sc in next st, sc in each st around, do not join–13 sc.
Rnd 18: 2 sc in next st, sc in each st around–14 sc.
Rnd 19: 2 sc in next st, sc in each st around–15 sc.
Rnds 20–22: Sc in each st around.
Fasten off, leaving a long tail for sewing. Stuff Arm. Set aside to join to Body.

BOOT SOLE (MAKE 4)

With **D**.
Rnd 1: Ch 5, sc in second ch from hook, sc in next 2, 3 sc in last, rotate to work on underside of chs, sc in next 3, 3 sc in last–12 sc.
Rnd 2: *Sc in next 3 sts, [2 sc in next] 3 times; repeat from * around–18 sc.
Rnd 3: *Sc in next 3 sts, [2 sc in next, sc in next] 3 times; repeat from * around–24 sc.
Fasten off first piece, but do not fasten off second piece. Trace Sole on a piece of plastic mesh. Place mesh between 2 Soles and continue to joining round.
Rnd 4 (Joining): Working in BLO through both thicknesses, with plastic mesh sandwiched in between, sc in each st around–24 sc.
Fasten off. Continue to Boot.

BOOT (MAKE 2)

Join with **E** at the center back of heel in BLO.
Rnd 1: With **E**, ch 1, working all sts in BLO sc in next 8 sts; with **D**, sc in next 9; with **E**, sc in next 7, join–24 sc.
Rnd 2: Ch 1, sc in next 8 sts; with **D**, sc in next 9; with **E**, sc in next 7, join.
Rnd 3: Ch 1, sc in next 8 sts; with **D**, [inv-dec, sc in next] 3 times; with **E**, sc in next 7, join–21 sc.
Rnd 4: Ch 1, sc in next 8 sts; with **D**, [inv-dec] 3 times; with **E**, sc in next 7, join–18 sc.
Drop **D**, continue with **E**.
Rnd 5: Ch 1, sc in next 6 sts, [inv-dec] 3 times, sc in next 6, join–15 sc.
Rnds 6–7: Ch 1, sc in each st around, join.
Drop **E**, pick up **D**.
Rnd 8: Ch 1, sl st in each st around, join.
Rnd 9: Ch 1, sc-BLO in each st around, join.
Drop **D**, continue with **E**.
Rnd 10: Ch 1, sl st in each st around, join.
Rnd 11: Ch 1, sc-BLO in each st around, join.
Rnd 12: Ch 1, sc in each st around, join.
Fasten off **E**, continue with **D**.
Rnd 13: Ch 1, sl st in each st around, join.
Rnd 14: Ch 1, sc-BLO in each st around, join.
Fasten off. Stuff. Continue to Leg.

LEG (MAKE 2)

Join with **B** to center back of heel.
Rnd 1: Ch 1, FPsc in each st around, join–15 FPsc.
Rnd 2: Ch 1 tightly, [sc in next 2 sts, 2 sc in next, sc in next 2] 3 times, do not join–18 sc.
Rnd 3: [2 sc in next st, sc in next 5] 3 times–21 sc.
Rnds 4–7: Sc in each st around.
Rnd 8: Inv-dec, sc in each st around–20 sc.
Rnds 9–10: Repeat Rnd 8–18 sc at end of Rnd 10.
Rnd 11: Sc in each st around.
Fasten off. Mark center of "inner thigh" of each Leg with a locking st marker.
Join to marked st of left Leg.
Rnd 12 (Joining): Ch 1, sc 18 around left Leg, sc in marked st of right Leg, sc in each st around right Leg, do not join–36 sc.
Continue to Body.

BODY

Continue with **B**.
Rnds 1–2: Sc in each st around–36 sc.
Rnd 3: 3 sc in first st, 2 sc in next, sc in each st around to last, 2 sc in last–40 sc.
Rnds 4–6: Sc in each st around.
Change to **C**.
Rnd 7: Ch 1, sl st in each st around, join.
Rnd 8: Ch 1, sc-BLO in each st around, join.
Rnds 9–10: Ch 1, sc in each st around, join.
Change to **B**.
Rnds 11–12: Repeat Rnds 7–8.
Rnds 13–15: Ch 1, sc in each st around, join.
Mark each "armpit" with a locking st marker, ensuring there are 19 sts between markers for the front of the Body and 19 sts between markers for the back of the Body.
Rnd 16 (Join Arms): Ch 1, sc in each st to first marked st, sc in marked st, holding Arm in line with Body sts and ensuring thumb is facing Body, sc in each st around first Arm, sc in each st to second marked st, sc in marked st, holding second Arm in line with Body sts and ensuring thumb is facing Body, sc in each st around second Arm, sc in each remaining st around, join–70 sc.
Rnds 17–19: Ch 1, sc in each st around, join.
Rnd 20: Ch 1, inv-dec, [sc in next 16 sts, inv-dec] 3 times, sc in next 14–66 sc.
Rnd 21: Ch 1, [inv-dec, sc in next 9 sts] 6 times, join–60 sc.
Rnd 22: Ch 1, [sc in next 4 sts, inv-dec, sc in next 4] 6 times, join–54 sc.
Rnd 23: Ch 1, [inv-dec, sc in next 7 sts] 6 times, join–48 sc.
Rnd 24: Ch 1, [sc in next 3 sts, inv-dec, sc in next 3] 6 times, join–42 sc.
Rnd 25: Ch 1, [inv-dec, sc in next 5 sts] 6 times, join–36 sc.
Rnd 26: Ch 1, [sc in next 2 sts, inv-dec, sc in next 2] 6 times, join–30 sc.
Rnd 27: Ch 1, [inv-dec, sc in next 3 sts] 6 times, join–24 sc.
Rnd 28: Ch 1, [sc in next st, inv-dec, sc in next] 6 times, join–18 sc.
Fasten off. Stuff Body firmly.

HEAD

With **F**, join to the center back of Body. Work in turned rounds to ensure a straight seam.
Rnd 1 (RS): With **F**, ch 1, working all sts in BLO sc in next 2 sts; with **A**, sc in next 15; with **F**, sc in next, join, turn–18 sc.
Rnd 2 (WS): Ch 1, sc in next st; with **A**, sc in next 15; with **F**, sc in next 2, join, turn.

Rnd 3: Ch 1, sc in next 2 sts; with **A**, sc in next 15; with **F**, sc in next, join, turn.
Rnd 4: Ch 1, sc in next st; with **A**, 2 sc in next 15 sts, with **F**, sc in next 2, join, turn–33 sc.
Rnd 5: Ch 1, sc in next 2 sts; with **A**, [sc in next 2, 2 sc in next, sc in next 2] 6 times; with **F**, sc in next, join, turn–39 sc.
Rnd 6: Ch 1, sc in next st; with **A**, [2 sc in next, sc in next 5] 6 times; with **F**, sc in next 2, join, turn–45 sc.
Rnd 7: Ch 1, sc in next 2 sts; with **A**, [sc in next 3, 2 sc in next, sc in next 3] 6 times; with **F**, sc in next, join, turn–51 sc.

Rnd 8: Ch 1, sc in next st; with **A**, [2 sc in next, sc in next 7] 6 times; with **F**, sc in next 2, join, turn–57 sc.
Rnd 9: Ch 1, sc in next 2 sts; with **A**, sc in next 54; with **F**, sc in next, join, turn.
Rnd 10: Ch 1, sc in next st; with **A**, sc in next 54; with **F**, sc in next 2, join, turn.
Rnd 11 (Nose): Ch 1, sc in next 2 sts; with **A**, sc in next 27, Picot-Sc, sc in next 26; with **F**, sc in next 2, join, turn–57 sts.
Rnd 12: Repeat Rnd 10.
Rnds 13–16: Repeat Rnds 9–10.
Rnd 17 (Arrow): Ch 1, sc in next 2 sts; with **A**, sc in next 27; with **F**, sc in next; with **A**, sc in next 26; with **F**, sc in next, join, turn.
Rnd 18: Ch 1, sc in next st; with **A**, sc in next 25; with **F**, sc in next, 2 sc in next; with **A**, inv-dec, sc in next 25; with **F**, sc in next 2, join, turn.
Rnd 19: Ch 1, sc in next 2 sts; with **A**, sc in next 25; with **F**, sc in next 3, 2 sc in next; with **A**, inv-dec, sc in next 23; with **F**, sc in next, join, turn.
Rnd 20: Ch 1, sc in next st; with **A**, sc in next 23; with **F**, sc in next 5, 2 sc in next; with **A**, inv-dec, sc in next 23; with **F**, sc in next 2, join, turn.
Rnd 21: Ch 1, sc in next 2 sts; with **A**, sc in next 23; with **F**, sc in next 7, 2 sc in next; with **A**, inv-dec, sc in next 21; with **F**, sc in next, join, turn.
Rnd 22: Ch 1, sc in next st; with **A**, sc in next 21; with **F**, sc in next 9, 2 sc in next; with **A**, inv-dec, sc in next 21; with **F**, sc in next 2, join, turn.
Rnd 23: Ch 1, sc in next 2 sts; with **A**, [sc in next 2, inv-dec, sc in next 2] 3 times, sc in next 4, sc-BLO in next 4; with **F**, sc in next 3; with **A**, sc-BLO in next 4, [inv-dec, sc in next 5] 3 times; with **F**, sc in next, join, turn–51 sc.
Rnd 24: Ch 1, sc in next st; with **A**, [inv-dec, sc in next 5] 3 times, sc in next; with **F**, sc in next 3; with **A**, sc in next 2, [inv-dec, sc in next 5] 3 times; with **F**, sc in next 2, join, turn–45 sc.
Rnd 25: Ch 1, sc in next 2 sts; with **A**, [sc in next 2, inv-dec, sc in next 2] 3 times, sc in next 2; with **F**, sc in next 3; with **A**, sc in next, [sc in next 2, inv-dec, sc in next 2] 3 times; with **F**, sc in next, join, turn–39 sc.
Add safety eyes between Rnds 13–14. Stuff and continue stuffing as work progresses.
Rnd 26: Ch 1, sc in next st; with **A**, inv-dec, sc in next 14; with **F**, sc in next 3; with **A**, inv-dec, sc in next 13, inv-dec; with **F**, sc in next 2, join, turn–36 sc.
Rnd 27: Ch 1, sc in next 2 sts; with **A**, [inv-dec, sc in next 3] 3 times; with **F**, sc in next 3; with **A**, [inv-dec, sc in next 3] 3 times; with **F**, sc in next, join, turn–30 sc.
Rnd 28: Ch 1, sc in next st; with **A**, [sc in next, inv-dec, sc in next] 3 times; with **F**, sc in next 3; with **A**, [sc in next, inv-dec, sc in next] 3 times; with **F**, sc in next 2, join, turn–24 sc.
Rnd 29: Ch 1, sc in next 2 sts; with **A**, [inv-dec, sc in next] 3 times; with **F**, sc in next 3; with **A**, [inv-dec, sc in next] 3 times; with **F**, sc in next, join, turn–18 sc.
Rnd 30: Ch 1, sc in next st; with **A**, [sc2tog] 3 times; with **F**, sc in next 3; with **A**, [sc2tog] 3 times; with **F**, sc in next 2, join, turn–12 sc.
Fasten off **A**, continue with **F**.
Rnd 31: Ch 1, [sc2tog] around, join–6 sc.
Fasten off, leaving a long tail for sewing. Sew remaining 6 sts closed. Weave in ends.

EAR (MAKE 2)

With **A** and leaving a long tail at start for sewing, make a magic loop.
Row 1: Ch 1, work 3 sc in loop, turn–3 sc.
Row 2: Ch 1, 2 sc in each st across, turn–6 sc.
Row 3: Ch 3, sl st in starting loop.
Fasten off, leaving a long tail for sewing. Sew Ears to sides of Head. Weave in ends.

COLLAR

With **B**.
Row 1: Ch 19, starting in second ch from hook sc in each ch across, turn–18 sc.
Row 2: Ch 1, sc in each st across, turn.
Row 3: Ch 1, sl st in each st across.
Fasten off, leaving a long tail for sewing. Sew Collar to FLO sts of Rnd 1 of Head. Weave in ends.

CAPE

With **C**.
Row 1: Ch 19, starting in second ch from hook sc in each ch across, turn–18 sc.
Row 2: Ch 1, [2 sc in next st, sc in next 2] across, turn–24 sc.

Row 3: Ch 1, [2 sc in next st, sc in next 3] across, turn–30 sc.
Row 4: Ch 1, [2 sc in next st, sc in next 4] across, turn–36 sc.
Row 5: Ch 1, [2 sc in next st, sc in next 5] across, turn–42 sc.
Row 6: Ch 1, [2 sc in next st, sc in next 6] across, turn–48 sc.
Row 7: Ch 1, [2 sc in next st, sc in next 7] across, turn–54 sc.
Row 8: Ch 1, [2 sc in next st, sc in next 8] across, turn–60 sc.
Row 9: Ch 1, [2 sc in next st, sc in next 9] across, turn–66 sc.
Row 10: Ch 1, [2 sc in next st, sc in next 10] across, turn–72 sc.
Rows 11–12: Ch 1, sc in each st across, turn.
Rnd 13 (Border): Ch 1, sc in next 72 sts, ch 1, rotate to sc 13 across row ends, ch 1, sc 18 across underside of starting ch, ch 1, sc 13 across row ends, ch 1, join–116 sc.
Fasten off, weave in ends.

Place Cape around neck and shoulders of Doll with Row 1 at the top and Row 13 (Border) at the bottom. Opening will be at center front of Body. Using a length of **C**, sew Cape closed at nape.

SLEEVE PIECE (MAKE 2)

With **C**.
Row 1: Ch 7, starting in second ch from hook sc across, turn–6 sc.
Row 2: Ch 1, sc in each st across, turn.
Rnd 3 (Border): Ch 1, sc in next 6 sts, ch 1, rotate to sc 3 across row ends, ch 1, rotate to sc 6 across underside of starting ch, ch 1, sc 3 across row ends, ch 1, join–18 sc.
Fasten off, leaving a long tail for sewing. Sew 6 sts to Rnd 13 of Cape in line with Arm. Sew to Arm at Rnd 15. Weave in ends.

"Everyone, even the Fire Lord and the Fire Nation, have to be treated like they're worth giving a chance."

—AANG (Book 3, Episode 6)

MONK GYATSO

Designed by
LIZETTE MEJIA

Skill Level:
INTERMEDIATE

A friend of Roku's and mentor to Aang, Monk Gyatso was a strong influence on the lives of the two Avatars, as well as an important figure among the Air Nomads. Known for his kindness and playful spirit, Monk Gyatso was always willing to not just teach the correct way of doing something, but to make it fun.

One hundred years after Aang's disappearance, the Avatar returns to the Southern Air Temple to try to discover what happened to his trusted friend and father figure. The reality of Monk Gyatso's passing devastates Aang and resolves his decision to embrace his role as Avatar and follow his master's teachings.

Monk Gyatso is wise, kind, and full of love. We think you can even see it on his face! Crochet this important teacher to the Avatar and be sure to give him his fantastic mustache!

"We can't concern ourselves with what was. We must act on what is."

—MONK GYATSO (Book 1, Episode 3)

FINISHED MEASUREMENTS
Height: 6¼ in. / 16 cm • Width: 2½ in. / 6.5 cm

YARN
Worsted weight (#4, Medium), shown in WeCrochet *Swish* (100% Superwash Merino Wool, 110 yd. / 101 m per 1.75 oz. / 50 g ball)
Color A: N4136 Shortbread, 1 ball
Color E: N4119 Curry, 1 ball
And DK weight (#3, DK), shown in WeCrochet *Cotlin* (70% Cotton / 30% Linen, 185 yd. / 169 m per 3.5 oz. / 100 g ball)
Color B: 25772 Hydrangea, 1 ball
Color C: 29492 Snow White, 1 ball
Color D: 24137 Crème Brûlée, 1 ball
Color F: 29531 Macchiato, 1 ball
Color G: 24138 Coffee, 1 ball
Color H: 29528I Lava Falls, 1 ball

HOOK
US C-2 / 2.75 mm, *or size needed to obtain gauge*

NOTIONS
Stitch markers • Tapestry needle • Polyester stuffing • 10 mm safety eyes • 16-gauge wire pliers • Wire cutters • Small amount worsted weight fuzzy white yarn • Small amount worsted weight blue yarn • Scissors

GAUGE
28 sc and 26 sc rounds = 4 in. / 10 cm; *make sure to check your gauge.*

ABBREVIATIONS
Back loop only (BLO), chain(s) (ch(s)), double crochet (dc), front loop only (FLO), half double crochet (hdc), magic ring (MR), single crochet (sc), skip (sk), slip stitch(es) (sl st(s)), stitch(es) (st(s)), two double crochet closed together (dc2tog), yarn over (yo).

SPECIAL ABBREVIATIONS
Popcorn (popcorn stitch): Work 3 dc in next st, drop loop on hook, insert hook from front to back in first of 3 dc, place dropped loop on hook, and draw it through the back of the first dc.
inv-dec (invisible single crochet decrease): Insert hook in FLO of each of next 2 sts, yo and draw through both sts, yo and draw through 2 loops on hook—1 st decreased.

NOTES

When referring to the "left" or "right," it is from the perspective of the Doll facing you.

◇◇◇◇◇◇◇◇◇◇◇◇◇◇◇◇◇◇◇◇◇◇◇◇◇◇

"Monk Gyatso, the greatest Airbender in the world. He taught me everything I know."

—AANG (Book 1, Episode 3)

ARMS

Do not stuff Arms.

LEFT ARM

Starting with **A**.
Rnd 1: MR, 6 sc in ring, pull tight to close–6 sc.
Join with **B**.
Rnd 2: With **B**, sc in next st; with **A**, sc in next 5.
Rnd 3: With **B**, sc in next 2 sts; with **A**, sc in next 3, Popcorn–6 sts.
Rnd 4: With **B**, sc in next 2 sts; with **A**, sc in next 4.
Rnds 5–14: Sc in next st; with **B**, sc in next; with **A**, sc in next 4.
Change to **E**.
Rnd 15: Sc in next 6 sts.
Rnd 16: Sc-BLO in next 6 sts.
Fasten off with a long tail. Set aside.

RIGHT ARM

Starting with **A**.
Rnd 1: MR, 6 sc in ring, pull tight to close–6 sc.
Rnd 2: Sc in next 3 sts; join with **B**, sc in next; with **A**, sc in next 2.
Rnd 3: Sc in next 3 sts; with **B**, sc in next 2; with **A**, Popcorn–6 sts.
Rnd 4: Sc in next 3 sts; with **B**, sc in next 2; with **A**, sc in next.
Rnds 5–14: Sc in next 3 sts; with **B**, sc in next; with **A**, sc in next 2.
Change to **E**.
Rnd 15: Sc in next 6 sts.
Rnd 16: Sc-BLO in next 6 sts.
Fasten off with a long tail. Set aside.

LEG (MAKE 2)

Stuff as you go.
Starting with **G** at shoe.
Rnd 1: MR, 6 sc in ring–6 sc.
Rnd 2: [2 sc in next st] twice, (hdc, dc) in next, (dc, hdc) in next, [2 sc in next] twice–12 sts.
Rnd 3: Sc-BLO in next 12 sts.
Rnd 4: Working all sts in BLO, sc in next 4 sts, [dc2tog] twice, sc in next 4–10 sts.
Rnd 5: Sc in next 10 sts.
Rnd 6: Inv-dec, sc in next 8 sts–9 sc.
Rnd 7: Inv-dec, sc in next 7 sts–8 sc.
Rnds 8–9: Sc in next 8 sts.
Change to **A**.
Rnds 10–18: Sc in next 8 sts.
Fasten off first Leg, do not fasten off second Leg.
Make sure feet are facing front when joining (dc are at front of Leg).
Rnd 19 (Joining): Ch 1, sc in 8 sts around first Leg, sc in ch-1, sc in 8 sts around second Leg, sc in opposite side of ch-1–18 sc.
Change to **E** for torso.
Rnd 20: Sc in next 8 sts, [2 sc in next] twice, sc in next 8–20 sc.
Rnds 21–22: Sc in next 20 sts.
Rnd 23: Sc-BLO in next 20 sts.
Rnds 24–25: Sc in next 20 sts.
Rnd 26: Sc-BLO in next 20 sts.
Continue to Body.

BODY

Continue with **A**.
Rnd 27: [Sc in next 4 sts, 2 sc in next] 4 times–24 sc.
Rnds 28–31: Sc in next 24 sts.
When attaching Arms in next rnd, be aware of their twist and ensure blue tattoo line is facing the same way for both Arms.
Rnd 32 (Joining): Sc in next 9 sts, line up left Arm with thumb facing forward, sc into closest st on Arm, sc into remaining 5 sts on Arm; starting in next unworked st on Body, 2 sc in next st, sc in next 8, 2 sc in next st; line up right Arm with thumb facing forward, sc into closest st on Arm, sc in next 5 sts on Arm; starting in next unworked st on Body, sc in next 5 sc–38 sc.
DO NOT CUT YARN.

Insert wire as follows: 1. Curl end of wire. 2. Measure and cut length needed for arm span and curl other end. Insert into both hands. 3. Continue stuffing Body as you go.

Continued from Rnd 32.
Rnd 33: [Inv-dec] 19 times–19 sc.
Rnd 34: Working all sts in BLO, [inv-dec] 9 times, sc in last st–10 sc.
Sl st into next st and change to **A**.
Rnds 35–38: Sc in next 4 sts; with **B**,

sc in next 2; with **A**, sc in next 4.
DO NOT CUT YARN.

COLLAR

Holding Doll upright, attach **D** with a sl st in front loop of second st from Rnd 34 of Body. Crochet over the tail as you go.
Row 1: Ch 1, sc in next 19 sts–19 sc.
Rows 2–3: Ch 1, turn, sc in next 19 sts.
Fasten off with a long tail. Weave in end.

Continued from Rnd 38 of Body.

HEAD

Rnd 39: With **A**, [2 sc in next st] 5 times; with **B**, 2 sc in next; with **A**, [2 sc in next] 4 times–20 sc.
Rnd 40: [Sc in next, 2 sc in next] 5 times, sc in next; with **B**, 2 sc in next; with **A**, [sc in next, 2 sc in next] 4 times–30 sc.
Rnds 41–47: Sc in next 16 sts; with **B**, sc in next 2; with **A**, sc in next 12.
Rnd 48: Sc in next 8 sts, inv-dec, sc in next 6; with **B**, sc in next 2; with **A**, inv-dec, sc in next 8, inv-dec–27 sc.
Rnds 49: Sc in next 3 sts; with **B**, sc in next; with **A**, sc in next 11; with **B**, sc in next 2; with **A**, sc in next 10.
Insert safety eyes between Rnds 44–45, 5 sts apart and centered on Head. Continue stuffing as you go.
Rnd 50: Inv-dec; with **B**, sc in next 3 sts; with **A**, sc in next 10; with **B**, sc in next 2; with **A**, inv-dec, sc in next 6, inv-dec–24 sc.
Rnd 51: With **B**, sc in next 5 sts; with **A**, inv-dec, sc in next 5, inv-dec; with **B**, sc in next 2; with **A**, sc in next 6, inv-dec–21 sc.
Rnd 52: Sc in next st; with **B**, inv-dec, sc in next; with **A**, [inv-dec, sc in next] twice, inv-dec; with **B**, inv-dec; with **A**, [sc in next, inv-dec] twice, sc in next–14 sc.
Rnd 53: With **B**, [inv-dec] 7 times–7 sc.
Finish stuffing. Fasten off and close remaining hole by sewing through front loops of 7 sc.

EAR (MAKE 2)

With **A**, make a magic loop.
Rnd 1: Ch 1, 5 dc in loop, join–5 dc.
Fasten off, leaving a long tail for sewing. Sew to side of Head approximately 5 sts away from eyes. Weave in ends.

SKIRT

With front of Doll facing and Doll upside down.
Row 1: Join with **E** in sixteenth front loop from Rnd 23 of Body with a sl st, ch 1, sc in each st around, working over tail–20 sc.
Row 2: Ch 1, turn, sc in next 20 sts, ch 14.
Row 3: Turn. Starting in second ch from hook, sc into next 13 chs, sc in next 20 sc–33 sc.
Row 4: Ch 1, turn, [sc in next 9 sts, 2 sc in next] twice, sc in next 13–35 sc.
Row 5: Ch 1, turn, sc in next 35 sts.
Row 6: Ch 1, turn, sc in next 34 sts–34 sc.
Row 7: Ch 1, turn, sk next st, sc in next 33–33 sc.
Row 8: Ch 1, turn, sc in next 32 sts–32 sc.
Row 9: Ch 1, turn, sk next st, [sc in next 10, 2 sc in next] twice, sc in next 9–33 sc.
Row 10: Ch 1, turn, [sc in next 11 sts, 2 sc in next] twice, sc in next 9–35 sc.
Row 11: Ch 1, turn, sk next st, sc in next 34–34 sc.
Row 12: Ch 1, turn, sc in next 34 sts.
Row 13: Ch 1, turn, sk next st, sc in next 33–33 sc.
Row 14: Ch 1, turn, sc in next 32 sts–32 sc.
Row 15: Ch 1, turn, sk next st, sc in next 31–31 sc.
Rows 16–17: Ch 1, turn, sc in next 31 sts.
Row 18: Ch 1, turn, sc in next 31 sts, sc in 17 row ends–48 sc.
Fasten off with a tail long enough to sew Skirt closed by wrapping it to the left. Weave in end.

BELT

With front of Doll facing and Doll upside down.
Rnd 1: Join with **D** in nineteenth front loop from Rnd 26 of Body with a sl st, ch 1, crocheting over tail, sc in same st as join, sc in next, 2 sc in next, [sc in next 2, 2 sc in next] 5 times, sc in next 2–26 sts.
Rnd 2: [2 sc in next st, sc in next 2] 8 times, 2 sc in next, sc in next–35 sc.
Rnd 3: [Inv-dec, sc in next st] 11 times, inv-dec–23 sc.
Rnd 4: Sc in next 23 sc.
Sl st into next st.
Fasten off and weave in end.
Tuck top edge of Skirt under Belt.

SLEEVES

Left Arm

With back of Doll facing and Doll upside down.
Rnd 1: Starting at center back of Arm, join **E** with a sl st in front loop from Rnd 16 of Arm, ch 1, 2 sc in same st as join crocheting over the tail as you go, [sc in next, 2 sc in next] twice, sc in next–9 sc.
Rnd 2: [Sc in next st, 2 sc in next] 4 times, sc in next–13 sc.
Rnd 3: [2 sc in next st, sc in next 3] 3 times, sc in next–16 sc.
Rnd 4: Sc in next 16 sts.
Rnd 5: [Sc in next 3 sts, 2 sc in next] 4 times–20 sc.

Rnd 6: Sc in next 20 sts.
Rnd 7: [2 sc in next st, sc in next 4] 4 times–24 sc.
Rnd 8: Ch 2 (does not count as dc in this section), dc in same st, dc in next 4, 2 sc in next, [sc in next 5, 2 sc in next] twice, dc in next 5, 2 dc in next, sl st in first dc–28 sts.
Rnd 9: Ch 2, dc in same st, dc in next 5, 2 sc in next, [sc in next 6, 2 sc in next] twice, dc in next 6, 2 dc in next, sl st in first dc–32 sts.
Rnd 10: Sc in next 32 sts.
Sl st to next st. Fasten off and weave in end.

RIGHT ARM

With Doll upside down.
Rnd 1: Starting at center front of Arm, join **E** with a sl st in front loop from Rnd 16 of Arm, ch 1, 2 sc in same st as join crocheting over the tail as you go, [sc in next, 2 sc in next] twice, sc in next–9 sc.
Repeat Rnds 2–10 of Left Arm. Sl st to next st. Fasten off and weave in end.

MUSTACHE

With **C**, ch 8, pull ends tight and cut close to knots on each end. Pin in center of face between Rnds 42–43. Attach to Head only at center, leaving ends to hang loose.

EYELID DETAILS

Cut a length of **A** long enough to stitch Eyelids. Use photos as a guide.
Bottom Eyelid: Make 1 stitch under each eye between Rnds 44–45.
Upper Eyelid: Make 4 sts above each eye, making sure edge of Eyelid is a straight, horizontal line. Monk Gyatso should look sleepy, not mad!

EYEBROWS

With **C** and starting at left Eyebrow, make 1 st at an angle starting between Rnds 48–49, lined up with inside edge of eye. Next, insert needle 3 spaces left and 1 rnd down. Come out 1 st right and 1 rnd up.

Make a tiny st to hold arch of Eyebrow. Make second Eyebrow in the same way, with 3 sts between them. Use photos as a guide.

NECKLACE

Starting with circle medallion using **F**.
Rnd 1: MR, 6 sc in ring, pull tight to close–6 sc.
Crochet over tail as you go.
Rnd 2: [2 sc in next st, sc in next] 3 times–9 sc.
Sl st in next st, ch 22 (adjust for your tension: Circle medallion should be at center of chest), wrap ch around neck, sl st into fourth st to the left of where ch began making sure not to twist ch. Fasten off and weave in end.

Tassels (Make 2)

Cut a 4 in. / 10 cm length of **H**. Using hook, pull yarn around Necklace and hook through as for a sl st. Use a tapestry needle to separate the plies. Trim Tassels to reach bottom of medallion.

AVATAR ROKU

Designed by
NICOLE ROGOWSKI

Skill Level:
ADVANCED

An Avatar known for his dedication to mediating conflicts between nations, Avatar Roku, the Fire Nation Avatar who preceded Aang, epitomizes a balance between strength and restraint. His diplomatic efforts, however, suffer from indecision, and when he's forced to choose between ending the life of his longtime friend Sozin and letting him pursue his political ambitions, Roku's forgiving nature leads to his own death and to an afterlife of deep regret. In his guidance to Aang, Roku tries to impart the perils of indecision and the need for swift and decisive action.

In the colors of the Fire Nation, and with magnificent flowing white hair, the noble, wise, and tremendously powerful Avatar Roku offers guidance and understanding. You can almost hear his helpful advice through this crocheted doll!

"Some friendships are so strong, they can even transcend lifetimes."

—ROKU (Book 3, Episode 6)

FINISHED MEASUREMENTS

Height: 12 in. / 30.5 cm • Width: 5 in. / 12.5 cm

YARN

Worsted weight (#4, Medium) yarn, shown in Lion Brand *Basic Stitch* (100% Acrylic, 185 yd. / 169 m per 3.5 oz. / 100 g ball)
Color A: 138L Pomegranate, 1 ball
Color B: 102W Clay, 1 ball
Color C: 100 White, 1 ball
Color D: 153 Black, 1 ball
Color E: 158I Mustard, 1 ball
Color F: 400G Red Heather, 1 ball
And worsted weight (#4, Medium) yarn, shown in Lion Brand *Color Theory* (100% Acrylic, 246 yd. / 225 m per 3.5 oz / 100 g ball)
Color G: 132AG Canyon, 1 ball
And DK weight (#3, Light) yarn, shown in Loops & Threads *Silky Soft* (100% Rayon from Bamboo, 240 yd. / 219 m per 3.5 oz. / 100 g ball)
Color H: HT-5862-3 Jet, 1 ball

HOOKS

US E-4 / 3.50 mm, *or size needed to obtain gauge*
US C-2 / 2.75 mm

NOTIONS

Stitch markers • Tapestry needle • Polyester stuffing • 6 mm black safety eyes • Scissors • Styrofoam dowel

GAUGE

With larger hook 20 sc and 24 sc rounds = 4 in. / 10 cm; *make sure to check your gauge.*

ABBREVIATIONS

Back loop only (BLO), back post single crochet (BPsc), chain(s) (ch(s)), double crochet (dc), front loop only (FLO), front post single crochet (FPsc), half double crochet (hdc), magic ring (MR), previous (prev), right side (RS), single crochet (sc), skip (sk), slip stitch(es) (sl st(s)), space (sp), stitch(es) (st(s)), three single crochet closed together (sc3tog), treble crochet (tr), two double crochet closed together (dc2tog), two single crochet closed together (sc2tog), wrong side (WS), yarn over (yo).

SPECIAL ABBREVIATIONS

inv-dec (invisible single crochet decrease): Insert hook in FLO of each of next 2 sts, yo and draw through both sts, yo and draw through 2 loops on hook–1 st decreased.
Lp(s) (loop stitch(es)): Pull out a loop of working yarn of indicated length down and slightly away from next st, without releasing this loop insert hook into next st and pull up a loop to begin a single crochet, yo and pull through both loops on hook.
Lp2tog (loop stitch two together): [Pull out a loop of working yarn of indicated length down and slightly away from next st, without releasing this loop insert hook into next st and pull up a new loop] twice (as for sc2tog), yo and pull through all 3 loops on hook.
Lp3tog (loop stitch three together): [Pull out a loop of working yarn of indicated length down and slightly away from next st, without releasing this loop insert hook into next st and pull up a new loop] 3 times (as for sc3tog), yo and pull through all 4 loops on hook.

NOTES

When instructed to join, join with a slip stitch in first stitch.

"Make sense of our past, Aang, and you will bring peace and restore balance to the world."

—ROKU (Book 3, Episode 6)

BOTTOM ROBE PANEL (MAKE 2)

With larger hook and **D**, ch 23.
Row 1 (RS): Working in back bump of chs, sc in second ch from hook and in each ch across, ch 1 and turn–22 sc.
Row 2: Sc in each st across, ch 1 and turn.
Row 3: Sc in next 2 sts; with **A**, sc-BLO in next 18; with **D**, sc in next 2, ch 1 and turn.
Rows 4–6: Sc in next 2; with **A**, sc in next 18; with **D**, sc in next 2, ch 1 and turn.
Fasten off and weave ends in.
Set aside for Body.

ARM (MAKE 2)

With larger hook and **A**, ch 11, join to back bump of first ch, ch 1.
Rnd 1: Sc-BLO in same ch as join and in each ch around–11 sc.
Begin working in continuous rounds. Use a st marker to keep track of rounds.
Rnds 2–5: Sc in each st around.
Rnd 6: Sc in next 5 sts, dc-FLO in next 6.
Rnd 7: FPsc in next 5 sts, sc in next, dc in next, [2 dc in next] 4 times, dc in next, sc in next–17 sts.
Next 8 rounds will create inner Arm shaping within the sleeve by skipping indicated sts every other round.
Rnd 8: Ch 2, sk 5 sts, sc in next 12–12 sts, 1 ch-2 sp.
Rnd 9: Sk ch-2 sp, sc-FLO in first 5 sts of Rnd 7, [dc in next, 2 dc in next] 6 times–23 sts.
Rnd 10: Sk first 5 sts of prev rnd, sc in next 2 chs of Rnd 8, sc in next 18–20 sts.
Rnd 11: Sk first 2 sts of prev rnd, sc-FLO in first 5 sts of Rnd 9, [dc in next 2, 2 dc in next] 6 times–26 sts.
Rnd 12: Sk first 5 sts of prev rnd, sc in first 2 sts of Rnd 10, sc in next 24–26 sts.
Rnd 13: Sk first 2 sts of prev rnd, sc-FLO in first 5 sts of Rnd 11, [dc in next 3, 2 dc in next] 6 times–35 sts.
Fasten off **A**. Change to **D**.
Rnd 14: Sk first 2 sts of Rnd 12, sl st-FLO in next 5, sl st-BLO in next 30.
Rnd 15: Sk first 2 sts of Rnd 12, sc-BLO in each st around, join to first st and FO. Weave all ends in before proceeding to next section.
Stuff Rnds 1–7.

Before proceeding to Hand, peel back opening of sleeve to see skipped sts of Rnd 12 and 5 unworked back lps at beginning of Rnd 13.

LEFT HAND

With WS facing, larger hook, and **B**, join to unworked back loop of first st of Rnd 12 of Arm and ch 1.
Rnd 1: Sc in same st as join, sc in unworked back loops of second, third, and fourth sts of Rnd 13, sc in unworked back loop of second skipped st of Rnd 12–5 sc.
Begin working in continuous rounds. Use a st marker to keep track of rounds.
Rnd 2: [2 sc-FLO in next st, sc-FLO in next] twice, 2 sc-FLO in next–8 sc.
Rnd 3: Sc in next 5 sts, sc in next, [ch 4, sc in second ch from hook and next 2 chs] (Thumb made), sc in next 2 sc–8 sc, Thumb.
Rnd 4: Sc in next 5 sts, 2 sc in next, sk Thumb and push it to RS, sc in next 2–9 sc.
Rnds 5–6: Sc in each st around.
Rnd 7: [Inv-dec, sc in next st] 3 times–6 sc.
Fasten off and close opening with tail.
Do not stuff Hand.
With Left Hand attached, this piece will be referred to as "Left Arm" in Body instructions.

RIGHT HAND

With WS facing, larger hook, and **B**, join to unworked back loop of first st of Rnd 12 of Arm and ch 1.
Rnds 1–2: Repeat Rnds 1–2 of Left Hand.
Rnd 3: Sc in next 2 sts, [sc in next, ch 4, sc in second ch from hook and next 2 chs] (Thumb made), sc in next 5 sc–8 sc, Thumb.
Rnd 4: Sc in next 2 sts, 2 sc in next, sk Thumb and push it to RS, sc in next 5–9 sc.
Rnds 5–7: Repeat Rnds 5–7 of Left Hand.
Fasten off and close opening with tail. Do not stuff Hand.
With Right Hand attached, this piece will be referred to as "Right Arm" in Body instructions.

BODY

The use of the front loops in this section will keep sts from slanting while working continuously in the round.

With larger hook and **A**, ch 13.

Rnd 1: Sc in second ch from hook, sc in next 10 chs, 2 sc in last ch. Rotate piece to work on opposite side of chain and resume working in last ch worked, sc in 11 chs, 2 sc in last–26 sc.

Begin working in continuous rounds.

Use a st marker to keep track of rounds.

Rnd 2: 2 sc in next st, sc in next 10, [2 sc in next] 3 times, sc in next 10, [2 sc in next] twice–32 sc.

Rnd 3: Sc in next st, 2 sc in next, sc in next 10, [sc in next, 2 sc in next] 3 times, sc in next 10, [sc in next, 2 sc in next] twice–38 sc.

Rnd 4: Sc in next 2 sts, 2 sc in next, sc in next 10, [sc in next 2, 2 sc in next] 3 times, sc in next 10, [sc in next 2, 2 sc in next] twice, join and ch 1–44 sc.

Rnd 5: BPsc in each st around.

Resume working in continuous rounds.

Use a st marker to keep track of rounds.

Rnds 6–11: Sc in each st around. At the end of Rnd 11, join, change to **D** and ch 1.

In next rnd, Bottom Robe Panels will be attached with their RS facing.

Hold Bottom Robe Panel in front of Body sts. Crochet through both thicknesses to join, always inserting hook into st on Panel first, then into BLO of st on Body.

Rnd 12 (Joining): With **D** and beginning in twenty-first st of Row 4 of first Panel, sc through both thicknesses; with **A**, sc in next 18 sts; with **D**, sc in next 2. Holding second Panel in front of Body, work as established: with **D**, sc in next 2; with **A**, sc in next 18; with **D**, sc in next 2, sc in last remaining st on first Panel–44 sts.

Resume working in continuous rounds.

Use a st marker to keep track of rounds.

Rnd 13: Sc in next st; with **A**, sc in next 18; with **D**, sc in next 4; with **A**, sc in next 18; with **D**, sc in next 3.

Rnds 14–18: Sc in next st; with **A**, sc-FLO in next 18; with **D**, sc in next 4; with **A**, sc-FLO in next 18; with **D**, sc in next 3.

Rnd 19: Sc in next st; with **A**, inv-dec, sc-FLO in next 14, inv-dec; with **D**, sc in next 4; with **A**, inv-dec, sc-FLO in next 14, inv-dec; with **D**, sc in next 3–40 sc.

Rnds 20–22: Sc in next st; with **A**, sc-FLO in next 16; with **D**, sc in next 4; with **A**, sc-FLO in next 16; with **D**, sc in next 3.

Begin stuffing Body.

Rnd 23: Sc in next st; with **A**, inv-dec, sc-FLO in next 12, inv-dec; with **D**, sc in next 4; with **A**, inv-dec, sc-FLO in next 12, inv-dec; with **D**, sc in next 3–36 sc.

Rnds 24–26: Sc in next st; with **A**, sc-FLO in next 14; with **D**, sc in next 4; with **A**, sc-FLO in next 14; with **D**, sc in next 3.

Rnd 27: Sc in next st; with **A**, inv-dec, sc-FLO in next 10, inv-dec; with **D**, sc in next 4; with **A**, inv-dec, sc-FLO in next 10, inv-dec, sc in next 3–32 sc.

Rnds 28–30: Sc in next st; with **A**, sc-FLO in next 12; with **D**, sc in next 4; with **A**, sc-FLO in next 12; with **D**, sc in next 3.

Rnd 31: Sc in next st; with **A**, inv-dec, sc-FLO in next 8, inv-dec; with **D**, sc in next 4; with **A**, inv-dec, sc-FLO in next 8, inv-dec; with **D**, sc in next 3–28 sc.

Continue with **D** for next 4 rnds.

Rnd 32: Sl st-BLO in each st around.

Rnd 33: Sc-BLO in each st around.

Continue stuffing Body.

Rnds 34–35: Sc in each st around. At end of Rnd 35, change to **A**.

Fasten off **D**. Next 16 rnds will be worked with **A** only.

Rnd 36: Sl st-BLO in each st around.

Rnd 37: Sc-BLO in each st around.

Rnds 38–41: Sc in each st around.

Rnd 42: [Sc in next 3 sts, 2 sc in next, sc in next 9, 2 sc in next] twice–32 sc.

Continue stuffing Body.

Rnd 43: [Sc in next 3 sts, 2 sc in next, sc in next 11, 2 sc in next] twice–36 sc.

In next rnd, Arms will be joined.

Hold Arm in front of Body sts. Crochet through both thicknesses to join, always inserting hook into unworked loop of starting ch on Arm first, then into st on Body. Rnd 44 will be worked across third to seventh starting chs of Right Arm and sixth to tenth starting chs of Left Arm. Rnd 45 will be worked across remaining starting chs of Arms.

Rnd 44 (Joining): Beginning in third starting ch of Right Arm and working through both thicknesses, sc in 5 sts

on Right Arm. Sc in next 13 sts of Body. Working through both thicknesses, sc in sixth starting ch of Left Arm, sc in next 4 sts of Left Arm. Sc in next 13 sts of Body only–36 sc.
Rnd 45: 2 sc in next ch on Right Arm, sc in 5 remaining chs on Right Arm, sc in 13 sts on Body only, sc in 5 remaining chs on Left Arm, 2 sc in last remaining ch on Left Arm, sc in 13 sts on Body–40 sc.
Rnd 46–47: Sc in each st around.
Rnd 48: [Sc in next 3 sts, inv-dec] 8 times–32 sc.
Rnd 49: [Sc in next 2 sts, inv-dec] 8 times–24 sc.
Continue stuffing Body.
Rnd 50: [Sc in next st, inv-dec] 8 times–16 sc.
Rnd 51: [Inv-dec] 8 times, join to first st, change to **B** and ch 1–8 sc.
Fasten off **A**. Remaining rnds of Body will be worked with **B**.
Rnd 52: Sc-FLO in same st as join and in each st around.
Rnd 53–54: Sc in each st around.
After Rnd 54, join to first st and FO with a long tail. Set aside for assembly.

CAPELET

With larger hook and **F**, leave a long tail and ch 10, join to first ch, ch 1.
Rnd 1: 2 sc in same ch as join and in each ch around–20 sc.
Begin working in continuous rounds. Use a st marker to keep track of rounds.
Rnd 2: [Sc in next st, 2 sc in next] 10 times–30 sc.
Rnd 3: Sc in next st, 2 sc in next, [sc in next 2, 2 sc in next] 9 times, sc in next–40 sc.
Rnd 4: [Sc in next 3 sts, 2 sc in next] 10 times–50 sc.
Rnd 5: Sc in next 7 sts, sc-FLO in next 11, sc in next 14, sc-FLO in next, sc in next 7.
Rnd 6: [Sc in next 4 sts, 2 sc in next] 10 times–60 sc.
Rnds 7–8: Sc in each st around.
At the end of Rnd 8 change to **D** and do NOT ch. Fasten off **F**. Remaining 2 rnds of Capelet will be worked with **D**.
Rnd 9: Sl st-BLO in each st around.
Rnd 10: Sc-BLO in each around, join.
Fasten off. Weave in **D** tail and set aside.

INNER CAPELET LAYER (MAKE 2)

With larger hook and **G**, join to unworked back loop of eighteenth st of Rnd 4 of Capelet with its WS facing, ch 1.
Row 1 (WS): Sc in same loop as join and in each loop across, ch 1 and turn–11 sc.
Rows 2–7: Sc in each st across, ch 1 and turn.
Row 8: Sc2tog, sc in next 7 sts, sc2tog, ch 1 and turn–9 sts.
Row 9: Sc3tog, sc in next 3 sts, sc3tog–5 sts.
Fasten off. Weave ends in. With larger hook and **G**, join to unworked back loop of forty-third st of Rnd 4 of Capelet with its WS facing, ch 1.

INNER CAPELET BORDER

With larger hook and **G**, and with RS of Inner Capelet Layer facing, join to back loop of eighth st of Rnd 4 of Capelet, ch 1.
Row 1: Working around Inner Capelet Layer, sc 8 across row ends, sc in 5 sts across Row 9, sc 8 across row ends, ch 1, join to back loop of eighteenth st of Rnd 4 of Capelet. FO and weave in both ends.
With larger hook and **G**, and with RS of Inner Capelet Layer facing, join to back loop of thirty-third st of Rnd 4 of Capelet, ch 1. Repeat Row 1, joining to back loop of forty-third st of Rnd 4 of Capelet.
Fasten off and weave in both ends.

FIRE INSIGNIA

With smaller hook and **H**, ch 5, join to first ch to form a ring, ch 1.
Rnd 1: Working into ring, make 2 sc, dc, [tr, ch 3, sl st in third ch from hook], ch 1, sl st, [ch 6, sl st in third ch from hook, sc in next ch, dc in next ch, sc in last ch], 2 dc, 2 hdc, join–9 sts, 2 flame points.
Fasten off with a long tail. Weave in starting tail. With tapestry needle and tail, sew Fire Insignia to bottom center front of Capelet, with flame points pointing to top of Capelet. Use pictures as a guide.

HEAD

With larger hook and **B**, create a MR and ch 1.
Rnd 1: 6 sc in MR and pull tail to close ring–6 sc.
Begin working in continuous rounds. Use a st marker to keep track of rounds.
Rnd 2: [2 sc in next st] 6 times–12 sc.
Lps created in this section should be 2 in. / 5 cm long.
Rnd 3: With **B**, [sc in next st, 2 sc in next] twice; join with **C**, [Lp in next, 2 Lp in next] 3 times; with **B**, sc in next, 2 sc in next–18 sts.
Rnd 4: [Sc in next 2 sts, 2 sc in next] twice; with **C**, [Lp in next 2, 2 Lp in next] 3 times; with **B**, sc in next 2, 2 sc in next–24 sts.
Rnd 5: Sc in next 8 sts; with **C**, Lp in next 2; with **B**, sc in next 3; with **C**, Lp in next 2; with **B**, sc in next 3; with **C**, Lp in next 2; with **B**, sc in next 4.
Rnd 6: [Sc in next 3 sts, 2 sc in next] twice, sc in next; with **C**, Lp in next; with **B**, sc in next 3; with **C**, Lp in next 2; with **B**, sc in next 3; with **C**, Lp in next; with **B**, sc in next 4, 2 sc in next–27 sts.
Rnd 7: Sc in next 11 sts; with **C**, Lp in next; with **B**, sc in next 8; with **C**, Lp in next, with **B**, sc in next 6.
Fasten off **C**. Remaining rnds of Head will be worked with **B**.
Rnds 8–16: Sc in each st round.
Insert safety eyes in sixteenth and twentieth sts of Rnd 12.
Rnd 17: [Sc in next 7 sts, inv-dec] 3 times–24 sts.
Rnd 18: [Sc in next 2 sts, inv-dec] 6 times–18 sts.
Rnd 19: [Sc in next st, inv-dec] 6 times–12 sts.

Firmly stuff Head.
Rnd 20: [Inv-dec] 6 times–6 sts.
Fasten off and sew remaining opening closed. Set aside.

NOSE

With larger hook and **B**, create a MR and ch 1.
Rnd 1: Dc2tog in MR, pull tail to close ring.
Fasten off with a long tail and weave in starting tail. With tapestry needle and tail, sew Nose vertically between safety eyes, between Rnds 9–12. Weave ends in.

HAIR CAP

Pull all Lps to the RS–especially when working last 4 rows of this section.
With larger hook and **C**, create a MR and ch 1.
Rnd 1: 7 sc in MR, pull tail to close–7 sc.
Next 3 rnds are worked continuously. Use a st marker to keep track of rounds.
Lps created in this section should be 4½ in. / 11.5 cm long.
Rnd 2: [2 Lps in next st] 7 times–14 sts.
Rnd 3: [Lp in next st, 2 Lps in next] 7 times–21 sts.
Rnd 4: [Lp in next 2 sts, 2 Lps in next] 7 times, join, ch 1–28 sts.
Begin working in rows.
Row 1 (RS): Beginning in same st as join, Lp2tog, Lp in next, Lp2tog, ch 1 and turn, leaving remaining sts unworked–3 sts.
Row 2: Lp in each st across, ch 1 and turn.
Row 3: Lp3tog, ch 1 and turn–1 st.
Row 4: Lp in next.
Fasten off with a long tail.

Attach Hair Cap to Head: With tapestry needle and tail of Hair Cap, sew Hair Cap on Head positioning it so top of Row 4 of Hair Cap is lined up with Rnd 16 of Head and in line with Nose. It is important to stretch Hair Cap down back of Head so edge of Rnd 4 of Hair Cap lines up with Rnd 12 of Head.Use remaining length of Hair Cap tail to embroider eyebrows onto face. Pull threaded tapestry needle through widow's peak (Row 4) to prepare for next section.

Hair Cap Finishing Steps: With tapestry needle still threaded. **Step 1:** Gather 8 long loops from Rows 1–4 into one hand, drawing them up and away from Hair Cap. **Step 2:** Cut at center point of loops to create 16 strands of hair. **Step 3:** Twist strands clockwise 180 degrees. **Step 4:** Wrap Hair Cap tail tightly around strands 2–3 times. **Step 5:** Fold strands in half toward back of Head so ends lie just past wraps. **Step 6:** Continue to wrap Hair Cap tail tightly around strands 2–3 more times to secure bun. Knot tail around wraps in back of bun and weave ends in. **Step 7:** Cut center points of remaining loops (Hair Cap Rnds 1–4).

Beard Finishing Steps: Cut center points of loops from Rnds 3–7 of Head.

Hair Cap and Beard Final Steps: Use a steamer to relax and straighten strands of hair from Hair Cap and Beard, and trim as desired.

Attach Capelet to Body: Thread a tapestry needle with starting tail of Capelet. Place Capelet on Body, with neck in ring opening. Align center front of Capelet with center front of Body at Rnds 44–45. Sew starting ch of Capelet to Body at the base of neck. Weave ends in.

Attach Head to Body: To keep Head from becoming wobbly, insert a Styrofoam dowel inside Body before attaching Head. Thread a tapestry needle with tail of Body. Sew top of Rnd 54 of Body to bottom center of Head at Rnds 1–2, aligning Nose with Fire Insignia. Weave ends in.

ROBE TIE

With **D** and larger hook, ch 60 and fasten off. Weave both ends in. Tie around waist at Rnds 32–35.

HAIRBAND

With **A** and larger hook, ch 10.
Row 1: Sl st in second ch from hook and in each ch across–9 sl sts.
Fasten off with a long tail. Weave in starting tail.

Attach Hairband to Hair Bun: Thread a tapestry needle with tail of Hairband. Wrap Hairband around wraps of Bun and sew in place, sewing short ends together before finishing. Weave ends in.

GOLDEN HAIR WING (MAKE 2)

With **E** and larger hook, create a MR and ch 1.
Rnd 1: Working into MR: sc, [sc, ch 4, sl st in second ch from hook and in next 2 chs], 2 hdc, sl st, join–5 sts, 1 ch-4 Wing tip. Pull tail to close ring. Fasten off with a long tail. Weave in starting tail.

Attach Hair Wings to Hair Bun: Thread a tapestry needle with tail of a Golden Hair Wing. Place Wing on side of Bun with Wing tip pointing up right above Hairband and sew into hair strands.
Once secured, weave in remaining end.
Repeat on opposite side with second Wing.

RAN AND SHAW

Designed by
LEE SARTORI

Skill Level:
ADVANCED

As the first Firebenders, dragons are crucial to Fire Nation history. They were believed to be extinct after Fire Lord Sozin's malicious initiative to hunt dragons for glory. But in an effort to discourage any further attempts to find them, Iroh falsely claimed that he fought and slayed the last dragons.

Ran and Shaw are believed to be the ancient dragons that originally taught humans to firebend. Under the protection of the Sun Warriors, these venerable creatures demonstrate the renewing, cleansing, and vitalizing spirit of fire, and only the few who are deemed worthy are imparted with this ancient wisdom.

These impressive crochet creations are an awe-inspiring project to make! One red, one blue, Ran and Shaw are twin crochet patterns, and super fun to stitch. The details make them come alive—but be sure to offer them protection.

"If you wish to learn the ways of the Sun, you must learn them from the masters, Ran and Shaw."

—SUN WARRIOR (Book 3, Episode 12)

FINISHED MEASUREMENTS
Length: 20 in. / 51 cm • Height: 8 in. / 20 cm • Width: 14 in. / 35.5 cm

YARN
Worsted weight (#4, Medium), shown in Lion Brand *Basic Stitch* (100% Acrylic, 185 yd. / 169 m per 3.5 oz. / 100 g ball)

RAN (BLUE DRAGON)
Color A: 406N Deep Denim Heather, 1 ball
Color B: 110AW Stonewash, 1 ball
Color C: 153 Black, 1 ball
Color D: 100 White, 1 ball
Color E: 109T Steel Blue, 1 ball

SHAW (RED DRAGON)
Color A: 400B Red Heather, 1 ball
Color B: 133A Pumpkin, 1 ball
Color C: 153 Black, 1 ball
Color D: 100 White, 1 ball
Color E: 138L Pomegranate, 1 ball

HOOK
US C-2 / 2.75 mm, *or size needed to obtain gauge*

NOTIONS
Stitch markers • Tapestry needle • Polyester stuffing • 12 mm yellow safety eyes • 10 chenille stems • Scissors

GAUGE
28 sc and 28 sc rounds = 4 in. / 10 cm; *make sure to check your gauge.*

ABBREVIATIONS
Back loop only (BLO), chain(s) (ch(s)), front loop only (FLO), right side (RS), single crochet (sc), slip stitch(es) (sl st(s)), stitch(es) (st(s)), wrong side (WS), yarn over (yo).

SPECIAL ABBREVIATIONS
inv-dec (invisible single crochet decrease): Insert hook in FLO of each of next 2 sts, yo and draw through both sts, yo and draw through 2 loops on hook–1 st decreased.
Basic Return: Ch 1, *yo and draw through 2 loops on hook, repeat from * until 1 loop remains on hook.
Tunisian Simple Stitch (tss): Insert hook under vertical bar of next st, yo and draw up a loop leaving loop on hook.
Whip Stitch: Align edges of 2 pieces to seam, thread a needle, and make angled stitches by bringing the needle in and out of the edges. Push needle through top layer, then bring it back through both layers at a slight angle and pull thread snug. Repeat this process across length of seam.

NOTES

Work in continuous rounds unless otherwise indicated. When instructed to join, join with a slip stitch in first stitch.

"My name is Zuko, Crown Prince of the Fire Nation. Or at least I used to be. I know my people have distorted the ways of firebending to be fueled by anger and rage, but now I want to learn the true way, the original way. When we came here, I never imagined the Sun Warrior civilization was secretly alive. I am truly humbled to be in your presence. Please, teach us."

—PRINCE ZUKO
(Book 3, Episode 17)

BODY

With **A**, make a magic loop.
Rnd 1: Ch 1, 6 sc in loop–6 sc.
Rnds 2–3: Sc in each st around.
Rnd 4: 2 sc in next st, sc in each st around–7 sc.
Rnds 5–6: Sc in each st around.
Rnd 7: 2 sc in next st, sc in each st around–8 sc.
Rnds 8–9: Sc in each st around.
Rnd 10: 2 sc in next st, sc in each st around–9 sc.
Rnds 11–12: Sc in each st around.
Rnd 13: 2 sc in next st, sc in each st around–10 sc.
Rnds 14–15: Sc in each st around.
Rnd 16: 2 sc in next st, sc in each st around–11 sc.
Rnds 17–18: Sc in each st around.
Rnd 19: 2 sc in next st, sc in each st around–12 sc.
Rnd 20: Sc in each st around.
Rnd 21: Sc in each st around, sl st in next st.
Stuff and continue stuffing as work progresses.
Begin Short Rows.
Short Row 22 (RS): Ch 1, sc in next 6 sts, turn leaving remaining 6 sts unworked–6 sc.
Short Row 23 (WS): Ch 1, sc in next 6 sts, turn.
Rnd 24 (RS): Ch 1, sc in 6 sts across previous Short Row, sc in skipped sts 2 rows below, join, **do not turn**–12 sc.
Rnd 25 (RS): Ch 1, sc in each st around, join, **do not turn**–12 sc.
Short Row Section will be repeated 2 more times below.
Rows/Rnds 26–33: Repeat Rows/Rnds 22–25.
Continue in joined, turned rounds.
Rnd 34: Ch 1, 2 sc in next st, sc in each st around, join, turn–13 sc.
Rnd 35: Ch 1, sc in each st around, join, turn.
Rnd 36: Ch 1, 2 sc in next st, sc in each st around, turn–14 sc.
Rnd 37: Ch 1, sc in each st around, join, turn.
Rnd 38: Ch 1, 2 sc in next st, sc in each st around, join, turn–15 sc.
Rnd 39: Ch 1, sc in each st around, join, turn.
Rnd 40: Ch 1, 2 sc in next st, sc in each st around, join, turn–16 sc.
Rnd 41: Ch 1, sc in each st around, join, turn.
Rnd 42: Ch 1, 2 sc in next st, sc in each st around, join, turn–17 sc.
Rnd 43: Ch 1, sc in each st around, join, turn.
Rnd 44: Ch 1, 2 sc in next st, sc in each st around, join, turn–18 sc.
Rnd 45: Ch 1, sc in each st around, **do not turn**.
Begin Short Rows.
Short Row 46 (RS): Ch 1, sc in next 9 sts, turn leaving remaining 9 sts unworked–9 sc.
Short Row 47 (WS): Ch 1, sc in next 9 sts, turn.
Rnd 48 (RS): Ch 1, sc in 9 sts across previous Short Row, sc in 9 unworked sts 2 rows below, join, **do not turn**–18 sc.
Rnd 49 (RS): Ch 1, sc in each st around, join.
Short Row Section will be repeated 4 more times below.
Rows/Rnds 50–65: Repeat Rows/Rnds 46–49.
Continue in joined, turned rounds.
Rnds 66–76: Ch 1, sc in each st around, join, turn.
Begin Short Rows. Note: This section is worked starting with WS to make the hump twist the other way.
Short Row 77 (WS): Ch 1, sc in next 9 sts, turn leaving remaining 9 sts unworked–9 sc.
Short Row 78 (RS): Ch 1, sc in next 9 sts, turn.
Rnd 79 (WS): Ch 1, sc in 9 sts across previous Short Row, sc in 9 unworked sts 2 rows below, join, **do not turn**–18 sc.
Rnd 80 (WS): Ch 1, sc in each st around, join, **do not turn**.
Short Row Section will be repeated 8 more times below.
Rows/Rnds 81–112: Repeat Rows/Rnds 77–80.
Continue in joined, turned rounds.
Rnds 113–124: Ch 1, sc in each st around, join, turn–18 sc.
Rnd 125: Ch 1, [2 sc in next st, sc in next 5] around, join, turn–21 sc.
Rnd 126: Ch 1, sc in each st around, join.

Rnd 127: Ch 1, [sc in next 3 sts, 2 sc in next, sc in next 3] around, join, turn–24 sc.
Rnd 128: Ch 1, sc in each st around, join, **do not turn**.
Begin Short Rows.
Short Row 129 (RS): Ch 1, sc in next 12 sts, turn leaving remaining 12 sts unworked–12 sc.
Short Row 130 (WS): Ch 1, sc in next 12 sts, turn.
Rnd 131 (RS): Ch 1, sc in 12 sts across previous Short Row, sc in 12 unworked sts 2 rows below, join, **do not turn**–24 sc.
Rnd 132 (RS): Ch 1, sc in each st around, join, **do not turn**.
Short Row Section will be repeated 10 more times below.
Rows/Rnds 133–172: Repeat Rows/Rnds 129–132. Turn at end of Rnd 132 so WS is facing for next section.
Begin next section of Short Rows facing the opposite direction.
Short Row 173 (WS): Ch 1, sc in next 12 sts, turn leaving remaining 12 sts unworked–12 sc.
Short Row 174 (RS): Ch 1, sc in next 12 sts, turn.
Rnd 175 (WS): Ch 1, sc in 12 sts across previous Short Row, sc in 12 unworked sts 2 rows below, join, **do not turn**–24 sc.
Rnd 176 (WS): Ch 1, sc in each st around, join, **do not turn**.
Short Row Section will be repeated 5 more times below.
Rows/Rnds 177–196: Repeat Rows/Rnds 173–176. Turn at the end of Rnd 176 so RS is facing for next section.
Continue to Head.

HEAD

Continue with **A**.
Rnd 1 (RS): Ch 1, [2 sc in next st, sc in next 3] around, join, turn–30 sc.
Rnds 2–10: Ch 1, sc in each st around, join, turn.
Rnd 11: Ch 1, sc in next 15 sts, [inv-dec, sc in next 3] 3 times, join, turn–27 sc.
Rnd 12: Ch 1, sc in each st around, join.
Rnd 13: Ch 1, sc in next 15 sts, [inv-dec, sc in next] 4 times, join, **do not turn**–23 sc.
Begin working in joined but unturned rounds.
Rnd 14: Ch 1, [inv-dec] twice, sc in next 11 sts, [inv-dec] 4 times, join–17 sc.
Add safety eyes between Rnds 10–11 on either side of face using photos as a guide.
Rnd 15: Ch 1 tightly, inv-dec, sc in each st around, do not join–16 sc.
Rnd 16: Inv-dec, sc in each st around–15 sc.
Rnds 17–19: Repeat Rnd 16–12 sts at the end of Rnd 19.
Rnd 20: [Inv-dec] around–6 sc.
Fasten off, leaving a long tail for sewing. Sew remaining 6 sts closed. Weave in end.

EYELID (MAKE 2)

With **A**.
Row 1: Ch 8.
Fasten off, leaving a long tail for sewing. Sew around top half of eye using photos as a guide. Weave in end.

EYEBROW (MAKE 2)

With **B**.
Row 1: Ch 8.
Fasten off, leaving a long tail for sewing. Sew in a straight line above inner edge of eye and back toward forehead using photos as a guide.

EAR (MAKE 2)

With **B**, make a magic loop.
Rnd 1: Ch 1, 6 sc in loop–6 sc.
Rnd 2: [2 sc in next st, sc in next] around–9 sc.
Rnds 3–4: Sc in each st around.
Rnd 5: Inv-dec, sc in each st around–8 sc.
Rnd 6: Inv-dec, sc in each st around–7 sc.
Rnd 7: Inv-dec, sc in each st around–6 sc.
Fasten off, leaving a long tail for sewing. Flatten piece. Sew to top of Head where Eyebrow ends. Weave in ends.

HORN (MAKE 2)

With **C**, make a magic loop.
Rnd 1: Ch 1, 3 sc in loop–3 sc.
Rnd 2: 2 sc in next st, sc in each st around–4 sc.
Rnd 3: 2 sc in next st, sc in each st around–5 sc.
Rnds 4–13: Sc in each st around.
Fasten off, leaving a long tail for sewing. Sew Horns directly behind each Ear. Weave in ends.

BACK SPIKE

With **D** and leaving a long tail at start for sewing. Note: Spikes are worked in one continuous piece.
Row 1: Ch 4, sl st in second ch from hook, sc in next, hdc in next (1 spike made), *next Spike [ch 5, sl st in second ch from hook, sc in next, hdc in next, skip last ch]; repeat from * 43 more times–45 Spikes.
Fasten off, leaving a long tail for sewing. Using finishing tail, secure end of Spikes to end of Body and weave in this end. Using starting tail, secure start of Spikes between Ears. Weave in this end. Pin remaining length of Spikes across spine of Body. Using a long length of **A**, whip stitch between each Spike to secure it to the body. Weave in ends.

BELLY PATCH

With **E**.
Note: In Tunisian crochet, the loop on your hook counts as the first stitch.
Row 1: Ch 3, starting in second ch draw up a loop in next 2 chs, complete Basic Return–3 tss.
Rows 2–100: Tss across, complete Basic Return–3 tss.
Fasten off, leaving a long tail for sewing. Using photos as a guide, sew to bottom of Body. Weave in ends.

TOE (MAKE 12)

With **D**, make a magic loop.
Rnd 1: Ch 1, 3 sc in loop–3 sc.
Rnd 2: 2 sc in next st, sc in each st around–4 sc.
Rnd 3: 2 sc in next st, sc in each st around–5 sc.
Rnd 4: 2 sc in next st, sc in each st around–6 sc.
Rnds 5–6: Sc in each st around.
Fasten off **D**, change to **A**.
Rnd 7: Ch 1, sl st in each st around, join.
Rnd 8: Ch 1, sc-BLO in each st around, join.
Fasten off. Stuff lightly. Continue to Foot.

FOOT (MAKE 4)

With **A**, join 3 Toes together in next round.
Rnd 1 (Joining): Sl st in any st of first Toe, ch 1, sc in next 3 sts on first Toe, holding second Toe in line with previous Toe sc in next 3 sts on second Toe, holding third Toe in line with previous Toe sc in next 6 sts on third Toe, sc in next 3 sts of second Toe, sc in remaining 3 sts of first Toe, join–18 sc.
Rnds 2–9: Ch 1, sc in each st around, join.
Fasten off, leaving a long tail for sewing. Stuff Foot. Set aside to join to Legs.

LEG (MAKE 4)

With **A**, make a magic loop.
Rnd 1: Ch 1, 6 sc in loop–6 sc.
Rnd 2: [2 sc in next st, sc in next] around–9 sc.
Rnd 3: [Sc in next st, 2 sc in next, sc in next] around–12 sc.
Rnd 4: [2 sc in next st, sc in next 3] around–15 sc.
Rnd 5: [Sc in next 2 sts, 2 sc in next, sc in next 2] around–18 sc.
Rnd 6: [2 sc in next st, sc in next 5] around–21 sc.
Rnd 7: [Sc in next 3 sts, 2 sc in next, sc in next 3] around–24 sc.
Rnd 8: [2 sc in next st, sc in next 7] around–27 sc.
Rnd 9: [Sc in next 4 sts, 2 sc in next, sc in next 4] around–30 sc.
Rnd 10: [2 sc in next st, sc in next 9] around–33 sc.
Rnd 11: [Sc in next 5 sts, 2 sc in next, sc in next 5] around–36 sc.
Rnd 12 (Separate for Foot): Sc in next 18 sts, join to first st leaving remaining 18 sts unworked–18 sc.
Rnd 13: Ch 1 tightly, sc in each st around, do not join.
Rnds 14–20: Sc in each st around.
Fasten off, leaving a long tail for sewing. To make Back Legs, sew Foot to unworked sts of Rnd 12. To make Front Legs, sew Foot to Rnd 20. Stuff Legs. Sew to front and back sides of Body using photos as a guide. Weave in ends.

WING FRAME (MAKE 2)

With **A**, make a magic loop.
Rnd 1: Ch 1, 6 sc in loop–6 sc.
Rnd 2: [2 sc in next st, sc in next] around–9 sc.
Rnds 3–72: Sc in each st around.
Rnd 73: [Sc in next st, 2 sc in next, sc in next] around–12 sc.
Fasten off, leaving a long tail for sewing. Twist 5 chenille stems together tightly for thickness and insert into Wing Frame. Bend Wing Frame gently in center to form a V.

WING MAINSAIL (MAKE 2)

With **E**.
Row 1: Ch 2, (sc 2, ch 2, sc 2) in second ch from hook, turn–4 sc.
Row 2: Ch 1, 2 sc in first st, sc in each st across to ch-2 space, (sc, ch 2, sc) in ch-2 space, sc in each st across to last, 2 sc in last, turn–8 sc.
Rows 3–13: Repeat Row 2–52 sts at the end of Row 13.
Row 14 (Edging): Ch 1, rotate to sc 27 evenly across row ends–27 sc.
Fasten off, leaving a long tail for sewing. Sew Mainsail into Wing Frame, with Row 1 at the top and Row 14 at the bottom of the Wing unsewn. Weave in ends.

WING INNER BONE (MAKE 4)

With **A**.
Row 1: Ch 50 tightly.
Fasten off, leaving a long tail for sewing. Loop the Bone through the top of the Wing at the bend, leaving a length of Bone on the inside and on the outside of the Wing. Secure the ends of the Bone at the bottom of the Wing using photos as a guide. Trim ends.

WING CLAW (MAKE 2)

With **D**, make a magic loop.
Rnd 1: Ch 1, 3 sc in loop–3 sc.
Rnd 2: 2 sc in next st, sc in each st around–4 sc.
Rnd 3: 2 sc in next st, sc in each st around–5 sc.
Rnd 4: 2 sc in next st, sc in each st around–6 sc.
Rnds 5–6: Sc in each st around.
Fasten off **D**, change to **A**.
Rnd 7: Ch 1, sl st in each st around, join.
Rnd 8: Ch 1, 2 sc-BLO in each st around, join–12 sc.

Fasten off. Sew Claw to top of Wing at bend. Weave in ends. Sew completed Wing to either side of Body above front Legs.

FU MANCHU

With **C**.
Row 1: Ch 100 tightly.

Fasten off. Thread the Fu Manchu through the side of the nose about 3 rnds away from the last rnd of the Head. Trim the ends.

FINISHING

Using **B**, cut approximately 12–15 strands of hair measuring roughly 5 in. / 13 cm. Loop strands at bottom of last round of Head for beard. Brush strands out gently. Do the same for sides of Head below Ears. Using **A**, add another set of strands behind **B** at sides of Head. Using a length of **E**, embroider a mouth starting from under the eye and around the nose to underneath the opposite eye using photos as a guide. Weave in ends. Using **B**, cut approximately 20 more strands of hair measuring roughly 6 in. / 15 cm. Loop strands through bottom of tail. Brush strands out gently.

ABBREVIATIONS

BLO = Back loop only

BPsc = Back post single crochet

ch(s) = Chain(s)

dc = Double crochet

FO = Fasten off

FLO = Front loop only

FPsc = Front post single crochet

hdc = Half double crochet

inc = Increase

MR = Magic ring

prev = Previous

RS = Right side

sc = Single crochet

sk = Skip

sl st(s) = Slip stitch(es)

sp(s) = Space(s)

st(s) = Stitch(es)

tr = Treble crochet

dc2tog = Two double crochet closed together

hdc2tog = Two half double crochet closed together

sc3tog = Three single crochet closed together

sc2tog = Two single crochet closed together

WS = Wrong side

yo = Yarn over

YARN RESOURCES

Lion Brand Yarn: www.lionbrand.com

WeCrochet: www.crochet.com

Furls Crochet: www.furlscrochet.com

AUTHOR BIO

Lee Sartori is the crochet designer behind CoCo Crochet Lee. Author of several popular crochet books, she can be seen as a guest host on the popular PBS/ CreateTV show *Knit and Crochet Now!* and as a featured instructor on Skillshare, where she demonstrates fun crochet skills and patterns. Lee's passion is designing modern, wearable garments and adorable amigurumi. Lee lives in Halifax, Canada, with her two children, Noël and Conan, her amazing husband, Sean, her adorable bunny, Neville, and four cats. You can find her work on her blog and on social media, where she posts fun and whimsical takes on crochet.

ACKNOWLEDGMENTS

Creating this book would not have been possible without the help of my fellow designers Sarah Csiacsek, Valérie Prieur-Côté, Lizette Mejia, and Nicole Rogowski. Thank you for lending your talent to this project! I would also like to thank Mark at Lion Brand Yarn, Pam at Furls Crochet, and Katelyn at WeCrochet for their continued support for my work.

INSIGHT EDITIONS

PO Box 3088
San Rafael, CA 94912
www.insighteditions.com

Find us on Facebook: www.facebook.com/InsightEditions
Follow us on Instagram: @insighteditions

nickelodeon

ISBN: 979-8-3374-0257-4

Publisher: Raoul Goff
SVP, Group Publisher: Jeff McLaughlin
VP, Manufacturing: Alix Nicholaeff
Associate Publisher: Thom O'Hearn
Senior Art Director: Stuart Smith
Senior Designer: Judy Wiatrek Trum
Designer: Kayleigh Hutcheson
Associate Editor: Sami Alvarado
Editorial Assistant: Melissa Santoyo
Managing Editor: Shannon Ballesteros
Production Editor: Ivy Long
Production Manager: Deena Hashem
Strategic Production Planner: Lina s Palma-Temena

Photographs by Stacy Ventura
Styling by Bethany Martin

Exclusive patterns can be found at *https://insighteditions.com/pages/atlaamigurumi*

ROOTS of PEACE   REPLANTED PAPER

Insight Editions, in association with Roots of Peace, will plant two trees for each tree used in the manufacturing of this book. Roots of Peace is an internationally renowned humanitarian organization dedicated to eradicating land mines worldwide and converting war-torn lands into productive farms and wildlife habitats. Roots of Peace will plant two million fruit and nut trees in Afghanistan and provide farmers there with the skills and support necessary for sustainable land use.

Manufactured in China by Insight Editions

10 9 8 7 6 5 4 3 2 1